"Stirring and more worldly than similar works by other medicine men, this is instructive reading for those wishing to understand what it is like to be a Native American today."

—*Publishers Weekly*

"This compelling memoir recounts the making of a modern medicine man. . . . In graphic, sometimes hilarious, sometimes heartbreaking detail, he recounts his experiences. . . . It's a thought-provoking look at ancient spirituality authentically expressed in a modern context."

— *Yoga Journal*

"This wonderful book is not for those looking for some quick, shamanic weekend formulas, but rather for those who are interested in learning more about the complex, intriguing traditions of modern Indians still deeply rooted in the mysteries of their age-old cosmology. It is also for those simply looking for some good wise tales, told by a man with a warm heart and a pinch of strong medicine."

—*Prout Journal*

"[Erdoes] has always had a special way of communicating the essence of the way of life of the Lakota, and his newest book, *Gift of Power*, is no exception. This book continues the high standard set by the others that have preceded it. It would make a great gift . . . "

—*Body, Mind & Spirit* magazine

"An excellent addition to any collection concerned with spirituality or Indian traditions."

—*Booklist*

" . . . a unique and powerful story . . . The candor, detail, and magical power of Native American spirit life is presented in a way that will move the reader to a greater understanding of the Plains "Indian" culture than most books available. It is not flowery prose, but plain talk in the style of a talented storyteller."

— *Transformation Times*

GIFT OF POWER

Also by Richard Erdoes

The Pueblo Indians

Lame Deer, Seeker of Visions

The Sun Dance People

The Rain Dance People

The Sound of Flutes

Picture History of Ancient Rome

Saloons of the Old West

The Woman Who Dared

American Indian Myths and Legends
(with Alfonso Ortiz)

A.D. 1000: Living on the Brink of Apocalypse

Crying for a Dream

Lakota Woman

Tales from the American Frontier

Gift of Power

THE LIFE AND TEACHINGS OF A
LAKOTA MEDICINE MAN

ARCHIE FIRE LAME DEER
& RICHARD ERDOES

introduced by
Alvin M. Josephy, Jr.

BEAR & COMPANY
PUBLISHING
SANTA FE, NEW MEXICO

LIBRARY OF CONGRESS CATALOGING-IN-PUBLICATION DATA

Lame Deer, Archie Fire, 1935-
    Gift of power : the life and teachings of a Lakota medicine man /
by Archie Fire Lame Deer and Richard Erdoes.
        p.   cm.
    ISBN 1-879181-12-6
    1. Lame Deer, Archie Fire, 1935-   . 2. Dakota Indians—
Biography. 3. Shamans—South Dakota—Biography. 4. Dakota
Indians—Religion and mythology. 5. Dakota Indians—Medicine.
I. Erdoes, Richard. II. Title.
E99.D1L23 1992
978.3'004975—dc20   92-10493
                                                                    CIP

Bear & Company, Inc.
Santa Fe, NM 87504-2860

Cover photo: Veretta © 1992
Cover & interior design & graphics: Angela Werneke
Erdoes photo: W.W. Koopman,
The Light, A Magazine of the Heart
Editing: Brandt Morgan
Typography: Buffalo Publications
Printed in the United States of America by R.R. Donnelley

5 7 9 8 6 4

To our teachers
and spiritual leaders who have gone to the spirit world,
but whose thoughts and wisdom still live:
Henry Quick Bear, John Fire Lame Deer, George Poor Thunder,
Frank Fool's Crow, Henry Crow Dog, Bill Schweigman Eagle Feathers,
Ellis Chips, Chest, Good Lance, and George Eagle Elk.

My friend,
They will return again.
All over the Earth,
They are returning again.
Ancient teachings of the Earth,
Ancient songs of the Earth,
They are returning again.

—*Crazy Horse*

C O N T E N T S

F O R E W O R D

Gift of Power is a wondrously magical book—an accessible, highly readable introduction to the beauty of the ancient Lakota religion and way of life, as well as a fascinating human story of Archie Fire Lame Deer, a modern-day Lakota spiritual man.

Coauthored with Richard Erdoes, a Vienna-born author, artist, and photographer who for thirty years has worked in friendship with Native Americans, assisting them in their struggles against racism and injustice, Archie's autobiography is something of a sequel to his father's book, *Lame Deer, Seeker of Visions*, which was also coauthored by Erdoes and is now a well-established classic. But the horizons of father and son—both full-blood Sioux traditional medicine men—differed greatly. Old John's horizon was that of the reservation; Archie's encompasses the whole world.

And what a story Archie has to tell of the long, rocky trail he followed on the way to becoming a spiritual man and teacher of Indian culture! Raised on Rosebud Reservation in South Dakota by his maternal grand-father, Quick Bear, a traditional, non-English–speaking healer, Archie did not meet his father until he was eleven years old, when he discovered old John performing as a rodeo clown. Growing up, Archie was a hell-raiser and proud of it, moving in an alcoholic haze from one career to another and compiling a record of 185 arrests for drunken fights and other diffi-culties in many parts of the world. During that time, he was a ranch hand, bartender, paratrooper with the U.S. Army in Korea, the chief rattlesnake catcher of the state of South Dakota, and the best-known Indian stuntman in Hollywood.

In a splendid, crisply written narrative, full of detail and vivid anec-dote, Archie and Richard recount these chapters in the life of a seemingly aimless and lost young Sioux man. But abruptly, some twenty years ago, Archie went on the wagon and since then has not tasted a drop of liquor.

He settled down, married a Chumash Indian woman with practical wisdom and a great sense of humor, and with her has raised a family of three children.

After his marriage, Archie became a counselor to Indian alcoholics and prison inmates, and played a leading role in bringing the Pipe and sweatlodge to Native Americans in federal penitentiaries. Finally, when Archie's father, old John Fire Lame Deer, was in his eighties, he passed on his power, wisdom, herbal knowledge, and sacred objects to Archie, who has followed in John's footsteps as a spiritual leader in the United States and Europe, lecturing on Lakota religion and culture, performing traditional ceremonies, and co-directing at Rosebud the annual Sundance, the most important of all Lakota rituals.

In chapters far more lucid and compelling than most anthropological writings, Archie takes the reader through the traditional Lakota world of spirituality, lore, and custom, explaining and describing ceremonies and the different kinds of "medicine men" as best he can and making clear that there is much that simply cannot be explained satisfactorily to the English-speaking non-Indian. Through it all, we continue to follow the mind-boggling career of this evolving, worldly wise Sioux spiritual man of the late twentieth century. Archie gives sweatlodges for his friend the Dalai Lama of Tibet, discusses religion with the pope at the Vatican, takes part in sacred bear rituals with the Ainus on the northern Japanese island of Hokkaido, philosophizes with Druids at Stonehenge, explores prehistoric caves with Celtic-speaking Frenchmen, and conducts ceremonies with Laplander shamans in Norway.

And that is not the half of it. But read the book, and enjoy and learn from its many moods of lightheartedness, seriousness, and, above all, Lakota power, mystery, and beauty.

Alvin M. Josephy, Jr.
Joseph, Oregon
June 1992

Alvin M. Josephy, Jr., is the author of The Indian Heritage of America, Now That the Buffalo's Gone, *and many other books about Native Americans and the American West.*

A Meeting of Minds

Perhaps the reader will wonder how I came to collaborate with Archie Fire Lame Deer on this autobiography. The story is fascinating even to me, many decades after my first contacts with the Sioux people.

I came to the United States from my native Vienna in 1940. Before I met Archie's father, John Fire Lame Deer, I had made my living in New York as an artist—particularly as a magazine illustrator. In 1964, *LIFE* and *American Heritage* magazines sent me out to the reservations to do a painting portfolio and a photo essay. I met John, and we took a shine to each other—after all, we were both artists.

Then, in 1967, Old John, intending to "break through the buckskin curtain," led a delegation of twenty-one Lakota men and women to take part in one of Martin Luther King's civil rights marches in New York. All twenty-one of them later wound up at my apartment for a celebratory feast. As a result, my place was henceforth known as "Sioux East."

A few weeks later, Old John showed up in New York again, unannounced. He knocked on my door, saying, "I like you and your family. I think I stay for a while." He shared my studio, grabbed my paints and canvases, and quickly proved himself to be a great artist with a gift for rendering a scene with only a few brush strokes.

John had a great time in the Big Apple. He seemed to need no sleep. He spent whole nights standing on Broadway and Forty-Second Street, in front of Whelan's drug store, taking in the scene, the lights, the strange characters who populated the Times Square area, and shaking hands and engaging passersby in conversation. He was a great storyteller with a sometimes wicked sense of humor and was very popular with the New York ladies.

John and I became close friends. We started visiting back and forth— he to New York and I to the Sioux Reservation in South Dakota. He even invited me to my first Sundance, which he ran in Winner, the small prairie town in which he had his humble home with no running water and a toppling privy in back, next to his sweatlodge.

After a year or so, John began urging me to help him write his life story. I told him, "John, I am an artist, not a writer." He brushed this aside. "My medicine tells me that you'll write this book," he said.

I protested: "John, not only am I not a writer, but English is my second language." He insisted: "My medicine tells me you'll do it."

Finally I gave in. Our book, *Lame Deer, Seeker of Visions*, became a classic, a modern *Black Elk Speaks*. Thus, I quite unexpectedly became a writer, and I will be forever grateful to John and his medicine for urging me on to an improbable new vocation.

When the book came out, our publisher sent us from coast to coast to promote it. Old John was a sensation. In Cleveland, a television interviewer badgered him: "Come on, Lame Deer. You say you can speak with animals. Don't put us on. Don't try to con us." John looked at her sternly for a while and then came up with this: "Lady, in your Good Book, a woman talks to a snake. I speak with *eagles*!" It brought down the house.

Our tour wound up in San Francisco and finally Los Angeles, and it was there that John introduced me to his son Archie. I was immediately impressed with Archie. At the time, he was running a rehabilitation program for Indian alcoholics and was bringing comfort in various ways to Native American inmates inside federal penitentiaries.

I asked him what had made him choose this career and whether he had studied psychology. He grinned and said, "No, I had on-the-job-training!" Meaning, of course, that in his younger years he himself had suffered from a drinking problem that had repeatedly landed him in jail.

Archie took John and me to Lompoc prison, where he and his father taught young Indians native culture and traditions. I found out that Archie was instrumental in bringing about legislation that enabled Indian inmates to meet with their tribal medicine men, just as white or black inmates had access to a priest, minister, or rabbi. Archie had also obtained for his people the right to keep and smoke their Sacred Pipe. He also was able to perform sweatlodge and other ceremonies inside prison walls.

Later, I was introduced to Archie's wife, Sandy, a Chumash Indian. I took an instant liking to her as well, admiring especially the way in which she handled the ups and downs of life without ever losing her wry sense of humor.

Finally John took me back to South Dakota. There, during a Yuwipi ceremony, he gave me my Indian name. He also tried, with fair to middling success, to teach me the Lakota language. When the Indian struggle for civil rights began in earnest, we all became heavily involved in the movement, though John was never a great radical. Instead of foaming at the mouth like many militants at the time, he used gentle, sometimes humorous persuasion to rid his white audiences of their racial prejudices. We went to a few confrontations together, and John always used his Gandhi-like approach to overcome all opposition. I was much less patient and considerably more belligerent than he.

After Old John's death in 1976—a loss that I still feel strongly—my friendship with his son Archie consoled me. As John himself had often done, Archie now visited me off and on, both in New York and later in Santa Fe.

Much to my delight, I soon discovered that he was an even better storyteller than his father, with a treasure of tales flowing from his rich and colorful life experience. Unlike his father, whose home had been the reservation, Archie's home was the whole world. Today he lectures in many countries on Lakota culture and tradition.

I accompanied Archie on one such lecture tour and was enchanted with the way he could, sometimes seriously and sometimes with humor, bring the beauty of Indian tradition, spirituality, and beliefs to white audiences. Never did he try to play the big medicine man or con his listeners by implying that he could make them into Native American shamans in one weekend for a thousand dollars, as some fake medicine people do.

In the summer of 1991, I was privileged for the first time to witness Archie running a Sundance at Rosebud. It was an unforgettable experience. As Archie is a traditional spiritual Lakota like his father before him, but also very different from his father, it was logical to follow up Old John's story with that of his son, passing on the old wisdom mingled with the new, passing on what Old John called "the flame, the Fire Without End."

Mitakuye Oyasin.

Richard Erdoes

Gift of Power

CHAPTER 1

The Seed Beneath the Snow

As my father lay dying, he gripped my hand. I felt his power flowing into me until it filled my whole being. At that moment, my life changed altogether from what it had been. My future became something I could only partly sense, like looking at a distant mountain range half hidden in a blue haze. At that moment, the man I had been died, and a new man took his place.

As my father's life was ebbing away in the hospital, he did not recognize me at first. He had recognized all his other relatives and friends, talking and joking with them, but to me, his eyes were blind; I seemed invisible to him. He also seemed not to hear me. His eyes would get wider as he tried to understand what I was saying, but it was just as if I had not been there.

I had traveled fifteen times from my home in Santa Barbara to Denver in order to visit my father in his sickroom, and he seemed to look right through me. I wept. But finally, when I came to visit him for the sixteenth time, one of the girls came running out of his room, telling me, "Grandpa is asking for you to come in."

So I walked in, and he smiled at me and said, "Where have you been? Why didn't you come?" He had no memory of the many times I had visited him. Even so, I felt as if something tremendous was about to happen. I felt as if he was about to pass on his power and his burden to me. He said, "Ask everybody to leave the room."

At that point, all the other visitors went out, leaving the two of us alone. My father said, "Pick me up from the bed and put me on that soft chair over there. I want to talk to you." I lifted him up, put him on the easy chair, and sat beside him.

For a long time, neither of us spoke. Finally he said, "Sit down on the floor and let me put my hand on your head." So I sat at his feet, and he began to talk, his hand always resting on my head.

The first thing he said was, "Son, you will never be the man that I was."

I thought he was trying to put me down, trying to arouse my anger. Some of the old resentment that I had nursed as a young man came back— the sort of resentment that comes naturally to a strong-willed son at a certain time in his life. I told him, "I have done more things than you have ever done, and I have done some of them better."

Ignoring me, he calmly repeated, "You will never be the man that I was."

"Why are you talking like this?" I asked him. "Are you not done with that kind of boasting yet?"

He went on as if he had not heard me. "You will never be the man that I was," he said, "because no son can ever be like his father—and no daughter like her mother. We all come from the same root, but the leaves are all different. Now my path is coming to an end, and yours begins where mine leaves off. If we teach our children in the right way, their footsteps go on from the point where ours end. That is what I am trying to tell you.

"I have taught you many things," my father went on, "but they were way beyond you. You never listened, so I taught the sons of others to become medicine men. But I always knew that sometime you would come back to me. Now you are here."

My father's hand seemed to grow heavier and heavier on my head. He kept on, as if talking in a dream: "Those young men I taught are now teaching others. So in case I gave them something that I should have given you, I said to them, 'Return this to my son when the time comes.'"

That time did come. After my father died, several medicine men came to me and showed me something in the spiritual way, telling me, "Your father gave this to me to keep for you." Some of them even told me of my father's visions and prophesies about myself—prophecies that later came true.

On the day my father parted from me, he gave me his Pipe, telling me, "Take care of this Sacred Red Pipe. Use it for yourself and your people. In that way, you will always have me with you, and my *nagi*, my spirit, will walk alongside you. I have sent for my sacred bonnet and my beaded buckskin outfit; they are yours. You are now me. You must teach your son. Teach him the language, the prayers, the ancient ways, and your seed will go on. That is the main thing—that the spirit of Lame Deer will go on."

Then my father told me of a vision he had had—his last vision, as it turned out. He said, "I went to another place, and there I saw our grandfathers—our ancestors—as far as the eye can see, and they all had chiefs' bonnets on their heads. My own father touched me and turned me around, and I asked him, 'Where is my son? I do not see him.' And my father's ghost told me, 'Look up on that hill. There he stands with his wife and three children. Now go back and do what you have to do. You are not finished yet. You must pass your power on.' So now I am back, doing what I have been told."

Now, at that time, I did not yet have three children, so my father's vision was a true one.

I sat in that hospital at my father's feet for four hours. During that time, I received precious gifts of power and wisdom from him. I cannot relate what he taught me. I will repeat it only once, to my own son, at the end of the path *I* have to travel.

Though I teach what my father taught in the traditional Lakota way, I am different from him. My father's horizon was the reservation and the Indian country, the prairie and hills covered with buffalo grass. He spoke English badly. He was, in body and mind, of another time—the time of Sitting Bull and Crazy Horse. Time stood still for him. For him, the clock had stopped at Wounded Knee more than a hundred years ago. He rode in cars and flew in airplanes, but such things were just like horses to him— spirit horses. My father spent his whole life in a crumbling, wooden shack without electric lights, tap water, or plumbing, with his sweatlodge in the back yard and his little dog rubbing against his worn-out cowboy boots.

In contrast, fate dumped me into the world of the white man. It made me a creature of the nuclear age, the age of TV and computers. It also made me a teacher—a teacher not only among my own Indian people but also among men and women of faraway countries. So, while I am in many ways like my father, I am also unlike him.

At last my father said, "I am tired. I want to rest. Pick me up and put me on the bed." I gathered him up in my arms and placed him on his bed for the last time. He suddenly smiled and said in a faint whisper, "Tell the people not to cry. Tell them to be happy." He took hold of my hand and held it for a long time in a strong grip. Then he let go and closed his eyes.

I looked upon him lying there with a great sadness deep inside me. During the night, he went on to the unknown, on the path guarded by Hinhan, the great Owl, which leads to the spirit world. For this last journey, I dressed him in his fringed and beaded buckskin shirt, leggings, and moccasins. But I kept his Pipe and bonnet, as he had asked me to do.

C H A P T E R 2

Corn Creek

My father, John Fire Lame Deer, had been many things during his long life. He always told me, "I was a roamer. I had to roam all over this Turtle Continent." He also taught me that to be a medicine man, you have to experience everything, live life to the fullest. "If you don't experience the human side of everything," he said, "how can you help teach or heal? To be a good medicine man, you've got to be humble. You've got to be lower than a worm and higher than an eagle." One of the last things he said to me was, "Be happy. Be happy." He always said that he could not die until he had created twelve other medicine men. I guess I was the twelfth.

In his youth, my father had been a *hlete*, a "hell-raiser"—the delight of women, a bullrider, a rodeo clown, a soldier, a sign painter, a bootleg-ger, a tribal policeman, and a spud picker. But always, like a seed beneath the snow, there had lain deep within him the knowledge that, like his ancestors, he would someday be what the whites call a "medicine man," or what we Lakota call a *pejuta wichasha*, a "spiritual man." He knew, too, that he would become a *heyoka*, a "contrary" or "sacred clown." And so, after midlife, he ceased his roaming and finally began his journey as a *wichasha wakan*, a "holy man."

In many ways, my life resembled my father's. I, too, was a hell-raiser. I was a sawmill worker, a rattlesnake catcher, a circus performer, a para-chutist, a prisoner of war in Korea, a ranch hand, a bronc buster, a bar-room brawler, a bartender, and the one-and-only Indian stuntman in Hollywood. But, as with my father, my roaming years were only prepara-

7

[handwritten annotations in margins: "hlete -", "hell - raiser", "father", "spiritual man"]

tion for becoming a medicine man. And, like him, I carried this spiritual seed within me from childhood on.

That I followed so closely in my father's footsteps—"walking in his moccasins," as the Lakota elders say—is strange, because I never met my father until I was eleven years old. That was in 1946, the year my grandfather Quick Bear died. At the same time that I lost the old man whom I loved so much, I finally found my father. Was this merely a coincidence? I do not know.

Like many Lakota children, I was raised by my grandparents. It was my maternal grandfather, Mato Ohanko, Henry Quick Bear, who brought me up at Corn Creek, in the northwest corner of the Rosebud Reservation. Corn Creek was an isolated place at the edge of the Badlands, a place of moonscapes strewn with the petrified skeletons of long-extinct animals— a haunted spot full of magic. It was Grandpa who instilled in me the knowledge of our people's old beliefs and way of life.

Grandpa was one of those Lakota men of old who kept the flame of tradition alive. When I was old enough to understand, he told me, "When the last of us traditional elders stands on the face of this Earth, and the Earth swallows him up, the Earth will go down with him." Grandpa was the light of my life—sun, moon, and stars all rolled into one.

I was born in 1935, on a night when a warm chinook wind swept over the reservation, bringing rain, thunder, and lightning—a *heyoka* night. I was born when the night was short, so my first name was Hanhepi-Chikala—Little Night. Later my grandfather told me, "Boys born on such nights have a seed of spirituality implanted in them. They are born to become medicine men."

I remember the one-room log cabin where I was born. I remember that it had an earthen floor. I remember my grandmother, who helped bring me into this world. And I remember my mother, whose Indian name was Rising Morning Star Woman. (Her white-man's name was Josephine.) She was a proud, beautiful woman. She was a Mato Ohanko, a Quick Bear. To this day, I consider myself a Quick Bear, too. I also remember that later my mother and I lived in a tipi.

One day, when my mother was still young, an old Model A with two men in it drove up to the tipi and took my mother away. They put her on a stretcher and then drove away with her. I never saw her again. She had been suffering from tuberculosis, a disease that at that time took a heavy toll among the Lakota people. Her lungs had been all but destroyed.

Man's death

I did not understand what was happening to her. I was only five years old. I cried and cried, "Don't take my mother away! Mother, come back! Please come back! Don't leave me!" But there was no answer.

Mother did come back—in a coffin. They told me my mother was in that box. I remember when they took her to the cemetery. I tried to stop them when they put her in the Earth. They dragged me away to the house of some relative. Again I cried and cried. Then, when nobody was looking, I sneaked out of the house and ran back to the cemetery, which was far away. I sat down at her grave, weeping and crying, "Mother, come out of there! Mother, where are you?"

My relatives were looking for me, but none of them guessed that I had run all the way back to where they had buried her. I was later told that I stayed at my mother's graveside for four days and nights. I almost died there myself. So that was my first Vision Quest, trying to bring my mother back to life again.

Grandpa Quick Bear found me. He figured out where I had gone; he had that gift. He told me, "Takoja, Grandson, your mother is gone."

"Where has she gone?" I asked. "To another world," he said. "She has gone there on Tachanku, the Spirit Trail, which is the Milky Way, up there among the stars. You will meet her again many years from now. You will find her waiting for you at the end of that trail."

Grandpa hugged and consoled me, saying, "Grandson, your human mother is gone, but you still have a mother. You're walking on her back. Your mother is Unchi, the Earth. Look for her in the trees, the grasses, the rocks. Grandson, I will raise you myself. I will bring you up in the way of our people. I will teach you all the things I know that you must also know. You have a home with me. Come."

With that, he picked me up in his arms and carried me to his log cabin. And so I came to live with Grandpa Quick Bear at Wagmeza Wakpa, at Corn Creek.

This is the country where our ancestor, the old chief Mato Ohanko, the first Quick Bear, made his camp over a hundred years ago, and we still live there. The creek after which the area is named starts in the north as an offshoot of Black Pipe Creek, five miles south of that stream. It loops into the Little White River near the town of Belvedere. Corn was grown in the valley, and that gave the place its name. To the west is the Corn Creek Dam near Wamblee. This is no longer a part of the Rosebud Reservation, but of the neighboring Pine Ridge Reservation where our Oglala brothers live.

The valley is surrounded by the Badlands, or the "Mako Sicha," as we call the area. This is a haunted country of fantastic geological formations. Seen from afar, some of them look like medieval cities with strange, eerie castles and twisted spires. Others look like ghostly ships with masts and sails of crumbling clay. All this was once water, part of a vast ocean that covered this land millions of years ago. The Badlands range all the way up to around Murdo and beyond, going as far as Reliance, South Dakota.

To the Lakota people, the Mako Sicha is a place of legends, the home of Unktehi, the Great Water Monster. Grandpa told me many ancient tales about it. Tunkashila, the Grandfather Spirit, so he said, had once raised up a great, all-destroying storm that swept everything before it, stripping the area of trees, bushes, grass—all the green things—leaving nothing but the bare earth. Grandpa explained that the Great Spirit had done this to create a barrier of wasteland that no one would dare to cross, protecting our people from powerful enemies bound to invade our old hunting grounds.

"They call the Mako Sicha 'Badlands,'" Grandpa said, "but they should call them Mako Washte, 'Good Lands,' because Wakan Tanka, the Everywhere Spirit, put them there as a wall to shield us."

Some people are afraid of being lost in the Badlands, a place where the desert heat can change to numbing cold within an hour and where great, raging winds and storms sweep through the canyons and gullies. But to me, they were a magic playground through which I liked to roam.

Throughout this strangely beautiful land, long-extinct creatures have left their remains. Whenever I went exploring, I found the ground strewn with fossils of many periods—shells, teeth, bones, and the imprints of leaves and feathers. First, about a hundred million years ago, came the creatures out of ancient oceans—large seashells called ammonites, still covered with shiny, rainbow-colored mother of pearl. Sometimes, at the moment when I cracked a boulder full of such fossils, there was a strong smell of oil and the sea. There are places along the Red River, where it hooks into the

Cheyenne River, where fish have turned into stone. Some of them have broken apart, and you can still make out their petrified intestines. In some spots, I found the whitened shapes of long-extinct turtles up to ten feet long.

Then came the dinosaurs. During a thunderstorm on a moonless night, my father was once caught on top of a sharp ridge. He got scared. He couldn't see what was to the right or left of him, and he was afraid of falling down one of those hundreds-of-feet-deep ravines that crisscross the Badlands. So he sat down, straddling the ridge, cautiously edging his way along it. When dawn came, he found himself straddling the enormous spine of a huge, dinosaurlike creature. "I rode the Great Water Monster," he used to say whenever he mentioned this adventure.

Later came the warm-blooded animals—long-extinct tiny horses and camels, and an Ice Age bison much bigger than the buffalo of today. Once my father found the oversized, petrified skull of such a bison, and he kept it for many years. I also came across the bones of big-fanged cave bears and saber-toothed tigers.

Once I stumbled upon the bones of an animal that must have been eight feet tall at the shoulder when walking on all fours. "These belong to the Thunder Horse," Grandpa told me when I showed him one of those huge leg bones.

When the ice cover melted about ten thousand years ago, the glacial water just disappeared beneath the Badlands, forming a vast underground lake beneath an area bordered by the towns of Wall, Interior, and Kadoka. One of the biggest reservoirs of good water is down there. So, when the great air force base at Ellsworth ran out of water, they drilled down eight thousand feet and tapped the lake, getting an abundance of good water.

When white people look at the barren, bleached Badlands, they think that nothing grows or lives there. But we Indians know that the Mako Sicha teems with life. On the grassy tableland, antelope and mule deer graze; in the caves, one can still find bears and mountain lions; and the air is filled with the cries of hawks and eagles.

When I say that this country is Quick Bear land, I mean not only the people called Quick Bear, but our whole clan, the *tiyospaye* or "extended family" of people descended from the many sons of the first Quick Bear. Once, when I was about seven years old, my grandfather took me to the top of a mountain called Cross Butte, which overlooks Corn Creek Valley.

"Look around you, Takoja," he told me. "Look to all the four directions as far as you can see. There your relatives live. To the east are the Singing Gooses and the Standing Bears; to the south, the Quick Bears, the Eagle Bears, the Lone Warriors, and the Neck Shields. To the north live the Wood Knives, and to the west the Dog Eyes, the Sleeping Bears, the Red Fish, and the Horned Antelopes. These are all relatives and good friends—people living in the old way—and there are many medicine men among them." Then he added, "Takoja, this land you stand on is sacred. Look upon it deep and hard and well."

I looked upon that valley, the place where I was born. Far down, I could make out the little log cabin where Grandpa and I lived. This was my world, the world in which I spent my childhood.

This world revolved around Grandpa Henry Quick Bear; he stood at its center. At the time he took me to live with him he was already getting on in years. At a time when most Sioux men wore suits and ties and cut their hair short to impress the white government people and the missionaries with how civilized they were, Grandpa still kept his two long braids wrapped in strips of red cloth and walked around in moccasins. I wish I had a picture of him, but Grandpa never allowed himself to be photographed. In that respect, he was like Crazy Horse, who likewise never let a white man take his picture. In a way, that was strange because I have seen quite a few pictures of Grandpa Henry's own father and grandfather (taken around 1900), and one of them looks almost exactly like him. Picture or no picture, I will carry Grandpa's image in my mind until the day I die.

In his own way, Grandpa was very forceful and straightforward. He taught me to respect the ways of our people, to respect their beliefs, and to respect our elders, whom he called the "firekeepers." He was strict about this, but very gentle. Also, serious as he was, he laughed a lot. He was about five feet and eleven inches tall, and very lean. His body was all muscle and sinew, without fat. He had a deeply etched, full-blood face that mirrored the hardships of his life, but the fine lines and wrinkles around his eyes came from laughter. He stayed physically very fit until the day he died.

On the day Grandpa was eighty-eight years old, his heart gave out. Even then, his hair was still coal black, and he still had all his teeth. Physically he had only one problem: during his last years, he was hard of hearing. I had to shout when I wanted to talk to him. So eventually I learned sign language, and we communicated that way. There were only the two of us, because my grandmother had died around the time I was born. The years I spent with Grandpa Quick Bear were the happiest years of my life.

Grandpa was a *pejuta wichasha*, a "medicine man," like most of his ancestors before him. He did not believe in hospitals, white doctors, or their pills. "Grandson," he used to say, "those white doctors try to cure one disease by giving you another one. They pile sickness upon sickness. The more sick they make you, the more it costs. They are not interested in your health but in the *maza ska*, the "white metal," the thing they call money. They say they can make a sick person well, but it was the white man who brought us the diseases we never had before, diseases that have wiped out many Indian nations: smallpox, chicken pox, measles, diphtheria, tuberculosis, and the worst disease of all—whiskey."

[handwritten margin note: grand's views on doctors]

Grandpa cured the sick with his knowledge of herbs, of bones and skin, and of how the human body functions. Just by looking at a person, he would have a good idea of what ailed him. Besides this practical knowledge, Grandpa also had spiritual power, and he used both. Grandpa also healed people with a certain buffalo horn that contained his special medicine. This was his *wopiye*, a "thing to do good with," and it was very powerful. He never used the Pipe for his doctorings. To him, it was too sacred, and only to be used in ceremonies.

Looking back at some of the cures Grandpa performed—and which I was allowed to watch—they now seem to me almost miraculous. He healed people who were paralyzed and got them to walk again. He doctored one man who had a stroke that left half his face wrenched out of place. The left part of the man's mouth was lower than the right one, and so was his left eye. His face was not good to look at. I have seen such faces in horror films. Yet after Grandpa straightened it out, the man could smile again. Grandpa was good at setting fractured bones, too, and he taught me how to set the broken wings and legs of animals.

Grandpa was also honest—unlike some medicine men of today who promise a sick person a cure while knowing full well that they do not have the knowledge or power to make good on their promise and thinking only of the money they can get out of the sick one. Grandpa never took money for his doctoring, but he might accept a gift of food. And often I heard him say to a man or woman who came to him for help, "I cannot cure you, but I know someone who can."

This was because, just as among white doctors, there are "specialists" among Indian medicine men. One is a bone setter, another can counteract a snakebite, and still another has an herb that can bring on an abortion to save a woman's life. And then there is the *wapiya*, the *hmugma wichasha*, the "conjurer" or "magician," who may cure your sickness but who may also give you a sickness. There is evil in such a man, and it is best to avoid such Jekyll-and-Hyde characters.

Grandpa sometimes said to a person, "You have a sickness that was brought to this country by the white man. For this I have no medicine, and neither have the other healers that I know of." He might even tell such a person, "Go to a white doctor for this white man's illness."

As I said, Grandpa's name was Quick Bear. Many of our relations had names that included the word *Bear*, and there used to be medicine men who got their power from this animal. The Bear is fierce and can be dangerous, but it has the knowledge of herbs and how to use them. It also has the claws to dig up medicinal roots and is known as the "medicine man among animals." It is said that if a man dreams of Mato, the Bear, he will acquire its knowledge of secret herbs to use in doctoring. Was Grandpa also a Bear medicine man? I do not know. It is one of those things one never talks about. At any rate, it is said that the last *pejuta wichasha* with Bear power died many years ago.

Before Grandpa died, he left his buffalo horn to me. With it, he also left herbs of understanding and truth, the teachings of the buffalo horn. I did not want it then—I was still roaming and raising hell; I did not yet understand what it meant. I resisted it for a long time. For a while, I even forgot where I had put it. But at the proper time, I found it again—and also the wisdom of how to use it.

The house we lived in was a log cabin, the typical reservation dwelling of the twenties and thirties. It was a two-room cabin with the bedroom and kitchen combined. (Some lucky families had a third bedroom.) The cabin had a dirt floor made of tamped earth. It had been stepped on so long and so often that it was as hard as cement. There was one door, one window to the east, and two windows to the south.

We had no electric lights; no one did. Instead, we used kerosene lamps with large, sheet-metal reflectors that we bought from the store. We had no tap water, either. It was my job to get water from the creek, half a mile away, and to keep a bucket in the kitchen freshly filled, with a dipper hanging from a hook close by. We had no indoor plumbing, of course: just a wooden privy in back of the house. To keep wind and rain from coming through the cracks between the logs, we filled them with white clay mixed with straw and water. We had to do that every year.

The roof was made of rather thin wooden boards covered with black tarpaper. A thick layer of earth was put on top for insulation. Grass grew in that dirt until the whole roof was covered with it. From the air, you could not have seen the house, as it blended in with the vegetation around it. For heat, we had an old iron stove in the front room. In the bedroom, an old- fashioned wood-burning range served for both cooking and warmth.

We slept on rickety iron bedsteads. For mattresses, we had sacking filled with corn husks and corn cobs. Every evening I had to move the corn cobs this way and that in order to be comfortable. We also had two old chairs, a table, a wash basin, and an old camelback trunk in which Grandpa kept his few possessions. Instead of a closet, we had plenty of nails stuck in the walls to hang things on, and that was all.

I was happy in that house. I knew of no other kind. All the homes in our neck of the woods were like that. Later, the government introduced better houses with shingles on the side and even electricity. But these were only for the half-blood politicians and councilmen, not for poor full-bloods like us.

The foods we ate were just staples—things we got on "purchase order," as it was called. This government-issue food was mostly starch; it included very little protein and never any fresh vegetables. Once a month, we went to Norris in a horse and buggy to pick up a purchase order. They gave us a slab of bacon, raisins, flour, and a few dried fruits. They never gave us canned fruits, canned meat, or canned pork like they hand out now to reservation Indians. Once every two months, we received a quarter of beef, which was part of the agreement the tribe had with the government. We ate a lot of fry bread, or "skillet bread," baked in a skillet on top of the stove. Luckily, Grandpa kept a ten-acre garden so that we had fresh vegetables. We had cucumbers, cantaloupes, watermelons, carrots, lettuce—everything we needed, with enough left over to give to our friends and relatives.

Grandpa also taught me how to recognize and where to find wild fruit. In late spring and summer, we picked wild onions, plums, and parsley. We dug up the kind of wild turnips called *timpsila* and other edible roots that, when cooked, make a delicious soup. We picked all kinds of berries. The first to ripen were the juneberries, then came the currants, gooseberries, raspberries, buffaloberries, and wild grapes. We filled whole buckets with chokecherries. Grandpa was the fastest cherry picker in Corn Creek. We gathered all of the wild things Grandpa knew. We kept what we needed for ourselves and took the rest to the store at Norris, where we exchanged it for white man's groceries such as rice, flour, and dried prunes.

In the wintertime, we drank a lot of tea made from the bark of different trees, sipped a drink made from fragrant dried mint, and drank cherry juice made from the inner bark of cherry trees. During the summer, my aunts would hang up meat to dry in the sun. This so-called "jerk meat" they would pound together with kidney fat and berries to make *wasna*, or pemmican. We ate that in the winter. It was sweet and delicious, and a handful could keep a person going for a whole day.

Sioux people are meat eaters. Grandpa taught me, and my cousins, the Spotted Owls, how to trap. Grandpa liked to trap. He never shot an animal with a gun, and he never used firearms, but he could trap anything—rabbits, ducks, pheasants, beavers. We ate everything that walked, crawled, hopped, or flew. Rattlesnake meat was good; it tasted like chicken. Turtle soup was a delicacy. In a pinch, gophers and squirrels would do. Grandpa always used a bow and arrow to hunt. Instead of flint or metal points, he used arrows with big knots on the ends, which stunned his game. Grandpa did all his hunting in the old manner. This way, he saved money on shells—money we didn't have, anyhow.

Some people think you need commercial steel traps, but Grandpa always improvised his traps from whatever was handy. He might make a noose or a deadfall. Once he showed me how to trap raccoons without a store-bought trap. Raccoons are forever curious—they like to stick their hands into everything—so he hollowed out a piece of wood and put sharp wooden stakes through it. When the coon stuck its hands in there, it couldn't pull them out. Luckily, we had no microwave ovens, but we had the old wood-burning range. Grandpa put a whole beaver in there with its innards taken out and the cavity filled with all kinds of good-smelling plants. A few hours later, it was just sizzling with the juice of all those herbs. Now *that's* food! Or, instead of the oven, you can just put it into hot coals; that's even better. The best part of the beaver is its tail. You barbecue it over a low fire, and it tastes great.

Once, in Germany, I was invited to a feast where they had two whole, roasted beavers in honor of my birthday. They tasted exactly like those Grandpa used to cook for me. You can imagine my surprise. I thought that the beaver had died out in Western Europe long ago. I even ate skunk a few times when there was nothing else. Meat is meat. But you've got to take the scent bag out first, or you'll be sorry.

As skilled a trapper as Grandpa was, sometimes he caught nothing for a day or two, and we went hungry. The meat we ate was not like the steak you get from a big Safeway. Their meat is dyed red to make it look good, but you can smell that it is bad already. You are looking at fifth-hand meat; it has already been sold five times before getting to the supermarket. You have to have an Indian nose to recognize it for what it is.

Before Grandpa took the life of an animal—and also after he had killed it—he prayed and gave thanks to the four-leggeds who give their flesh so that the two-leggeds can survive. He always told an animal he had killed, "Forgive me, Brother, but the people have to live." He taught me never to kill for pleasure, but only for food, and to take only one animal at a time. He also taught me to eat all of it, not just cut the head off to hang on the wall for a trophy and throw away the rest. Also, after a kill, Grandpa would take a part of it to offer to the spirit world as food for those who have "gone south."

My father, John Fire Lame Deer, did the same. At every meal, Old John would put a little morsel aside for his dead friends. I even remember him spilling a spoonful of wine for his drinking companions who had passed on, saying, "There, you old wino, have a little *mni-sha*. Have a sip of that good red stuff. Enjoy it!" And Grandpa did the same after gathering plants, herbs, or red-willow-bark tobacco. He would make a tobacco offering to the spirits and thank Wakan Tanka for having given us those healing herbs, and say a prayer for all the living green things—the trees, bushes, grasses, and flowers. In the Indian belief, all food and all healing herbs are sacred.

Grandpa carried the whole history of our people in his head. He did not believe in book learning and the written word. He had been raised in the oral tradition and was a fine speaker and storyteller. Grandpa made me proud of my Quick Bear ancestors.

White historians keep confusing us Quick Bears with the Swift Bears. They are forever crediting my Grandpa's grandfather's deeds to a nonexistent Chief Swift Bear. The Swift Bears are Oglalas from Pine Ridge, while the Quick Bears are Brulés from Rosebud. *Brulé* is a French word meaning "burnt." The Sioux word for our tribe is *Sichangu*. Our English name is "Burned Thighs." Our tribe got its name when enemies set fire to the prairie around them. They managed to fight their way out through the flames but got their legs and moccasins burned.

On my father's side, I come from the Mnikowoju tribe (often called "Minneconjou" by the white man), the "Planters by the Water." Big Foot's band, victims of the 1890 Wounded Knee massacre, were Mnikowojus. They now live mostly on the Cheyenne River reservation. Oglalas, Brulés, and Mnikowojus all belong to the seven western Sioux tribes—to the Oceti Shakowin, the "Seven Sacred Campfires." They all speak the same Lakota language and have the same beliefs and ceremonies.

The first Quick Bear was a great warrior. As a young man, he earned his eagle feathers fighting white soldiers who were trying to build a road through our ancient hunting grounds, in violation of treaties that bore Quick Bear's thumbprint. This was the "Bloody Bozeman Trail," which the Indians called "The Thieves' Road."

Quick Bear fought alongside such famous chiefs as Red Cloud and Crazy Horse against Captain Fetterman's troopers. Fetterman was a fire eater like Custer. He had boasted that, with eighty men, he could ride over all the Indian nations on the plains. He had exactly eighty men when he came up against Red Cloud and Quick Bear, and not one of the whites escaped.

Quick Bear was also one of the old treaty chiefs. No treaty was considered valid without his signature. He even went to Washington to "touch the pen." Of course, he signed in the Indian way, with his "mark" beside his thumbprint. Later, after the Sioux had been driven onto reservations, Quick Bear labored for the welfare of his people. He was head chief of the Wazhazha band and later became chief of the Black Pipe district. He is still remembered for always having given of himself. One of his sons, Reuben, later became postmaster at Norris, South Dakota. History was running at full speed then; from warrior to postmaster was just one step.

Grandpa told me about the great chiefs he had known among our people—men like Red Cloud, Spotted Tail, American Horse, Crow Dog, Two Strikes, and Iron Shell who had been great in peace and in war. Grandpa carried their stories in his mind. He recounted the names, places, years, and even the coups each had counted. He was the Brulés' living history.

Even so, he did not tell me about the greatest of my ancestors, the first Chief Lame Deer, who led the Mnikowojus into battle against "Long Hair" Custer and who was later killed in a fight with General "Bearcoat" Miles at Lame Deer, Montana, a place named after him. But the first Chief Lame Deer was neither a Quick Bear nor a Brulé, and his story did not belong to Grandpa. It belonged to my father, John Fire Lame Deer.

Building a Person

Grandpa Quick Bear was both father and mother to me. Nature was my teacher, and the prairie was my classroom. When I was about six or seven years old, we had a day school at Corn Creek. There were two white boys there called Larry and Stanford. I never thought of them as white. They had freckles all over. I thought it was some kind of disease.

I went to that school for only two or three days. They didn't want to keep me; I was too wild. They said I was a creature out of the mountains and woods, rambunctious and obstinate. They said, "This boy is not civilized; he can't fit in. He is one of those kids who was raised in a tipi or earthen-floor cabin by folks who went back to the blanket. They're little savages; you can't do anything with them."

So I stayed away and that was fine with me. It was also all right with Grandpa and my uncle, Philip Quick Bear, a tribal policeman. He told me, "You have the greatest teacher there is: your Grandpa Henry. You don't have to go to school, which could make you into someone who's neither red nor white. You can't learn anything from pieces of paper."

Later, a bunch of white ranchers, with the help of Asa Lone Warrior, moved the day school to Norris, where most of the children were white—one more reason to stay away. Some of my friends went to school and liked it. They also liked one of the teachers, a Mr. Anderson, one of the few who made an effort to relate to Indian children. From these friends, I picked up a little learning secondhand, even a little English. But my real school was the woods—the mountains, streams, and animals.

Corn Creek was an Indian paradise. There were about ten or fifteen beaver dams along the creek, creating natural reservoirs so that we had a never-ending supply of water. They might have droughts in other places, at He Dog or Parmelee, but never at Corn Creek. The streams and lakes were teeming with fish, big bullheads and catfish in particular. Along the creek grew an abundance of red willows and red osier dogwood, whose bark supplied us with plenty of *chan shasha*, better known as kinnikin-nick, our sacred tobacco. There was also lots of sweetgrass, cedar, and sage four or five feet high. All these plants are what we call "holy herbs," which we use in our ceremonies. That's why so many medicine men settled in this area with their families.

The valley is always green and the climate warmer than elsewhere, because the Badlands and the mountains to the west and north break the winter storms and form a barrier against the blizzards that sweep the un-protected plains. For probably the same reason, we never had tornadoes come through Corn Creek, though they tear up the country around Spring Creek and He Dog. When I was a boy, the country was still unfenced, and all the roads were dirt. Barbed wire and blacktop didn't come to our area until 1947 or 1948.

This valley, nestled between the mountains and the Badlands, is the place where I have my roots. Grandpa's old log cabin is gone now, but the land is still the same. Every morning, before the first glimmer of light touch-ed the darkness, when sky and mountains still formed one black mass, Grandpa got up and sang for the night creatures, for the dark side of the moon, for the morning star and the approaching dawn, and for a new cir-cle. There was a sadness in his song that sometimes brought tears to my eyes, but there was strength in it, too, and words of comfort. It announced the coming of Tunkashila, the Grandfather, whom the whites call "the Great Spirit."

> Take a look over there,
> Take a look over there.
> Your Grandfather is coming to see you.
> Take a look over there,
> Take a look over there.

To the west, a black spirit rock
Is looking my way.
Friend, I am sending a voice in anguish—
Listen.

To the north, a red spirit rock
Is looking my way.
Friend, I am sending a voice in despair—
Listen.

To the south, a white spirit rock
Is looking my way.
Friend, I am sending a voice in sadness—
Listen.

Above, a spotted eagle is my friend.
Friend, I am sending a voice in anguish—
Listen.

On Earth, a mole brother is my friend.
Friend, a voice I am sending—
Listen.

This song is very ancient. It goes back to a time before the coming of the white man and before we had horses. Grandpa also sang and prayed to the sacred Four Directions, and to a fifth—the Above Spirit, and to a sixth—Unchi, Grandmother Earth. Today's generation thinks of the Four Direction colors as black, red, yellow, and white. But ancient songs that were handed down for generations say that to the west the color is black, to the north it is red, to the east it is brown, and to the south it is white. The color for Tunkashila, the Everywhere Spirit above, is blue, which stands for the sky. Tunkashila, or Wakan Tanka, the Great Sacredness, is represented by the eagle, who is a messenger between Wakan Tanka and us humans. Green is the color of the sixth direction, the Earth with its plants and trees. Unchi is represented by the mole people. My grandfather never missed a single morning singing in this way.

At night, when the sun went down, Grandpa sang other songs, thanking Wakan Tanka for the good red day he had given us. These songs were "silent" teachings. I was meant to hear and absorb them. It was Grandpa's way of setting my feet upon a spiritual path. He did not want me to become "white-man-ized." He said, "Don't be an eagle that turns into a crow or a pigeon." Had he lived today, he would have said, "Don't be an apple—red outside and white inside." He also taught me to get up at 4:30 or 5 every morning, and as soon as I was on my feet to drink a glass of water and thank Wakan Tanka for the new day. I still get up early. I am suspicious of some who call themselves medicine men but who are still in bed at 9 a.m.

Grandpa knew how to bring up a young boy. He never got angry at me. Once in a while, he would say, "Don't do this" or "Don't do that." Most of the time, he just looked at me in a certain way when I did something wrong.

We had few store-bought things. The toys I had were all homemade. Grandpa made them out of horse and cow bones or out of wood. He carved figures of humans, horses, buffalo, and other animals for me. He also made me a toy bow and arrows. The arrows had big knots on the ends instead of sharp points. When I was older, I got a real bow and hunted rabbits. If I killed one for food, I prayed over it like Grandpa had taught me. Grandpa also made me an old-time Lakota sled out of huge buffalo ribs and leg bones. Whenever it snowed, I rode on it, coming down the mountainside at top speed. He also made me flutes out of reeds and white willow stems and taught me how to play them. Often I took the toys Grandpa had made for me, the bone horses and cows, and went up the hills with my friends to play like we were ranchers. We made ourselves a toy corral. We also made animals out of clay and shot at them with our toy bows.

I didn't miss the elaborate playthings white children have because I didn't know they existed. I got no Christmas presents because Christmas was not a traditional Indian feast. One time, when I was nine years old, Uncle Francis Quick Bear bought me a windup Charlie McCarty toy. This doll wore a black hat and a monocle, and when I wound him up, he would walk as if he were drunk. He could also chew, and I used to put sticks in his mouth so he could munch on them while he tottered around. That was the only mechanical thing I ever had. It was the grandest, most magical thing I had ever come across, and I played with it constantly until it fell apart.

We had no radio, for the simple reason that we had no electricity. Also,

Grandpa didn't want to have any of those foolish "white-man things" around. I saw, and heard, my first radio at Uncle Norris Quick Bear's place. I could not believe the strange gibberish (someone speaking in English) that came out of that little box. There had to be a *wapiya*, a "conjurer," hidden somewhere—a belly talker or ventriloquist, as the whites call it.

We didn't have any money. I didn't see a dime or a dollar bill until I was sent to the Catholic boarding school at St. Francis. Grandpa said we didn't need the white man's green "frogskins" to survive. I did not have overshoes and gloves like the half-blood kids. During those famous South Dakota winters, when temperatures can drop to fifty below, Grandpa would wrap gunny sacks around my feet to keep them warm. Sometimes I was lucky enough to have a pair of gloves, but mostly I used a pair of socks for mittens. Grandpa also made me a fur hat and a coat out of animal skins. He was a great improviser.

He was also a great storyteller. Whenever word got around that Grandpa was about to tell stories, all the kids in our neighborhood would pile into our little log cabin to listen. Grandpa had an inexhaustible supply of wonderful, old-time tales—such as the one about We Ota Wichasha, the "blood-clot boy," who was kicked into life by a rabbit; or the one about the woman who swallowed a pebble and gave birth to a stone boy who rescued his brothers from an evil witch. Our favorite funny stories were about Iktome, the Spiderman, a smart-ass trickster who always outsmarts himself. Iktome is greedy, always hungry, always scrounging around for something to steal or trying to get a woman under his blanket.

Of course, Grandpa would also relate to us the sacred legends upon which our religion is founded, such as the tale of Ptesan Win or White Buffalo Calf Woman, who brought the Sacred Pipe to our people and then transformed herself into a white buffalo calf. Grandpa also told many stories about real-life men and women, about ancestor warriors who went on horse-stealing raids against Pawnees or Crows and about their battles with the Mila Hanska, the "Long Knives," which is what we called the U.S. Cavalry.

I still remember the story of one young Lakota brave who rode north all the way to the Little Bighorn and crept right into the center of a large Crow camp and took one of their women out of her family's tipi. Bareback, the two of them jumped on one horse and took off at a dead run. The whole camp was in an uproar. All the Crow warriors jumped on their ponies and took after them. But even though the young Lakota and his captive were doubling up, the Crows could not catch them. They were just too fast.

The pursuers finally came to a halt on top of a hill, totally exhausted, with their horses about to collapse under them. They could only watch the fugitives disappear a long way off amid a cloud of dust. "I guess that Crow *winchinchila* didn't resist being captured very much," Grandpa concluded with a grin.

Once, on our way back from Pine Ridge, Grandpa showed me where the Crows had chased the young warrior and his stolen beauty—through the outcroppings of the Black Hills and the forbidding Badlands. "From Crow country to ours was a long, hard ride," Grandpa told me. "Our Sioux ponies had such speed and endurance in those days that the Crows could not catch up to those two, even though the Crows were riding single and that young man and woman were riding double. He risked his life for love. Had he been caught, they would have killed and scalped him. It was a good thing for that brash, young fellow that he had such a fine horse. Men will do just about anything for love, but you're too young to know about such things. One day you'll find out."

Grandpa also told us how some of the places in our part of the country got their names: "When Big Foot and his band of Mnikowojus came through here on their way to Wounded Knee, where they were massacred by the white soldiers of Custer's old regiment, they stopped in our neighborhood for a while, close to the creek. Suddenly, one woman went completely out of her mind. She ranted and raved with foam on her mouth and started running in circles, faster and faster, without stopping, until she dropped dead from exhaustion. They buried her right over there, near that old dead cottonwood. From that time on, they called that stream Witko Win Wakpala—"Crazy Woman's Creek."

As I said before, Grandpa was a *pejuta wichasha*, a "medicine man" who used many different plants and roots to heal the sick. He always taught me that in order for these herbs to work, there had also to be power— spiritual power. "Takoja, Grandson," he said, "I treat the whole person— spiritually, mentally, and physically—while doing my doctoring. I use the power given to me and the power of the plants, and there must also be a little power on the side of the sick man or woman to bring about a cure.

The sick person plays a big part in the healing process. He must have good thoughts and use whatever he finds that is *wakan*, or "holy," within himself. I don't just treat a little part of him; I have to treat his whole body and all of his mind."

People knew about Grandpa's healing power and came from all around to get his help. He also made "house calls," as a white doctor would have put it. Grandpa had a wagon and a team of buckskin horses, which he used to visit the sick. Often he drove more than 100 or 150 miles to do his doctoring—all the way to Standing Rock and beyond, into Montana; or toward the northeast to Cheyenne River or Eagle Butte; or even all the way to the Santee Reservation on the Missouri River. At that time, there were hardly any white doctors at all in that vast prairie country. There were only Grandpa and a few other traditional medicine men.

Many were the times when Grandpa took me along on his travels. During the long hours of driving along rutted dirt roads (which often disappeared altogether), Grandpa kept me amused by telling me stories—tales of laughter, of sadness, and of magic. Sometimes nightfall would catch us in the middle of nowhere. Then we would make our camp, kindle a fire, and have a mug of *pejuta sapa*—"black medicine," our word for coffee. When it rained, he spread our bedroll underneath the wagon and we went to sleep that way.

When word reached my grandfather that Grandma Lizzie had suffered a stroke, he hitched up his team at once, and we drove over to her place. Many of her family members and friends were waiting there when we arrived. The stroke had left one of Grandma Lizzie's sides paralyzed, and she had lost the power of speech. Grandpa had someone heat a rock over a fire while he and I went to pick certain herbs that were needed for the healing.

When we returned with the herbs, Grandpa took his buffalo horn, which was his most powerful medicine, and went into Lizzie's room. He wrapped her in a buffalo robe, put the heated rock under the small of her back, and purified her with cedar incense, using his eagle wing to fan the fragrant smoke toward her. Then he asked all of us present to leave the house. Standing outside, I heard him singing sacred songs at Lizzie's bedside.

When he had finished his doctoring, Grandpa came out of the house. He said he was hungry and asked the women to cook up something for the two of us. As he and I sat eating, barely half an hour after the doctoring began, Grandma Lizzie came out of the house. She was walking around and chatting as if nothing had happened.

This made a great impression on me, as I fully realized Grandpa's power to heal and the strength of his spirituality. On the other hand, such healings were everyday happenings to me, parts of a life I considered normal and in no way out of the ordinary. I was used to seeing Grandpa perform cures a white doctor might have called miraculous.

Young as I was, Grandpa sometimes allowed me to help him—for example, by holding a broken leg straight while he set it. Every time, after letting me watch his doctoring, he would ask me, "Takoja, did you learn something?"

Back then, we Indians still suffered from diseases that had almost been eradicated among white people. As a boy, I caught smallpox. Grandpa said, "Takoja, these are white man's diseases for which we have no herbs or roots, but I will pray and sing over you, cedar you, and fan you with my eagle wing. I will use the power of my buffalo horn to make you well." I don't know whether it was my strong constitution or the buffalo horn that pulled me through, but I survived.

Grandpa took no money for his doctorings. He asked for no reward, but sometimes a grateful family, thankful for a "house call" involving a round trip of maybe two hundred miles, would present him with a horse. This he would accept after a little coaxing. I remember one occasion when, after making a huge circuit around the whole countryside visiting dozens of sick people, there were six fine horses tied to our wagon as we slowly rumbled home.

My father often told a funny anecdote about how he met his first white man, and I also have a story about how I met my first white man. It happened when I was seven years old. My friends and I were on our way to our favorite swimming hole. We were all barefoot and shirtless. When we came to the top of the hill, we could see that the makeshift bridge had collapsed. Somebody had laid a big log across the creek, and my friends, who were all older than I, walked across on it. They did quite a balancing act. I was afraid of falling into the water and searched for a safer way to cross. Nearby, I discovered a wide plank over a narrow part of the stream. I was about to walk across it when I saw a strange human creature sitting on the bank on the other side. I had never seen a person like that before: he had no hair on the top of his head but lots of it on his face, and he was wearing strange-looking, blue-and-white-striped pants that went up to his armpits and down to his ankles.

I stood open-mouthed, watching him as he sat chewing on something and looking at me. This strange human being never stopped spitting into our swimming hole. He was munching on a sandwich and spitting at the same time, so I figured that maybe he didn't like what he was eating. The stuff he was spewing forth landed in the water, and the fish would come up hopefully and then swim away disappointed. He reached into his sack, pulled out another sandwich, and offered it to me as he waved at me to come across to him. He spoke to me in a gibberish I could not understand. I spoke only Lakota then and did not know a single word of English. He motioned again for me to come to him, but I was afraid.

When he stood up, he looked like a giant. We must have looked like David and Goliath standing at opposite sides of the creek, and I was glad that there was that much deep water between him and myself. He had no shirt beneath his strange pants, and I noticed that his body was covered with hair, which looked like the stuffing coming out of a mattress. I was dumbfounded because I had never seen a man with that much hair on his chest; we Indians have very little body or facial hair.

When he started toward me with the sandwich in his outstretched hand, I turned and ran back up the hill as if the Great Water Monster had been after me. I never looked back to see whether he was following me, but I am sure he couldn't have caught me if he was.

I later learned that the man's strange pants were bib overalls and that the yellow stuff he was spitting into our water hole was chewing tobacco. That man had an extraordinary talent that enabled him to eat sandwiches and chew tobacco at the same time, but it's a talent I wouldn't want to develop. That man left quite an impression on me.

I realize now that I must have met a few white men before that, but if I had, it just hadn't registered with me. Up to the moment I came upon this giant tobacco chewer, I had not been concious of the fact that there were any other people in this world except Lakotas. And so for me, this hairy man in overalls was my first white man.

One man who was a regular visitor at Grandpa's place always came in a black coat with a high, stiff, white collar. He wore an old battered hat and had a short, grizzled beard. I took him for one of our medicine men. It never occurred to me that he was a white man because he used to sit cross-legged on the dirt floor of our cabin, chatting with Grandpa in a singsong voice, speaking fluent Lakota. He always talked about spiritual things, religion and ceremonies. He often stayed for hours and never stopped asking questions. He also spent a lot of time discussing the fine points of our language.

As I grew older, I would come to know him as Father Eugene Buechel, a Jesuit priest from Germany who for many years was head of the Catholic mission at St. Francis on our Rosebud Reservation. He later put together the definitive Lakota-English dictionary, a big, heavy book with over forty thousand words. He also wrote books on Sioux grammar and systematically photographed all his parishioners with his old Kodak box camera.

Grandpa combined his curing trips with going to various traditional ceremonies, and I usually went along. He drove his wagon cross country, straight over the prairie and through the buffalo grass. At that time, the country was not yet fenced in and there was nothing to stop you. The different ceremonies were performed in secret, out of sight of the missionaries and government people because our old beliefs were still being suppressed. We were surrounded on all sides by relatives, members of the extended Quick Bear clan who were traditional spiritual people living in the old Indian way and running the ancient Lakota rituals. Among them were John Singing Goose, Paul Sleeping Bear, Horn Chips, and George Poor Thunder, all of whom were what we call "*yuwipi* men," medicine men who performed the ancient Yuwipi ceremony. Jack and Sam Chasing Horse were singers, always chanting for the people who ran the ceremonies. Moses Bull Tail, Granduncle Spotted Owl, Grover and Abraham Horn Antelope, and Leslie Wood Knife were all spiritual people and medicine men.

One day, Grandpa went into town for groceries and left me at home with my friends. Inspired by my visits to our medicine men relations, and having watched some of the ceremonies, I decided, on the spur of the moment, to run an Inipi, or Purification ceremony, in the sweatlodge. Of course, I was just a young boy, probably about seven years old. Some of my friends were a little older, but not by much. We were all children of traditional families who looked up to and admired our spiritual elders. In our minds, each of us picked one of the medicine men we knew and pretended to be him for our sweat.

The older boys got the fire started and were heating the rocks in the flames. Because I was the youngest and smallest, they sent me with the bucket to bring the water from the creek. I wasn't strong enough to carry a full bucket, so I brought it less than half filled, which was as much as I could carry. We did not have a Pipe to pray with, so we got an L-shaped stick, and that was our pipe.

When we had everything ready, we all piled into the little beehive-shaped lodge we had made out of willow sticks and covered with blankets. We all hunkered down in a circle, sang Purification songs, and poured the cold water over the red, glowing rocks. Enveloped in white-hot steam, we were having a real good Inipi when we ran out of water. The other boys got mad at me for not bringing enough.

We knew enough not to creep out and go to the creek for more water in the middle of the ceremony, which would offend the spirits and bring bad luck. One of the boys decided to solve our water-shortage problem by urinating on the hot rocks. It was not a good idea. The stench was awful and, in that tiny enclosed space, was suffocating us. I knew I shouldn't leave but thought, considering our predicament, that the spirits would forgive me if I just lifted the cover a little and stuck my head out to get some fresh air. So I lay down on the ground and raised the blanket and took a couple of deep breaths.

This felt very good until, peeking out from under the cover, I caught a glimpse of something awful that made my teeth chatter: a pair of brown, hairy, cloven hooves and a skinny tail with a tassle at the end. I dropped the cover pretty fast. "Wakan Sicha, the Devil the missionaries always talk about, what does he look like?" I asked.

One boy said he heard that the Devil had cloven hooves. "Does he have a tail?" I asked.

"Yes, the Devil has a tail for sure."

"Then that's him standing right out there," I said, breaking out in goose pimples in spite of the heat.

Another of my friends peeked out from under the cover, and he, too, saw the Devil's feet and tail. He said, "That's Wakan Sicha, all right. Who-ever peed on those rocks during our ceremony has done wrong, and now the white man's Devil has come to get us for playing with the Inipi."

Now we got really scared. I yelled, "Get me out of here!" I opened the flap and began crawling out when my little friends, in a hurry to get away, ran over me. I jumped up again and tore after them. We were all in a panic to get back to Grandpa's log cabin.

"On the roof! Get on the roof where the Devil can't get at us!" somebody yelled. We were all trying to climb up on the roof, hanging on to each other as we tried to pull ourselves up—and in the frantic scramble pulling each other down instead. We finally managed to get up there, and as we sat shivering on the roof, we grew brave enough to look back toward the sweatlodge. Instead of a terrifying vision of Old Nick himself, we saw a shaggy Highlander bull slowly walking away, swishing his tail behind him. And there we were, sitting on top of the house, mother-naked with dirt clinging to our sweaty bodies. I think we must have looked very foolish. We all were conscious that we should have known better.

That night, when I was going to bed, Grandpa asked me why the blankets were wet. I told him everything. He didn't say anything then, but the next day he told the parents of the other children, and we all caught hell. They took us to Jack Chasing Horse's place, where some of the older men put on a proper Inipi for us so that we could purify ourselves after having done this bad thing. This taught me never to play hard and fast with our religion or ceremonies.

Another time, when I was older, Grandpa had taken off on some business. A friend of his came by and asked me to break a young horse for him. I was already good at this kind of work and had the colt ready for riding in a few days. My friend Rudi and I took the horse back to its owner, Wilson Plenty Bull. When we got to his house, we found many people gathered there for a peyote ceremony. We visited for a while until it began to get dark. Rudi said that he was not ready to go home but wanted to stay for the ceremony. I didn't know anything about peyote, but Rudi's family belonged to the Native American Church, the "Peyote Church." He said they would have oranges, apples, and a lot of sweets at the end of the meeting, so we had better stay. I agreed.

I had no idea about what was going to happen, but I was curious. They offered me some peyote tea, which tasted bitter and had a strange smell. I also ate some chopped-up peyote buttons. I gagged on them but was able to swallow this medicine all the same. Toward morning, the whole world looked yellow to me. My horse seemed to be made of gold. The peyote whirled me around so that I could not gather my thoughts.

After morning water, I got on my horse only with great difficulty. I lost my sense of balance and fell off a couple of times on the way home. For some time, I rode in a circle, not knowing where I was. When I finally reached our log cabin, Grandpa had gotten there ahead of me, and he already knew what had happened.

The peyote cult is not native to the Lakota people. It came to us from the south in the 1920s. Peyote does not even grow anywhere near Sioux country. Grandpa was among those who said that we should not mix peyote with our other ancient rites. He looked at me and said, "You have wandered away from your teachings. You must concentrate on your spiritual teachings and hold on to your knowledge of herbs. Don't be sidetracked." That was all the punishment I got—a few kind words of advice.

At about this time, I also saw my first movie. Grandpa had taken me to visit relatives in a small town called Midland. My cousins there took me to see a film. It was a war story. I hadn't learned English yet, so I couldn't make heads or tails of it. Tanks and armored cars seemed to be headed straight for me, so I got scared and averted my eyes.

When we got back to our relatives' house, my uncle asked me what I had seen. I told him that I had seen huge iron wagons shooting at each other, that one man had killed a lot of people, and that at the end they had put safety pins all over his chest. My uncle laughed and explained that these were ribbons and medals the white men gave to their warriors for brave deeds instead of eagle feathers.

A few other childhood happenings stand out in my memory—funny and ridiculous things. There was, for instance, the great egg smash-up. I did not know about Easter, a white man's festival that Grandpa wanted nothing to do with. Nor did I know about Easter eggs or about eggs in general. I had never eaten a chicken egg, for the simple reason that Grandpa wouldn't have any chickens around the place. In his opinion, they were sorry critters bred by the white man—indecent caricatures of wild birds.

Well, one day, my uncle and auntie came to have a proper Easter feast. They lived close to Norris and had adopted some of the white man's customs. Grandpa grumbled something about white-man foolishness and made himself rare, leaving the field to my aunt. She had brought a whole crate of eggs, intending to boil and color them. Of course, she was going to hide them to have an Easter-egg hunt for the children, but I didn't know that.

All of a sudden, my aunt remembered that she had forgotten all kinds of things she needed for her big Easter festival, and she and her husband went off again in their wagon to get the stuff. They left the crate of eggs by the cabin door. I looked at these strange white things and picked one up. It slipped from my fingers and broke. I looked at the yellow yolk spreading out on the earth. It looked beautiful. Then I set the eggs out on the ground in a row and started throwing them, one after another, against the side of our log cabin. I marveled at the sight of them smashing, turning the whole side of the little house yellow, their yolks dripping down like paint. I felt like an artist creating something beautiful.

After I had thrown the last egg, I just stood there for a long time, admiring my work. When my uncle and aunt came back, Auntie threw a fit. I couldn't understand why. All I could say was, "Isn't it beautiful?" After a while, Grandpa appeared. He had one look at the whole mess and all those eggshells, and he just laughed.

Another time, Grandpa hitched up his team to go to Norris for supplies. As usual, I went along. It was late in the day, and Grandpa was in a great hurry. He got the horses to go faster and faster until we were racing along on that rutted road like a movie stagecoach pursued by outlaws. Suddenly we hit a rock, a wheel came off, and Grandpa went over one side in a great arc while I flew through the air in the other direction.

I landed, rolled over on the grass, and wasn't hurt at all. Grandpa had skinned one side of his face, but he laughed as if the whole mishap had been one great joke. The hub had come off the wheel, and it took some time to get it back on again. It was now too late for getting to Norris, so we turned around toward home again. Grandpa was still beside himself with laughter.

"Takoja, Grandson," he said, after getting his breath back, "you must learn to have a good laugh at yourself when you make a mistake." So that was another lesson Grandpa taught me.

One of my aunts took me to a box social at the church. For that occasion, all the girls of the whole valley of Corn Creek had made boxes, stuffing them with cakes, cookies, or whatever else they made. On the boxes were the names of the girls who made them. And there were a lot of boys there, older than I, who were more interested in the girls than in the boxes.

The boxes were auctioned off, and the auctioneer would always say, "This comes from Ruth," or "from Francine," or "from Twila." The bids went from a penny to a nickel to a dime. When a boy heard the name of a girl he liked, he would bid sometimes the enormous sum of a quarter. But sometimes there was only a little bit of old, dried fry bread in a box. The whole thing bored me. I was still too young to be interested in girls. Besides, I did not have even a single penny.

Sometimes, when I asked Grandpa questions he said he could not answer, he would tell me that I must find the answer for myself. He would point to a mountain called Cross Butte and say, "Go up there. There you'll find the answer." So I would climb to the top of that mountain, and I would lie there and think and dream. Up there my mind would often wander, and sometimes I would reach a point where I seemed to be floating in space. I could look down and see my body lying there on the mountain. I seemed to be traveling through the universe, through time and an infinite variety of colors, to places I had never seen, places that existed only in visions.

Sometimes I seemed to travel as a thumb, or even as a fingernail. After returning once again into my body, I would go down and tell Grandpa what I had experienced. He said that, for me, Cross Butte was a sacred place and that I should climb it whenever I felt the need, for on that mountaintop, I would gain much of the power I would need in years to come.

From the ages of seven to fourteen, my grandfather taught me. I have used much of his practical wisdom all my life, but only after I turned forty did I start drawing from his bank of spiritual knowledge.

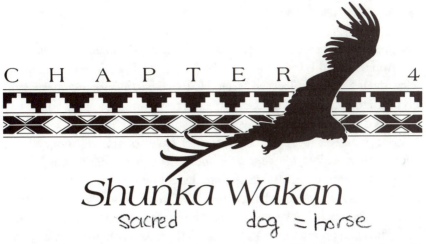

C H A P T E R 4

Shunka Wakan
sacred   dog = horse

Shunka wakan means "sacred dog." It is our Lakota word for "horse." There were no horses in America until the white men brought them from across the oceans, one of the very few good things they brought us. Before we had horses, dogs were our only beasts of burden. We harnessed two sticks to their shoulders and tied bundles to them, which the dogs dragged along. This was called a dog travois. So when the Lakotas got their first horses, they had no word for this wonderful new animal. The horse could carry burdens like the dog, only much better, so they called it the "holy dog" or "sacred dog."

When I was a kid, it was said that we Sioux learned to ride before we learned to walk. Everybody had horses, and we kids knew how to ride them. Nowadays, Chevy, Ford, and Toyota are the names of our ponies. There are fewer horses and fewer men or women who can ride, but when I was a young boy, horses were my pride and joy.

Grandpa always had some nineteen or twenty horses around. He constantly gave horses away at honoring feasts and similar occasions, but people always gave him more ponies as a way to thank him for having cured them. The horses changed, but the number remained more or less the same, so I had a whole remuda to choose from.

In the old days, during a battle, a warrior could hang on to the side of his pony so that the body of the horse shielded the body of the man. All an enemy could see of the rider was one foot clinging to the withers. That way, the warrior could avoid being shot at or getting an arrow between his ribs. He could suddenly pop up, fire his own weapon, and, quick as a flash, disappear again behind his pony's flank. He could do all that at a dead run.

And so could I. One day, somebody was having a Yuwipi ceremony a few miles from our place. My friend Curtis Chasing Horse came over on his pinto to pick me up, but Grandpa did not want me to go. "You're too young for that," he said, "too young for staying out all night."

But I wanted to go. I was curious, and I was also thinking about all that good food they always have at a ceremony: *wojapi* or "berry soup," sweet *wasna* or "pemmican," and beef soup. I went behind the trees where the horses were tied and picked a fast one. We didn't have any saddles because they cost too much, but I was used to riding bareback. I let Curtis ride ahead, then I jumped on my horse and hung on the side, with just one foot and one hand sticking out. I started after Curtis, away from the cabin so that Grandpa wouldn't see me, but just when I thought I was well clear of the place, that damn horse turned around and headed for home.

I was still hanging on to the side when the horse came to a dead stop in front of our cabin, with Grandpa sitting outside on a bench. He could see me as plain as day, and he hollered, "Hey, get off that horse! What do you think you're doing? It's getting dark. It's no time to be clowning around. Leave that horse alone!" So I didn't make it to that ceremony. I put it down to Grandpa's medicine power that had turned that horse around.

At that time, the country was still full of horses. There were horses everywhere you looked, in all directions. Once there was a big horse drive that came through our valley from Nebraska. We were told that some outfit was moving those horses from Texas all the way to Canada. As far as I could see, there were horses moving in a great sea of dust, the Earth trembling beneath their hooves.

The herd stopped at Grandpa's place to water at the nearby reservoir. There, the wranglers told us that the young foals couldn't make the trip— that some were dying because they were too young to keep up. They told us that if we could catch them, we could keep as many as we wanted.

Every Indian at Corn Creek was grabbing anything that could be used to catch colts: ropes, the driving reins from harnesses, even clotheslines. We caught dozens of young horses and cared for them as best we could. We lost some that were too young to be away from their mother's milk or that had been driven beyond what their little bodies could stand, but we saved most of them and added them to our pony herds.

When my mother died, she left me a big overland wagon, a matched pair of buckskin team horses, and their offspring—a mare and a colt. These were my own personal horses, not Grandpa's. In time, the mare gave birth to a foal, which I named Ribbon. She was the one horse I loved above all others. I raised her as if she had been a human baby, and she became a part of me.

Ribbon was a strawberry roan. To me, she was the most beautiful being in the world. She had a long, snakelike body, and her movements were as graceful as those of a deer. She was affectionate, playful, and fast—the fastest horse within a hundred miles. As Ribbon and I got older, I entered her in every race in the valley. And when she got going, it seemed like all the other horses were standing still.

Ribbon and I were inseparable. Wherever I went, she went. One night, I was coming home late. It was pitch dark, and I was riding bareback. Ribbon was ambling along at a slow walk when we went from soft ground onto a hard gravel road. Suddenly, I heard a sound behind me, like someone walking after me with a cane. It made me uneasy. Who could be walking there in the middle of nowhere on a night as dark as this?

I kicked the horse into a trot, trying to get away from the ghostly sound, but the "tap, tap, tap" of that damn walking stick kept right after me. I kicked Ribbon again. Now she was trotting so fast I was almost sliding off her back. I grabbed her mane, pulled myself up, and listened, but the cane was coming on even faster.

"Ribbon," I said, "now you're going to run home as fast as your legs can go. Hiyupo!" I closed my eyes and just turned her loose and held on. When we went over the wooden bridge near home, Ribbon's hooves and the cane together made a noise like somebody running a stick very fast along a picket fence. The tap, tap, taps were no longer distinct but just blended into one rattling sound, like a machine gun.

Ribbon was running, and I knew I was getting close to the house. By now, I could see the tipi I was living in at the time. (The little log cabin had become too small to hold both Grandpa and me.) Inside the tipi, a kerosene lamp was lit. I made a run for it. We got there panting, Ribbon and I. I dismounted so fast that I took the bridle off at the same time. Then I tripped over a tent pin and went flying. Inside the tipi was a wood stove, and it was red hot. The edge of my left hand hit the stove, and to this day I have a big scar there to remind me of my clumsiness.

Grandpa heard my scream. "What's going on?" he yelled.

"There's a ghost chasing me!"

He came to the door and looked. "It's Ribbon," he said. "She's standing outside. I think I can show you what that ghost is."

But I refused to leave my tipi. All night I was shivering. That was the first time I had been chased by anything that was as fast as Ribbon.

When I woke up, it was daylight, and Ribbon was still standing outside my tipi. I petted her and thanked her for having carried me safely home. Then I jumped on her back and guided her with my knees to the well and the nearby watering trough. As I rode, I heard that cane again, and I realized that what had chased me hadn't been a ghost after all. The sound was coming from inside Ribbon's hipbone. Every time she took a step, it clicked; it was the strangest thing. I watered Ribbon and turned her loose to join the other horses. Then I went home to tell Grandpa.

I found him chatting with one of my uncles. "That ghostly noise is coming out of Ribbon's hip," I said.

Grandpa laughed. "I could have told you that last night," he said, "but you were too scared to listen."

"How did you know?" I asked.

"Takoja, Grandson, when a horse eats too much alkali dirt, its bones dry up in the hip socket. Ribbon is too young to know not to eat that white stuff. Just keep her away from it. She'll be OK in a week. Don't ride her until then." It seemed to me then that Grandpa knew everything there was to know.

Ribbon and I stayed together for years, even after Grandpa died. But then my uncle put me in the Catholic boarding school at St. Francis, and I could not take her there with me. I hated that school.

But one day I saw Ribbon near the school. I don't know how she got there. She recognized me at once and came running, putting her soft, velvety muzzle against my cheek. At first I was mad at my uncle, who was supposed to be taking care of her, but Ribbon's being there suddenly gave me the idea of running away. I jumped on her back, and off we went.

I am still sorry I did not take her back to Corn Creek to stay. Instead, I took her back to my uncle's. Of course, I was caught and sent back to school, and later my uncle went and sold Ribbon. He also sold or gave away everything else I had in this world—the things my mother had left me: the buckskins, the wagon, and my harnesses. I did not mind losing these things, but the loss of Ribbon crushed me. I felt as if my life had ended.

I think when my uncle saw how hard I took it, he felt sorry for what he had done, because the summer after he sold Ribbon, he came to St. Francis. I heard him calling, "Archie, come here, I have something to show you."

I went outside, and there stood a gray horse. He was beautiful, but his ears were cropped. My uncle said, "I have brought you a horse. Try him out."

I got on and pulled on the reins. The horse tore down the hill, right through Rosebud where my uncle lived, thundered along on the blacktop and across the bridge, and then raced up the hills on the opposite side. I couldn't stop him until I got clear to the fairgrounds. He galloped furiously for over over four miles.

I brought the runaway back and gave the reins to my uncle. "No, no," he said, "he's yours. Now you have a horse again."

"*Pilamaye*," I said, "but no, thank you." Out of resentment that he had sold Ribbon, I did not accept the gray. My uncle was sad for not being able to make it up to me, and he got rid of that horse, but I could never get Ribbon out of my mind. I can still see her long, graceful, honey-colored body in my dreams. I can still see her eyes looking at me, shining like dark crystals.

Naturally, I also had dogs. My favorite was Jack. I don't know who gave him his name. He was already four years old when I was born, and he became my dog and grew up with me. Jack was black with long hair, white around the neck and brown around the nose. He followed me wherever I went—barefoot, shirtless, and free.

Whenever we came across a rattlesnake, Jack would pounce on it, grab it behind the neck, bite its head off, and shake it to pieces. He killed rattlers but never any other kind of snake. He seemed to know that the water snakes and garter snakes I used to play with were harmless. He thought of himself as my protector. He was the best dog I have ever known, and he was also gentle with the other pets I raised. I had another dog named Duke. I loved him, too, but he was never as close to me as Jack. Duke died from a rattlesnake bite.

When I went after rabbits, Jack always came along, but he was the better hunter. If I came home with five rabbits, four of them had been caught by

Jack. Whenever we came back from hunting or trapping with a bunch of rabbits, Grandpa would look at me and smile, asking "Which ones are Jack's?" And I would have to admit that *most* of them were. Then Grandpa would tease me: "Takoja, I guess that dog is a better man than you."

It annoyed me that I found myself in competition with Jack, and it annoyed me even more that he always beat me. One morning I thought, "Today I shall win out." I tied Jack up so that he couldn't hunt while I trapped. But I didn't catch anything that day. When I came back, I untied Jack. He didn't greet me as usual but walked away from me because he knew that I had pulled an unfair trick on him. I was standing there with the rope in my hand when Grandpa came up. He said, "It seems there's some dog hair on that rope."

"It sure looks like it," I agreed.

"Well, Grandson, what good things did you bring us today?"

"I didn't have any luck today, Tunkashila."

"Well, that's all right," he said. "We have enough. I think somebody tied Jack up by mistake, so I let him loose, and he came back with two rabbits in his mouth. Then I tied him up again. Give thanks to Wakan Tanka that we have at least one good hunter in the family to provide for us." Grandpa ambled off, grinning from ear to ear.

After my Easter egg flop, I developed a taste for eggs. Grandpa still would not keep chickens, those unholy creations of the white man, but there were always wild duck eggs. I could never take Jack along when I was going after ducks because he always beat me to them. He always got there first, lapped up the eggs, and sometimes got a duck, too. I didn't want him to catch the ducks because the eggs have to be picked up in the middle of the night, somewhere between 3 and 4 a.m., before sunrise. By midday, they're no longer good for eating because there's already the beginning of a little duckling in them.

Good old Jack shared all my growing-up years with me. Even after Grandpa's death, when I lived with my uncle at Rosebud, every time we visited the old homestead, Jack was there. He was a survivor. He didn't need anyone to feed him; he hunted for himself. For years, he lived near the old log cabin all by himself. Some of my relatives who lived three or four miles away left some bones and scraps for him once in a while. They might not have seen him, but they knew he was there.

In August of 1955, after four years in the military, I felt a great need to see the old log cabin again. I still had my uniform on. Grass and weeds had grown up around the place. I sat down among them, leaning against the cabin's side with sun in my face, trying to recapture the old days, ten years gone, when Grandpa had still been alive.

At that moment, Jack came around the corner. Most of his teeth were gone. He was blind in one eye, his hair was falling out, and he was limping badly with age. But he recognized me, smelled me, wagged his ancient tail, and put his head in my lap. I was twenty years old and knew exactly how old Jack had to be: twenty-four. He had grown that old living his last years all by himself.

Jack's death

I sat there for a long time with Jack's head in my lap, stroking and talking softly to him. Then suddenly I noticed that he had stopped breathing. He had died right there in my lap. I think he had stayed alive until then because he was determined to see me one more time. Today, there is no one living near the old place, and the cabin is falling apart, but there are still a lot of spirits around. Whenever I go there, I can feel their presence.

Grandpa looked on all animals, big and small, as relatives, not much different from humans, and he instilled in me the same love for all wild creatures. So I had many wild pets. One of Grandpa's friends once brought me a fawn that still had white spots on its reddish-brown skin. We fed it milk from a bottle. Of course, we had no refrigerator, so we used powdered milk. Later, Grandpa made a kind of mush out of the milk, mixed with grains and herbs. I raised the fawn until he became a full-grown buck.

I also had a pet skunk. Its name was Gleza, which means "striped." Grandpa took the scent bag out and sewed up the wound as if he had been a veterinarian. Gleza was very affectionate, but one day he met a lady skunk and went off with her. I guess he preferred her company to mine.

One day I was hunting for duck eggs at Corn Creek, at the bottom along the stream, when I saw a big owl sitting in her nest in a treetop. Hinhan, the Owl, means bad luck. Her hooting at night means that someone is dead or dying. So, as a boy, I was afraid of owls, particularly at night. But this was full daylight, when owls have no power, and I decided to find out what she had in her nest.

I climbed up the tree, and the owl flew away. In the nest were three little balls of down feathers with big yellow eyes—three small, fuzzy owlets with their beaks wide open. The mother owl made a dive at me and I ducked to protect my eyes. Soon her mate arrived, and the two big birds tried to knock me off the tree. I grabbed the three little ones, stuffed them into my shirt, and shinnied down. The parents followed me for about half a mile and finally gave up.

I ran home with those fluffy things in my shirt screeching, making baby owl noises. They couldn't fly or hop or walk yet. Their beaks were always open—"Gimme, gimme, gimme!" So I had to hunt for them. I was running all over the place, catching grasshoppers and feeding them to my new pets. The more I fed them, the more they wanted.

Grandpa looked at my owls, then brought out an old washtub and put straw and dry grass in it. He told me, "That will be their new nest. You've created quite a job for yourself. You're going to be father and mother to these owls. And you're going to work hard for them because they eat around the clock. They never stop. You won't get much sleep now. You'll be busy all the time feeding them worms, bugs, and grasshoppers. That's all you're going to do. And in a few days, you'll start them on raw meat and maybe a dead bird or rodent, and they'll take bites out of your fingers if you don't watch out. Well, hop to it! They're already screeching for their grub again."

owls

All during the months of May, June, July, and August, I played the role of Mama Owl and Papa Owl. Every day I had to hunt for them, and they grew bigger and bigger and bigger. Pretty soon they came hopping out of the washtub, surrounding me, hooting away: "Gimme, gimme, gimme!"

A friend of Grandpa's, the medicine man Abraham Horn Antelope, came to visit us. "You've got yourself quite a passel of owls," he said, "Do you have names for them?"

"Yes," I answered, "their names are Wanji, Nunpa, and Yamni," which mean "One," "Two," and "Three" in Lakota. I was the only one who knew which was One, which was Two, and which was Three. To others, the owls looked the same, but I could tell them apart by little differences—especially the slightly different colors of their feathers, stripes, and faces.

By September, they were beginning to fly. I took them up to the roof and threw one up into the air. It flew around in a circle and came back. The others did the same thing. I taught them to fend for themselves, but for a week longer they depended on me, hopping around my feet or sitting on my shoulder with their beaks open. In October, a night came when the leaves started to fall. I was sitting outside the cabin with my owls around me, and I said, "OK, that's it. You birds are on your own. You're old enough to fend for yourselves and to give me a vacation."

I think they understood, because after waiting in vain to get their goodies from me, they flew off into the trees. And all night they hooted. Before that time, I had been afraid of the hooting of owls, thinking they were ghostly spirits of dead people, but now I knew that these were my owls making their music, and I was no longer afraid.

Wanji, Nunpa, and Yamni stayed around the place for a while, dropping in for a visit now and then, but their visits got increasingly rare and finally stopped altogether. I think I started a whole owl population with my three birds. To this day in Corn Creek Valley, if you walk at night to where nobody lives, you can hear the hooting of many owls—maybe as many as a hundred, talking to each other. I feel that these are my grandchildren, the offspring of the three birds I raised. We have a few big prairie dog towns in the valley, and that's where the owls get most of their food, keeping the rodent population down.

One day I came across a magpie with a broken wing. I brought him to Grandpa, who fixed him up so that he could fly again. So now I had a magpie for a pet. He was beautiful—shiny black, with a long tail and big, white, oval patches on each side. He had round, very intelligent-looking eyes that sparkled like black diamonds. I thought maybe he was as smart as myself, maybe even smarter. He made himself a little nest in the rafters, where he kept this stolen loot—bits of glass and metal, a marble, a quartz pebble, anything bright or shiny. He would have stolen a man's gold watch, except that nobody in Corn Creek Valley had such a precious thing.

That magpie could talk. I taught him to say, "*Hau, witko?*" which means, "How are you doing, crazy man?" Then Grandpa split his tongue so he could talk even better. This magpie of mine would fly from tree to tree, or even to the homes of neighbors, screeching, "*hau, hau, hau*" ("hello, hello, hello") or "*witko, witko, witko*" ("crazy, crazy, crazy").

One day, one of Grandpa's friends, Adam Horn Antelope, dropped in for a visit. The magpie was sitting in the rafters of the log cabin looking down on us, but Adam had not noticed it. I was sitting at the table playing with some bone horses Grandpa had carved for me. The magpie screeched loudly, "*Hau, witko?*"

Adam looked hard at me. "What did you say?"

The magpie cried again, "*Hau, witko?*"

Horn Antelope was very annoyed. "You said a bad thing. You should not talk like this to old folks. Didn't your grandfather teach you to respect the elders?"

The magpie went on and on: "*Hau, witko? Hau, witko?*" I stuck my finger out, and the bird flew down onto the table and hopped onto my finger. I started feeding him bread and meat scraps. When old Adam realized that the magpie had called him crazy, he laughed and slapped his thighs. He thought it was the funniest thing he had ever heard. The strange thing about this was that Adam was stone deaf. Grandpa had to talk to him in sign language, but he had understood the magpie's high-pitched, piercing screech perfectly.

Grandpa always told me, "Look around, Grandson. If you see magpies hanging around a house, it means that the people there have meat. They have just killed a deer or rustled some cattle, some 'slow elk.' So if you're hungry, drop in where there are magpies, and you'll be fed."

These were my happiest years, living with Grandpa in his little log cabin, close to nature, surrounded by my four-legged and winged friends.

CHAPTER 5

Alien Gods

Grandpa always told me, "Takoja, pay attention to what I am trying to teach you while I am still here, for my time is not very long." I could not imagine a world without Grandpa. I thought he would always be there to protect and teach me. I was eleven years old when I saw him coming toward me for the last time. There was something in his walk and the way he looked at me that made me tremble. When he had nearly reached the spot where I was standing, he suddenly fell to his knees and reached for me. There were tears in his eyes. I grabbed his hand. He took hold of it and cried.

"Grandson, Grandson, watch yourself," he said. "Be a help to your people. Pray with the Pipe. I will watch over you always."

I wept, too, because I sensed that Grandpa was on his way to another world. He died holding onto my hand. His grip was so strong that, even after he was dead, it was hard for my uncle to pry his hand loose. Grandpa was gone. They laid him to rest next to my mother, the same earth becoming their blanket. Part of myself died with him, but he still lives with me. I could not fully measure my loss then, but I felt that a great emptiness had replaced him. I thought, "Grandpa, what will I do now that you are gone?"

A Sacred Pipe song my grandfather always sang to me began, "My son, you are going to travel a hard road." I started walking that road in 1947, the moment they laid Grandpa in his grave. My uncle Francis took me to live with him in Rosebud, and a short time later came the day all Lakota children hope will never come: *anpetu sicha*, the "worst of all days," the day of doom.

45

There is a kind of monster our women threaten disobedient children with called the *chichiye*. Nobody knows exactly what the *chichiye* is like, but it must be a truly horrible creature, because a woman will say, "*Hoksila*, little boy, behave yourself, or the *chichiye* will get you!" She might also say: "*Hoksila*, if you are bad, the white man will come and take you away—*wasichu amgnikte!*"

For me, the day of doom dawned when the *chichiye* appeared in the shape of a bearded white man in a black dress with a white collar. This was Father Buechel, whom I had already met and who could speak Lakota in a strange, singsong voice. When he talked, he sounded like a bell. Buechel had come to take me away from the world I knew to another, frightening world—the Catholic boarding school at St. Francis, some ten miles away from Rosebud.

For me, the distance might as well have been a hundred thousand miles, because children at St. Francis were totally cut off from their families. As far as I was concerned, St. Francis was as far away from Corn Creek as the moon. I was scared but somewhat reassured because Father Buechel seemed to be a nice man who could speak to me in my own language. I was soon to find out that the other priests and nuns were altogether different human beings.

I now had to live under strange, alien gods. There were three chief Christian gods, we were told: the Father, Wakan Tanka Chincha; the Son, whose name was Jesus; and Woniya Wakan, the Holy Spirit, who I thought must be something like Wakinyan, the Thunderbird, because he was depicted as some kind of pigeon. They also had a chief woman god, the mother of Wakan Tanka Chincha. She had a husband named Joe, but her son's father was Woniya Wakan, the strange pigeon god. Joe didn't seem to mind. There were also dozens of lesser gods, represented by plaster-cast statues with outstretched hands, as if they wanted to catch Indian souls. Some were painted in gaudy colors. One of them had birds all over him—obviously a god of swallows. We were supposed to kneel before these statues and pray to them, but when I did not want to pray to these plaster-cast figures that depicted only white men, they took the strap to me.

At St. Francis, we were forbidden to speak our language, to pray in Lakota to the Great Spirit with the Pipe, or to go to Inipi or on Vision Quests. They tried to make us forget Tunkashila, White Buffalo Calf

Interesting perspective on catholic religion

Woman, the Pipe—all our ancient beliefs. They wanted us to love their white gods. And, if we did not, they would try to beat that love into us with a strap or a ruler.

Every Sunday morning, they took us to Mass at about 10:30. Mass was read in Latin, and even some of the English-speaking kids complained that they couldn't make heads or tails of it. To me, it made no difference. I couldn't have understood it if they had done it in English. From the beginning, the priests always tried to keep the boys away from the girls—even the little ones. At Mass, the girls were always sitting on the left aisle and the boys on the right.

After Mass came lunch. About 5 p.m., they would take us back to church for benediction, where we would pray for another hour before supper. It was hard on the knees. I couldn't understand why these Catholics spent so much time on their knees. I had been taught to pray to my Indian Creator standing up, and to make it short and simple.

The first time I went inside the church, I noticed a bowl of water on the wall on the way in. I saw the boy in front of me dip his hand in the water. From where I was standing, it seemed to me that he drank it. So I cupped my hand, dipped it in, and took a drink. I spat the water out immediately because it tasted awful. A lot of other kids had already put their hands into it, and who knows what they had been doing before that?

The kid behind me said I was not supposed to drink it but to use my moistened fingers to touch my forehead and each shoulder. I asked him what that was for. He laughed and said it was the sign of the cross. I told him that he was wrong, that it was a sign of the Sacred Four Directions. I told him that these were the Four Winds bringing to us the powers of the Great Spirit.

This kid snitched on me, and a little later a priest took me up to the attic with his leather strap. I had broken the two biggest rules of the mission school: talking in my Lakota language and talking about Indian religion. I could not understand their rules.

At St. Francis, we all had to wear the same kind of clothes, including identical shirts, pants, jackets, and shoes. The heavy, stiff shoes were particularly hard on me, since I was used to moccasins or going barefoot. The priests and nuns tried to make us into little white people, and I began to suspect that their god loved white people more than he loved Indians.

The priests we were most afraid of were Father Fagan and Father Healy. On the spur of the moment, they would take you up to the attic. They would take along a tug, the thickest part of the strap used to hitch a horse to a wagon. They made us pull our pants down and then whipped us on the buttocks with a piece of tug. Sometimes they whipped us on the backs of our legs below the knees, giving us ten, fifteen, or twenty swats for little things like talking in class.

There is a harmless little children's game called *chanpa su on kichiopi* in which you take a handful of cherries and use a forked stick to shoot cherry pits at each other. Well, another kid and I did this, and we got a terrific beating. To me, this came as a great shock. I had never been beaten before. Indians never spank their children as white parents do. There were some kids, usually half-breeds, who acted as informers. If they heard anyone speak in Lakota or mention one of our ceremonies, they would run at once to one of the priests and snitch on us.

The ones most often beaten were myself, Collins Horse Looking, and the Long Pumpkins brothers, because we came from traditional families and spoke almost no English. We were beaten even for things we did not do. For very slight infractions, we were not allowed to see the Saturday night movies, were deprived of food, or given the worst kind of cleanup jobs. For the worst infractions, they had a cell in the attic where they might lock us in for twelve or even twenty-four hours, something akin to doing solitary inside a penitentiary.

Our little Indian sisters did not fare any better. They, too, had to take their panties down when getting a spanking from the nuns. The most feared among the nuns was the one who took care of the clothes. We called her "Sister Mouse," because she looked like a rodent. She had big, protruding buck teeth. To me, she looked like a rat. Her specialty was pulling on our ears. Sometimes I was afraid she would yank them clear off. She was also handy with a ruler. Once, the Mouse came after me for something or other, but in her ankle-length habit, she was not fast enough to catch me. Love comes through the heart; you cannot instill the love of Jesus through the buttocks.

One of the priests was Father Klaus, a man of German descent who had been an army chaplain during the Second World War. He made us march out there on the playground with sticks instead of rifles. He marched us around in cadence: "Left flank, right flank, about face, to the rear, march!" As far as he was concerned, we could have been in a military school. If we'd had blond hair and blue eyes, you might have taken us for Hitler youth in Nazi Germany.

Not all the priests were bad. The one we liked best was Brother Perry, who was in charge of the greenhouse where I worked for a time when I was in fifth and sixth grades. Perry taught me gardening and gave me a lot of popcorn as encouragement.

September was spud-picking time. The school was partly self-sufficient and owned big potato fields. We'd pick enough 'taters to last through the winter. The school also handed out hundred-pound bags of potatoes, carrots, turnips, and rutabagas to hungry families. There was a big root cellar where I worked. I'd go down there to sort out the rotten vegetables and keep the good ones. We cut out the bad parts and ate the good ones. The mission also had its own milk cows, and I got to milk some of them. They also had a bakery where the school's bread was made.

Each of us boy students was supposedly learning to be a farmer, baker, or shoe repairman. The priests would go to the nearest town to get old car tires, and some of the kids had to make shoe soles out of them. I was forced to learn shoe repair, but I was no good at it, so they gave up on me. They also had a carpentry shop. The priests thought that we Indians were only good at menial jobs. They did not prepare us to become teachers, lawyers, or doctors.

Much later in life, I learned about Christ's teaching and found it beautiful. To me, Christ seemed like an Indian, oppressed and killed by the Roman conquerors. Even so, I never accepted Christianity; it was too different from Lakota religion. For us kids, the word "Jesus" always conjured up memories of the leather strap.

Many times, I tried to run away, but I was always caught and brought back to get a beating. Once, one of the priests heard me singing an Indian song and whipped me badly. I was in despair. I went out into the field, lay down on the grass, and wept. I prayed in Lakota, "Grandfather Spirit, pity me. Must I live like this?"

Father Buechel, my grandfather's old friend, would console me when I had reached my lowest point. I think those priests like Buechel, who took the trouble to learn our language, absorbed some of our Indian ways and beliefs. He understood how hard it was for us to adjust to the white God's ways.

Once I asked Father Buechel, "In your religion, is there a Spirit World?"

"Let me tell you," he said. "Before we had cars here, I used to make regular trips to Parmelee, Martin, Black Pipe, Bad Nation, or Spring Creek. It was a long journey with horse and buggy. I would stop and drop in on the Indian families along the way, and they always welcomed and fed me as if I had been a Lakota myself.

"On one such trip, I was caught by bad weather," Father Buechel continued. "I was hungry, cold, and tired. Nearby was the house of a family I had been visiting for years. They had always been especially generous and hospitable to me, and I had a warm spot in my heart for them. I saw no one around, either outside or inside the house. I found that they had left a fire in the stove, and the table was set with a good meal that included freshly baked bread, still warm, and a pot of hot coffee. I warmed myself, relaxed a bit, enjoyed my meal, and got on my way again.

"On my return trip, I made a point of stopping again at this family's home, because I had missed them when I had come through before, but I found their house burned to the ground with nothing remaining but a heap of black ashes. I went to their nearest neighbors, told them of my previous stop, and asked where the family was now. I said I wanted to help them in any way I could.

"These neighbors looked at me in a very strange way and shook their heads. They told me that I could not have eaten there a few days before, that the house had burned down more than a month before, and that everyone in it had perished in the flames.

"I was quite shaken. I returned to the home of my dead friends and set up my portable altar and said Mass for them. It made me realize that this is Indian country, where things happen that cannot be explained by the white man's science."

When Christmas arrived, no one came to take me home. I was left at St. Francis with about six other kids who also were orphans. I was in the dormitory all by myself, and that was the loneliest time I ever had. I was glad when the other kids came back and school started again. I learned prayers by rote from their catechism and was baptized, but I didn't feel or think any different afterwards.

There was a kid in the eleventh or twelfth grade who always stuck up for the smaller boys and girls. His name was Zondo Swally, and he was not afraid of the priests—they were afraid of *him*. Once, during Mass, I got bored. To break the monotony, I took a rubber band and made spitballs from a page I had torn out of the prayer book. I was shooting some boys in the back of their heads, and when they turned around to find out who had done it, I looked very innocent. I was having a good time when one of the priests walked up the aisle. He managed to get in the line of fire, and I hit him in the back of the head. He spun around, but he wasn't fast enough to catch me.

I found that shooting priests was more fun than shooting the other kids. I reloaded and aimed at the priest's head again. Just as I let go, he turned, and I caught the side of his nose. This time he saw who had done it, and he came after me with a vengeance, looking so ferocious that I froze to the spot. He grabbed my ear and started to pull me out of my place when a fist came flying over my shoulder. It was Swally's. The blow knocked the priest off to the side. Swally jumped over a row of benches and grabbed the priest, and they got into it.

It was a terrific all-or-nothing fight, but the black-robed one was hampered by his long, flapping cassock. When it was over, the good Father was lying knocked out cold in the middle of the church aisle. The Mass went on as if nothing had happened.

After that, I lost all my privileges, and, every chance he got, that priest found some excuse to give me a beating. Nothing happened to Swally because they were too afraid of him. He also knew too much—like which of the priests overdisciplined the little boys.

Some of the older *winchinchilas* likewise were not afraid to take on the nuns, such as the Great Mouse, on behalf of the smaller girls. They did not mind getting into a kicking and hair-pulling free-for-all with the reverend mothers.

The priests tried to instill in us a sense of sin and a fear of the Devil and hellfire everlasting. They depicted Old Nick ("Wakan Sicha" in our language) as a nasty, vengeful fellow with horns, cloven hooves, and a hairy behind like a mountain goat, and a buffalo's tail. I thought this was an insult to the animals, our four-legged relatives. My father always said, "You whites invented the Devil; you can keep him." That was my feeling too.

One day, I had a sudden craving for sweets. I thought I'd go to town to get me some candy, but I never had any money in my pocket. I went into the church and knelt down before the big collection box. I made the sign of the cross and said, "I'm sorry, white man's God, but I need some of your money to buy some candy."

I managed to fish fifty cents out of that box and sneaked off to the store in town. In those days, fifty cents bought a lot of candy, and I spent the whole afternoon sitting in the shade of a big cottonwood eating it all up. I was a little apprehensive about what the white God might do to me, but he never noticed. I felt no sense of sin in the Christian manner, but I was ashamed of having stolen something that did not belong to me.

Father Buechel always told me, "Do not forget your old religion," but the other priests took me up to the attic to beat it out of me. I could not understand it; it just made no sense.

The next year, after school, they let us out for the summer. Uncle Francis came to get me and took me back to Corn Creek. I was the happiest boy alive to be in the place I loved once again. My dog, Jack, came to greet me. He stood on his hind legs, licking my face. I don't know who was happier, Jack or me. I acted like a frisky colt running all over the prairie. I felt so good and free. I went into the old log cabin. Grandpa's things were still there, exactly as he had left them. I took off my shoes and ran out barefoot, only to find that my feet had become quite tender from wearing shoes at school. I thought then that I would like to stay at Corn Creek for the rest of my life.

Uncle Francis said I could live with his brother, Uncle Norris, who was coming back from the war. He knew that I was happier at Corn Creek than at Rosebud. There was going to be a big celebration at Cedar Butte, so I rode over there to be part of it. They had a Yuwipi ceremony there, and I was happy to be away from Christians and among people who believed in the things Grandpa had taught me.

Right after the ritual, Uncle Norris suddenly appeared, still in his uniform. Everybody was happy to have him back in one piece. There was a welcoming feast for him that lasted for six days. Some cows were slaughtered, and there was good, belly-filling Indian food, singing, and dancing to the sound of the drum. Uncle Norris told of his experiences in the war, and I wondered why he had been fighting the white man's battles so far away from home.

One incident around this feast still stays in my mind. The people had made an arbor for shade and put the skull of one of the slaughtered cows on top of it. One of the dogs decided that he wanted that oversized bone, and he carefully climbed to the top of a ladder that had been left leaning against the arbor. He got all the way up and opened his mouth as wide as he could, managing to get a good hold on the nose of the skull. He started pulling on it, slowly dragging it to the arbor's edge. Then he carefully made his way down the ladder, feeling below him with his hind legs until he found them resting firmly on each rung. As he made his way down ever so slowly with his haul, the skull suddenly came completely free of the arbor, and its weight knocked the dog off the ladder. Both dog and skull hit the ground with such force that part of the skull got wedged in the poor critter's mouth, and he could not shake it loose. I could not help laughing at that pitiful hound until my uncle came and pried the skull loose.

A couple of days later, I was riding my stud, rounding up a herd of horses. I was riding both bareback and barefoot, and my stud tried to mount a mare who was in heat. The mare kicked back, missing the stud but knocking me off my horse. I was crouched there, doubled over and crying, when that same dog came running out of nowhere. He jumped on my back with all four feet and sent me flying. I could almost sense that he was laughing at me as he ran off. He not only got his revenge that day, but he also reminded me, rather rudely, of my grandfather's teachings not to make fun of animals but rather to help them when they are in trouble.

The summer quickly came to an end, and with it the good time I had enjoyed so much. In September, I had to go back to that damn mission school. It was much harder for me now, after my short period of freedom. The beatings and whippings started all over again, and the *iyeska*, the half-breed kids, laughed at me every time I came down from the attic rubbing my backside. They called me a dumb buck Indian who couldn't learn to speak English. I promised myself that this would be the last time I let the priest lay a strap on me.

In October, three of us kids ran away together. The priests tried to catch us but gave up after three or four miles. The three of us hid in a haystack, sharing a box of crackers. We lay there looking back at St. Francis and then fell asleep, almost suffocating from all that hay. Early the next morning, before daybreak, we headed toward the town and then went our separate ways.

I dreaded going back to Uncle Francis because I knew that would be the first place the "black robes" would be looking for me. I lay on top of the hill overlooking Rosebud and cried because I had no place to go and because I had no father to care for me. I hugged the grass and dug myself into the earth because my grandfather had often told me, "Takoja, whenever you feel sad and lonely and don't know what to do, lie down on the grass and get strength and power from Makoche, from Unchi, from Grand-mother Earth." I don't know how long I stayed on that hill, but I left with new strength flooding through my body.

It took me a few days to get back to Corn Creek. There I hid out, hang-ing around my relatives, the Singing Gooses, the First in Troubles, and the Sleeping Bears. Eventually, of course, I was caught and brought back to St. Francis.

The priest who had last whipped me was the first one to greet me. He tried to be friendly, saying, "I understand why you ran away." I didn't say anything. I knew I would run away again.

I stuck it out from January to March. Then a friend of mine and I took off across a field. One of the Rosebud Indian agents saw us and chased us. We split up. I didn't see how my friend made out, but the white man who was chasing me lost his glasses. I got away because he couldn't see without them.

I got as far as Parmelee and joined some other kids who were hitching. As always, I went to my grandfather's log cabin. I crawled through the win-dow and, as I looked around, it seemed like only a day since Grandpa and I had been happy there together. I found my grandfather's medicine pouch, his buffalo horn, and all the things he had used to cure people. I picked them up, wrapped them carefully, and took them out and buried them deep in the ground to keep them safe for future use. I vowed to return some day to use these sacred things again.

The place was falling apart. The windows looked like eye sockets without eyes, the door like a toothless mouth. Curled up in front of the door, I found a huge rattlesnake. I grabbed it behind the head and carried it half a mile to a spot where I released it, saying, "*Pilamaye*, thank you, Brother, for watching the place for me."

runs away to grandpa house

I told my uncles to tell the priests that the only way they could get me back to St. Francis was as a corpse. After that, they never tried to catch me again. I did not know what I would do or where my next meal would be coming from, but the white gods had lost their power over me. I was free at last.

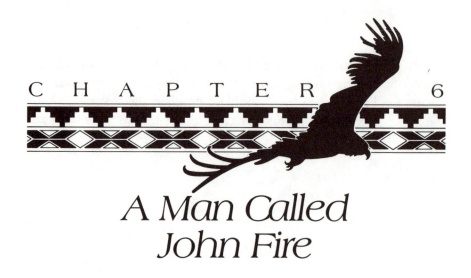

A Man Called
John Fire

A long time ago, the census takers came to the reservation to count heads. They could not make sense of our Indian names because they didn't understand the Lakota language. So they decided to give everybody English names. They made a big joke out of it, giving people whatever names came into their minds.

My grandfather Silas, son of the old Chief Lame Deer, was standing there to be registered. Among the Lakota at this time, Silas was known by the name "Let Them Have Enough" because of his generosity. He was always making sure people had food and other necessities. Just as Silas was about to be named and counted, a kerosene lamp tipped over and set fire to a tent. There was a big commotion, and someone was shouting, "Fire, fire!" The census taker looked at my grandfather and said, "That's it. Your name is *Fire*!" And he put it down in his big book. From that day on, my grandfather was known as Silas Fire. But his family name, by which all Indians knew him, was Tahcha Ushte—"Lame Deer." And so my father's name was John Fire Lame Deer.

There is an old legend handed down in our family that traces our family name back to the beginning of time, when humans and animals spoke to each other in a common language. A young man, so the story goes, was wandering among the mountains and forests when he heard a woman's sad wailing. He followed the sound and came upon a beautiful young woman with a little baby in her lap. He asked her, "Why are you crying?"

The woman answered, "I got lost from our tribe. I have not eaten for days. My milk has dried up, and I have nothing to feed my baby. It is dying. That is why I am crying." The man took pity on the mother and her child. He saw a deer nearby watching him—an old buck with one lame leg. When the buck moved, the man saw that he was limping badly. The man addressed the deer, "Friend, will you give your life so that others may live?"

The deer answered, "I am a four-legged and you are two-leggeds. Why should I sacrifice myself for a two-legged woman? She is of your kind. Why don't you give *your* life for her?"

"Because you are old, friend. I am young and still have my whole life to live."

"And I," said the deer, "wish to go on enjoying what little time I have left. This is no concern of mine."

Tunkashila, the Grandfather Spirit, who sees all and is everywhere, heard the argument. And Tunkashila spoke: "My four-legged friend, you are old and useless. You have only three legs to walk on. Why don't you give of your flesh so that these people can live?"

But the deer defied the Creator, saying, "It is up to you to feed them."

So the Everywhere Spirit told the man, "Take this wood and make a weapon. Take this creeper hanging from the tree and make a weapon. Take these two pieces of sharp flint and make a weapon."

The man instantly perceived what was in the Creator's mind. So he made the first bow and arrow. And the Creator again spoke to the deer: "From this day on, the two-leggeds will be your masters. And from this day on, you will no longer be able to speak to each other."

The man took his bow, brought down the deer, and fed its flesh to the woman and her child. And thus a nation was born.

The first Lame Deer we have certain knowledge of was my great-grandfather, the father of Silas Fire Lame Deer. He was a great chief and warrior. As a young man, he had counted coup in a big fight against fifty Crow Indians. He brought his Mnikowoju tribe—some fifty-one lodges—to the Little Bighorn and led his warriors against Custer's men, aided by his friends, Hump and High Backbone. Refusing to go to the reservation, in 1877 he moved with some ninety lodges of his people to Montana near the present hamlet of Lame Deer, named in his honor. He was the last holdout among the Lakota. Eventually, General "Bearcoat" Miles came up with a large force of white soldiers to force him and his people to surrender.

The proud chief knew that the end of the free-roaming life of the Lakota had come. He did not want a fight in which many women and children would be killed, so he rode up to General Miles with a white flag in his hand. He and Miles shook hands. By Lame Deer's side rode his young nephew, Big Ankle, wearing a beautiful bonnet. Bearcoat Miles told the chief that he and his people must give up their weapons.

Big Ankle said, "I am a warrior standing on my own land. I will not give up my gun." Two of Miles' Indian scouts started wrestling with Big Ankle, trying to take his gun by force.

Chief Lame Deer said, "My friend is young and proud. Do not shame him. Let him keep his weapons."

The scuffle, however, continued. One of the scouts jerked the gun around violently, and it went off. Big Ankle staggered, saying, "I am hit."

Then all hell broke loose. Lame Deer shouted, "*Hoka-hay*, Nephew!" and fired his Winchester at Miles. The bullet went through the general's coat and killed the orderly next to him. A sergeant fired at the chief and missed, but he killed one of the Mnikowoju warriors. Big Ankle shot the sergeant dead. Miles blasted away at Lame Deer with his six-shooter.

The chief disdainfully turned his back on the soldiers and walked slowly away to where the women and children were hiding among the trees. His nephew was limping alongside him, using his gun as a crutch.

Many soldiers now were firing at the two men walking proudly and without haste. Miraculously, all the bullets missed. Finally, Big Ankle was hit again. The Chief tried to support his nephew, letting him lean on his shoulders. He said, "Tonska, let us turn and fight." But Big Ankle was too badly wounded. He sank to the ground, still facing the enemy bravely, trying to reload, singing his death song.

Lame Deer grabbed his arms, trying to raise him. As he did so, a bullet pierced the chief's chest, killing him. Big Ankle still tried to fight back but was shot through the forehead. One of the scouts ran up and scalped both the chief and his nephew. Their bodies were stripped, and their guns, decorated warshirts, and feather bonnets were kept by Miles and his officers as souvenirs. Chief Lame Deer left a son whose name was Chante

Witko, "Crazy Heart." He was my grandfather in the Indian way, my great uncle by the white man's reckoning.

Of all this family history on my father's side, I knew nothing. I was fourteen years old but had never even met my father. My grandfather and all the other Quick Bears did not want him around. They looked upon him as a *hlete*, a "hell-raiser" and a no-good roamer, and as a *pisko*, a kind of bird that lays its eggs in other birds' nests and then flies off. Also, the Quick Bears belonged to the Brulé, or Burned Thighs, tribe on the Rosebud Reservation, while my father was a Mnikowoju, belonging to the "Planters by the Water" who live at Cheyenne River. I still thought of myself as a Quick Bear, not knowing that, in reality, my name was also Lame Deer.

In 1949, when I was fourteen, my uncle Norris took me to the Rosebud Fair. This was always a big affair with much feasting and dancing. The fairground was covered with tipis and hundreds of horse-drawn wagons, that, at that time, still outnumbered the cars. The biggest event was the All-Indian Rodeo, with the best riders from many tribes competing for prizes.

The most conspicuous figure at the rodeo was a strange woman who was tall, skinny, raw-boned, awkward, and very funny. She was dressed entirely in red. She had bright red hair, a red dress, red high-heeled shoes, red stockings, a red purse, and a red umbrella. The man at the loudspeaker announced, "Folks, give a big hand to Alice Jitterbug, our famous rodeo clown." There was a lot of yelling, whistling, and hand clapping. I thought, "So, this is the famous Alice Jitterbug everybody is talking about."

I watched Alice's grotesque antics and posturing. Everybody was laughing at the funny things she did. It was all so comic that one could easily overlook the fact that hers was the most dangerous job at the rodeo. Whenever one of the huge Brahma bulls threw its rider, that red-haired woman had to put herself between the man and the bull, diverting the enraged animal's attention from the fellow lying helplessly on the ground. Every time she intervened, she was risking her life; invariably, the bull tried to gore her with its enormous horns. Sometimes she saved herself by diving headfirst into a large wooden barrel, which the mad bull would promptly toss about like a soccer ball.

I said, "Lekshi, Uncle, that is the bravest woman I have ever seen."

Uncle Norris laughed and told me, "Look closely. That ain't a woman. It's John Fire, your dad!"

In this strange way, I finally met my father, the famous rodeo clown. He had chosen to do his act disguised as a woman because he was a *heyoka*, a Thunder Dreamer—a "forward-backward" man who had to act in accordance with his sacred clown nature. Uncle Norris also told me that when my father was in his twenties, he had been a well-known Brahma bull and wild-buffalo rider who'd had every bone in his body broken at least once.

After the rodeo was over, a gangling, good-looking man with fancy cowboy boots and spurs came over to me with a bag of cookies and some soda pop. There was laughter in his eyes and laughter in the way he moved. He had an easy manner. He spoke to me in Lakota, and I took an instant liking to him. It took a little while until I realized that this was Alice Jitterbug changed back into a man. Uncle Norris introduced us, and this was the first time I met my father. I had a hard time calling him "Dad."

I asked him, "Why do you do such dangerous work? You'll be killed."

He laughed and said: "Son, I used to make a good living as a bootlegger, but that damned repeal spoiled the business. Then I went into cattle rustling, but with those new-fangled radio cars and observation planes, that was becoming too risky. Then I became a tribal policeman, but all my old cattle-rustling and bootlegging pals were crying, "Unfair!" and I had to give it up. But this clown business keeps me in plenty of beer." I didn't know what to make of this.

Then I was introduced to John's wife, Ida, my stepmother, who spoke Sioux in a very funny way. I did not realize that she was Santee, from the Dakota branch of the great Sioux nation. The Santees can't pronounce an "l," using a "d" instead. It's like somebody saying "dove" instead of "love," or "damp" instead of "lamp." One of our old jokes goes, "What's a flat tire in Santee?" Answer: "A bdowout."

Ida's father, Joe Johnson, was a Christian preacher who brought his family to the Rosebud Reservation in 1910 and settled in the northern part of Corn Creek, where he built his church. He was the biggest man I ever saw. He had a drooping walrus mustache and a loud voice that made the windowpanes rattle—the voice of a hellfire-and-brimstone preacher. He still had a brother living at the Santee Reservation on the Missouri River.

Later that night they had a square dance, and it was my father with his hand-held loudspeaker who called the dances in Sioux and broken English:

Wachipi right, Wachipi left,
Rope your heifer, swing her high.
Don't get lost and away we go,
Swap your partner, do-see-do!

Swing your Injun, swing your squaw,
Swing your maw and swing your paw,
Don't forget your mother-in-law!

Allemande left and allemande right,
Love your *winchinchila* tonight!
Hiyupo, hopo, hoka-hay!
Sashay, sashay, sashay!

Up and down, and round and round,
Your old gal is lost and found.
Big pig, little pig, hog or die!
Hoksila, hoksila, let her fly!

Put your honey out to grass,
And don't fall on your big fat ass.
Up the middle, march home!

This was another one of my father's *heyoka* jobs that everyone enjoyed, but I soon found out that he had another, more spiritual side. Some elders told me, "Go with your father into a ceremony, then you'll see his strength."

One incident made a profound impression on me. A powwow was to be held near Rosebud, but the weather seemed to mock those who had come to sacrifice themselves. It rained and rained. The sky was dark gray and heavy like lead. Old Man Sam Moves Camp said, "Let's have some fun with that *heyoka*, John Fire. Let's tell him to stop that rain and make the sun shine. Let's see what he can do."

Everybody was laughing. I was embarrassed and sad seeing them make fun of my father. One of his closest friends, Godfrey Broken Rope, went over to my father and said, "John, can you do it? I know you have the power. You are a medicine man."

My father answered, "It's you who say that I'm a medicine man. I never said it, but I'll try to help you." With that, he went to his horse and came back with a bundle. He unwrapped the bundle, taking out his pipe and an eagle wing. He went to the center of the dance circle, raised the pipe, and prayed with it to the Four Directions. Then he waved the eagle wing and sang a song whose ancient words were known only to himself.

While he was singing this song, the wind started blowing. It got so strong that it blew one of the tents down. It scattered the clouds, making them fly like a flock of frightened birds. Everybody present looked up in awe as the sun began to come out. Within an hour the sky was clear, and it became so hot that three hours later the earth began to crack. Everybody kept staring at my father. He just smiled, wrapped up his pipe, went back to his horse, and rode away. At that moment, I was proud to be his son.

My father was a strange man among the Lakota, a *heyoka* and a *wapiya*, something of a magician. During his first Vision Quest, he had received power from the eagle and other birds. He sometimes said that at moments when he was "in the power," he could understand and speak with the winged creatures of the sky.

John Fire always did the unexpected. When his book *Lame Deer, Seeker of Visions* came out in 1972, my father went to New York, and one of the first things he did was to ask someone to take him to the ocean. On a raw November day, he was taken to Long Island Sound. There, he put on his full regalia—beaded and fringed buckskin shirt, leggings, moccasins, and chief's bonnet—and waded into the icy water until it was up to his knees. Raising his pipe toward the clouds, he sang a song.

When he had finished the song, he emerged from the surf, smiling broadly. "I already had the power from the Earth and the sky," he explained, shaking the water from his sleeves, "but now I also have the ocean power, the power from the creatures of the sea."

My father had a wicked humor. On a TV show in Los Angeles, he was interviewed by an overdressed dude in a white leather suit. "Lame Deer," the man said, "we have many women viewers who are interested in cooking and dieting. What is Indian food like?"

"The white man spoiled the Indian food," my father replied.

"How, Chief? In what way did the white man spoil the Indian's food?"

"Brought in them cans of beans," he said. "Air in tipi no good anymore." This brought an audible gasp from the white-clad man.

At a radio interview in Chicago, John Fire was asked, "Chief, what herbs do you use?"

"Them little black seeds that make old man's thing stand up in bed again," he said. The next morning, the hotel in which he was staying was surrounded by old geezers, some in wheelchairs, clamoring for little black seeds.

On TV in New York, my father shared billing with a two-headed turtle. The two heads were battling furiously over a piece of lettuce. He wagged his finger at them. "Don't fight, brothers," he said, "it's all going into the same stomach!"

In New York, he was again asked about what kind of food the Indians ate. "Well, I'll tell you," he said. "There were these two old Sioux for the first time in your big city. One of them noticed a big sign: 'HOT DOGS.' 'Look over there, Brother,' one of them said to the other. 'They're having our kind of food. Let's go over there and get ourselves one of them hot dogs.' They each bought themselves a frankfurter. The first one opened the roll, looked at the frank, and quickly slapped it together again, asking his friend, 'Brother, which part of the dog did *you* get?" My father always loved to give the white people a shock treatment.

When I first met my father, he was a puzzle to me. He was still in his roaming days, while mine had not yet begun. He would do a ceremony, praying with tears in his eyes, and the next day he would go and hit the bottle. I could not understand that. He saw my questioning look, grinned, and slapped me on the back. "Son," he said, "a medicine man must experience everything. He must creep as low as a worm and soar as high as an eagle. Some days he must humble himself. I'm still in my experiencing stage."

My father had the power of the Elk, the magnetic power, and it was strong. Women were attracted to him. They gathered around him whether he wanted it or not—white women, black women, brown women, yellow women; it did not matter. Even when he was past eighty, women flocked to him—especially young white women in search of the Indian life. I once saw him dancing with four women at each side. He had his arms around all eight of them.

He was very good looking. In his youth, he had a smooth, handsome, full-blood face. In old age, he had a face that artists loved to paint—a face, as he said, like the Badlands, all canyons and ravines. But it was not his looks that made women come to him; it was the way he had with them. It was his Elk power. When he was already an old man, I would walk with him, and here and there a white-haired grandmother would give him that silent love-wink, as if to say, "Hey, old man, remember me? Remember that summer night out on the prairie?" And he would smile at her, give a slight nod, and walk on.

To tell the truth, my relationship with my father at that time was strained. I probably had an unconscious resentment toward him for not being around when I was a child. He probably felt this and reacted to it. Also, we were too much alike. We both went through a roaming and searching period, drinking and fooling around, only to settle down in later life, accepting the tasks that fate had prepared for us. As I often say, "The teaching of Lame Deer lives on—from father to son to grandson."

Physically, my father and I were not alike. I have a Quick Bear body—heavy, stocky, and overweight—while he had a Lame Deer body, lean and light. But our minds ran in the same direction and went through the same stages.

I loved my stepmother, Ida. In 1955, when I was twenty and living with my father, I saw him going out with many different women. I got very angry, thinking that I had to stand up for Ida and that it was up to me to keep my father on the straight and narrow road.

I was drinking heavily at the time, and I went looking for my father, intending to beat him up. I looked for him for two days and could not find him. Luckily, Ida found me first. She took me home, fed me, and got a lot of black coffee down my throat to sober me up. When I told my stepmother that I wanted to fight my father for what he was doing to her, she got very mad at me, saying, "You leave your father alone!"

A year later, I found out that in 1952 my stepmother had undergone an operation that made it impossible for her to have marital relations with my father. We Sioux look upon marital sex as a beautiful, natural, even sacred thing, an essential part of human life, and Ida was a Sioux. She was compassionate and wise, and the two of them lived happily together like brother and sister. She knew that John's Elk nature needed an outlet and accepted that. When my adopted sister, Maxine, told me all this a year later, I regretted having felt such anger at my father. Ida could have told me all this, but she was too shy—especially since, in Sioux tradition, there is a reluctance on the part of a woman to speak to her stepson about such matters.

In 1962, when I was about twenty-seven, I went to live in California. Seven years later, in 1969, I returned to the reservation and met my father again at the Rosebud Fair. I told him that I had quit drinking, that I had not touched a drop of the stuff for several years. He turned to Ida and said, "You know Archie. You know how he is. He says he's quit drinking, and maybe he's been sober for a few weeks and then he'll be on the bottle again." I turned around and walked away.

In 1972, I went back to the reservation again, this time with my wife, Sandy. I showed her off to my father. We were sitting in the old shack he had been living in for all that time, a dilapidated clapboard house whose fading, white paint was peeling off. My father and Ida had just gotten electricity, and a naked light bulb hanging from the ceiling was all the illumination they had. The wooden floor was all splinters. They still had no plumbing, just the privy in back, leaning to one side like the Tower of Pisa, and the path to it ankle deep in mud. There was also a sweatlodge standing in the tiny yard, ready for use.

We were sitting by the huge old potbellied stove. As usual, there was a dog around, a tiny fellow who had been very succesful at widening the hole in the toe of one of my father's cowboy boots. John was looking Sandy over. He turned to Ida, who was busy as usual, cooking something up on her ancient wood range. My father said, "Ida, I think this young man is serious now." My acquiring and taking care of a wife was making an impression on him.

From that moment on, my relationship with my father changed. We became close and loving. We traveled together to ceremonies. He took me to Green Grass and introduced me to Stanley Looking Horse, the keeper of the Sacred Buffalo Pipe, the one that White Buffalo Woman brought to the Lakota people. He also began teaching me about Yuwipi, about herbs, and about the ways of a medicine man. I learned many songs that, if it had not been for him, would have been forgotten.

Spiritual men among the Sioux tribes are very individualistic. Each does things according to his own vision. But essentially, my father's teachings were not so different from those of Grandpa Quick Bear. They complemented each other. My father merely added to the treasure of wisdom my grandfather had left me. In fact, he doubled it.

When I told my father that maybe we could all pool whatever money we could raise to get him an indoor flush toilet, he said that his old shack and outhouse was exactly what he wanted. "I don't want to live in one of them fancy *wasichu* tipis: 'Watch the ashes, don't smoke; you'll stain the curtains. Wipe your boots; the floor's just been mopped. Watch the goldfish bowl. Don't breathe on the canary bird. Don't lean your head against the wallpaper; your head may be greasy. Don't spill your Jack Daniels on the coffee table; you'll ruin the varnish. Don't, don't, don't!' That's a lot of *ta-chesli*, 'buffalo shit.' I like a place where I can forget to put the cigarette out and let it burn a hole in the table. I like to be able to spill things on the floor. I like a rug my dog can chew on. If I had my way, I'd live in a tipi out on the hills."

When my own son John (named after my father) was born, my father came out to California to have a look at him. He stared for a while at my baby boy and then said, "That's the one!" I asked him what he meant. He said, "He's the one who will inherit the Lame Deer power—mine and yours—and who will carry it on."

As my father got older, his lungs started bothering him. Like many Sioux of his generation, he had suffered from tuberculosis in his younger days. He also got cataracts in his eyes and was growing deaf, so that he had to wear a hearing aid. But nothing seemed to bother him or stop his laughter or prevent him from being surrounded by adoring women. Not until a terrible car accident when he was in his eighties did death get a stranglehold on him.

Just before my father died, I noticed that he was not wearing his hearing aid. I asked whether I should go and find it for him. He grinned at me and said, "Son, did you ever see me buy batteries for that damn thing?"

"No," I said.

"I never needed that hearing aid," he went on. "I let people think that I could hear nothing without it. So whenever I had an argument with somebody, or when Ida got after me, I pretended to turn it off and shook my head to everything people said, as if I could not understand a word. So they had to give up badgering me."

My father was a *heyoka* to the last.

CHAPTER 7

Black Face Paint

When I ran away from school at the age of fourteen, I had to support myself. I got a job cleaning machinery for potato harvesting and then picked spuds. I stayed in a windowless shed with a crude bed and a wash basin and not much else. But to me it was a palace, because I was living on my own now and earning my own living. When the harvest was over, I had enough money to buy some warm pants and a wool sweater. I was very pleased with myself. I had come up in the world since the days when my grandfather used to put gunny sacks on my feet instead of shoes.

From the Indian school, I hitched a ride to Rapid City with a young Sioux who was driving a typical Indian car—no brakes, no windows, and no lights—but he got us there. I asked my new friend where the 'skins (short for "redskins") were hanging out, and he took me to Main Street, to a place called Fitzgerald's Bar, with a green shamrock and a harp painted over the door. There were, however, no Irishmen inside.

In those days, it was still illegal to sell liquor to us "aborigines," and many bars had signs like "No Indians or Dogs Around." But Fitzgerald's served booze to our people all the time. The first guy I met in there was one of my cousins. The second was one of my uncles, Melvin, who ran me out of there in a hurry.

My new friend and my cousin walked me to the Indian part of town, called "Omaha Camp." My Uncle Frank lived there, and he gave me a roof over my head. As it turned out, it was not much of a roof. Omaha Camp was a trash heap, and some of the trash was human. It was a home for junked cars and junked human beings. There was little sanitation but

67

a lot of smells—about a hundred different ones, all bad. Omaha Camp was the part of Rapid City that had been swept under the rug. There wasn't a single street lamp or fire hydrant in the place. The dwellings in the camp were mostly tarpaper shacks and crumbling hovels. No policeman or fireman ever showed his face in that "Asshole of the West," as some people called it.

Life was rough for the Indians in that camp. Most of them were unemployed, and those who had jobs were underpaid. A lot of them got drunk every weekend, and some didn't wait until the weekend. Even so, there wasn't as much drinking then as there is now, because it was illegal to sell alcohol to the "poor wards of the government." There was a lot of bootlegging, and some of the half-bloods passed themselves off as Mexicans in order to get their drinks. The liquor store owners always sold booze to these guys as long as there was no federal agent around.

Among those who got good and drunk every Friday or Saturday night was Uncle Melvin. On such nights, Uncle Frank always told me, "Hurry up with your dinner and get lost. Uncle Melvin will be coming home soon." Melvin raised so much hell when he was drunk that everybody would hide when he came around. He always wanted to fight when he had a load on, and he was not a man to tangle with. It was said that Melvin could fight his weight in wildcats. Whenever he came home from Fitzgerald's, he let out a tremendous war whoop, and all the lights in Omaha Camp went out as people locked and barricaded their doors, pretending to be not at home.

In order to get away from Melvin and the all-pervading misery, I moved into a tent in the back of Uncle Frank's place, which I shared happily with his dog, Blackie. I didn't think then that there could be a worse place in the world than Omaha Camp, but I found out later that almost all Western cities had "Indian Towns" that were in no way different from our Rapid City camp.

I worked for a short time in a sawmill and then got myself a job as a bus boy and bottle washer in a greasy spoon. As this didn't pay enough for even my most basic needs, I also got an evening job as a pin boy in a bowling alley. Even working two shifts, I couldn't make enough to live on, so I started working in a car lot where the pay was better. I survived almost exclusively on black coffee and hamburgers that had lots of gristle and lit-

"Omaha Camp"

tle meat. The more of that stuff I ate, the thinner I got. At six feet tall, I weighed only 115 pounds. I was looking for a way out, and thought that wearing black face paint might solve my problem.

In the old days, a young man going on the warpath painted his face
black. There was a war on in Korea, and a lot of my friends were talking
about joining up. For poor kids, the army is a way out. That's why most
of the fighting that the U.S. Army has done since World War II has been
done by blacks, Chicanos, and Indians. I thought it might be a way for me,
too, to earn eagle feathers and three square meals a day.

But I had a problem: I was still a year underage. So I put a few dollars
in my pocket and headed for Fitzgerald's bar. Sitting at the bar with his
girlfriend was a Pine Ridge Sioux I knew. I gave him enough money for a
case of beer and an extra fiver, and the two of them signed a paper as my
father and mother, attesting to the fact that I was over eighteen and enlisting
with their permission.

I was at the recruiter's office at eight the next morning. "Where are your
parents?" he asked me. I told him they had to be back on the "Res" and that
I had come alone with the papers. He grinned at me like a cat at a fat mouse
and said, "Son, you're now part of the U.S. Army. You'll make a fine soldier."
When my relatives saw me packing my bag, they thought I was heading
back to Corn Creek. They didn't find out I was going to war until I was
already well on my way.

I went to Sioux Falls for my physical. A few hundred others were already
there for the same purpose. First we were given a test to find out whether
we were educated enough to be soldiers. Some of us could neither read nor
write nor speak English, but we passed all the same. You don't need to be
literate in order to be shot at. It was, "Open your mouth, cough, bend over,
spread your cheeks, piss in this bottle." We might just as well have been cattle
parading in front of a meat inspector. The white boys took this in stride.
We 'skins did not. To us, the procedure seemed debasing and dehumaniz-
ing. We were too individualistic, lacking the required herd instinct. Later,
this would land many of us, including myself, in the stockade.

They gave me a ticket to get to Chicago and report to the base there.
In Chicago, I walked through what seemed like deep canyons of brick, glass,
and steel. I was totally bewildered. Here I was, a gangling, six-foot Indian
kid, with long hair, a black "Uncle Joe" hat, Levi's, and much-worn cowboy

boots, staring at the skyscrapers and huge crowds of people in a great hurry to get nowhere. The people, in turn, gawked at me. Their sheer numbers, the ear-splitting noise, and the traffic bewildered me. I was as confused as a deer caught on a subway platform. I went into a police station for help, explaining matters as best I could in broken English. They called the base, which sent an MP with a jeep to pick me up.

I found myself now in the belly of the beast. The first morning at the base was haircut time. They lined us up for their "GI Special." Everyone was laughing at me. "Hey, Chief, you're gonna get your long hair cut off." Six barbers worked double time. They did their job so quickly that a fellow would sit down with a full head of hair and, after a couple of passes with the clippers, would get up a minute later looking like a peeled onion.

I couldn't wait to look at myself in a mirror. When I put my black, wide-brimmed hat on, it immediately fell down over my eyes, almost down to my chin. There was nothing left to hold it up. I didn't like it.

Next, a fat three-striper barked at us: "Get rid of those cruddy, lousy duds!" To replace the stuff we had been wearing, we were issued uniforms, all two or three sizes too big. So there we were, a bunch of sorry-looking sad sacks.

Then came pin-cushion time. I got so many injections for so many strange diseases that my arms swelled up. After that, we were instructed on how to make up our beds in proper army style. What this had to do with fighting North Korean commies was a great puzzle to me. All orders were issued in bellows and roars, intermingled with curses, put-downs, insults, and obscenities. In all the time we were in basic training, none of the drill sergeants ever talked to us in a normal voice or in anything but abusive terms. The idea, obviously, was to reduce us to unthinking robots.

Already, most of the white kids were having trouble holding back their tears. I thought, "And with these poor guys, they want to fight a war?" I also thought that my grandfather had done rather well against Custer's cavalry, even though he had never drilled or learned to make a bed the right way.

That first night at the base, I ran into a Sioux from North Dakota who invited me to go to the PX with him. I was only seventeen and had never tasted alcohol before. The result can easily be imagined. My Sioux friend and a black buddy got me back to the base—how, I do not know, because I remember nothing. My head swam, and the ground under my feet rolled like a wave. They hoisted me onto my bunk. Some time later, I got sick and vomited all over the place, which made my black buddy in the bunk below me very unhappy. He hollered at me, "Get a mop and clean up this mess!" I climbed down in a haze, but I was still conscious enough to notice the head of a blonde, blue-eyed woman peeking out from under his blanket. I could never figure out how he had smuggled her in, let alone out.

From Chicago, we were sent to Camp Breckenridge, Kentucky. Thirty-five of us boarded the train—men from Arkansas, Texas, Missouri, and New Jersey. I was lying in my compartment listening to the wheels clicking on the rails, thinking how my life had changed from the time when I had been living with my grandfather at Corn Creek. I felt very lonely and was terrified at the thought of what the future might hold in store for me.

At Camp Breckenridge, I was assigned to the 502d Battalion, part of the 101st Airborne Division. At the time, it was a basic training outfit and not a real paratrooper division. It regained its jump status later. There, the drilling continued, as well as the incessant hazing, barking, and cursing.

Punishments for slight infractions were severe. Sometimes the officers would make a man lie on the ground, bury him up to his neck in sand, and leave him there for hours. I saw them make some guys march for hours in a circle carrying buckets of water. Some of my buddies who were caught smoking at the wrong time or in the wrong place were made to dig big holes, six feet wide, six feet long, and six feet deep. Then the sergeant would throw cigarettes into the holes and make the guys fill them back up again. Sometimes a sergeant would ask his poor victim what brand of cigarette it was. If he couldn't answer, he was forced to dig that damn cigarette up again, ascertain the brand, and rebury it.

I saw some guys spend two or three days shoveling. Others were made to run up and down a long, steep hill with a heavy bucket of sand in each hand. Some were made to sit with five-gallon buckets and blankets over their heads and forced to smoke a half dozen cigarettes until they became sick.

As for me, I talked back and wound up in the stockade for thirty days. The guys in there spent all their days in vicious fights. The whites called the blacks "niggers" and "coons," while the blacks called the whites "fucking honkies." Being neither white nor black, I was left alone most of the time.

This was one of the few instances in which being an Indian worked to my advantage.

There was one sickening incident, though, before I got out of the stockade. One day a bunch of us were taken out to chop wood. As we were sweating in the hot sun, some trainees came along and started making fun of us and calling us names. This put us in a foul mood, as we were engaged in the hottest, most hard-driving work I had ever done. There were six of us in the crew—three black men, two whites, and myself. And we had one guard, a young white recruit who carried a gun.

The guard made the fatal mistake of keeping after one of the guys, calling him a lazy black bastard. The black soldier straightened up and hurled his heavy axe at the guard, hitting him right in the center of his forehead above the eyes.The axe split the guard's skull wide open, just as if it had been an overripe watermelon.

I saw the sick, terrified look on the black man's face as he realized what he had done. He groaned and took off, disappearing over the hills. Horrified and sick to my stomach, I kept watching the guard squirming in a pool of blood. I couldn't move or even look away. An ambulance came and took him to the hospital, but he was dead on arrival.

Both of these men were kids, just out of high school. Now one was dead and the other a fugitive, sure to be caught and court martialed. And it had all happened because one was black and the other white, and because society and perhaps their parents as well had taught them how to hate.

One black fellow in the stockade had already seen combat in Korea. "Try to get out of going to that war," he told me. "You're just a kid. You are discriminated against, just as we are. Whitey has always kept us way in back, except when it comes to combat; then we're suddenly in front. When you get back, or rather *if* you get back, they'll still call you a lousy Injun."

After I was released from the stockade, things got serious: We were instructed in how to kill. At bayonet practice, they egged us on to scream like panthers as we drove our big knives into the dummy. Kill, kill, kill, and howl like a banshee while you're doing it. Learn to enjoy ripping the guts out of your fellow man. That was about the only time we were allowed to open our mouths and come out with a roar.

I was good with weapons, including the M-1, the heaviest rifle I ever carried; the Thompson submachine gun; the .30-caliber heavy machine gun; and the light machine gun. Our targets were human figures. We were told to aim at the head, heart, and guts. Always we were told, "Shoot to kill, you bastards!"

When I enlisted in the army, I had signed up to be a paratrooper, but I was too light at the time. So during my basic training, I did everything I possibly could to gain weight. After sixteen weeks of basic, I barely made it. So then I was sent to Fort Benning, Georgia, for six weeks of jump school and glider training.

My first sergeant and I were the only ones in a group of five hundred who, immediately after jump school, were ordered to go to Korea without the customary leave to say goodbye to our families. My orders were for Camp Stoneman in San Francisco.

Trying to find the base, I got lost in the city and passed a bar with the door wide open. Inside I saw a completely naked woman dancing on the bar. Curious to check out this aspect of the white man's culture, I paid my cover charge, sat down at a table, and ordered a beer. A waiter asked me how old I was. I told him seventeen. He told me I was too young to have a beer. I told him that if I was old enough to get myself killed for Uncle Sam, I was old enough to have a drink. The waiter told me to get the hell out of there. When I objected, they just threw me out bodily. I didn't even get my cover charge back.

I spent a week at Camp Stoneman and then was shipped out with a whole group of young soldiers destined to become human cannon fodder. We were taken by ferry to the main dock, where we were to board the ship that would take us to Korea. The other fellows were playing games, all running together to one side of the ferry until it was on the point of capsizing and then running to the other side, yelling like crazy.

While we were waiting to board ship, other soldiers were busy unloading the caskets of those who were coming back as corpses. We were surrounded on all sides by flag-draped coffins while a chaplain came to the loudspeaker and droned on and on about God and country. Then the air force band struck up "So Long, It's Been Good to Know You"—not exactly a heartwarming send-off.

Two weeks later, we landed in Yokohama and from there were shipped to Korea. There, as in all strange and faraway places where American soldiers fight, the prevailing motto was, "If you get them by the balls, their hearts and minds will follow." I found myself now among Asians who looked so much like Indians that I got the uncomfortable feeling I would be shooting at my own kind of people.

I cannot bring myself to speak about the horrors that awaited me in Korea. I do not even want to think of it, much less put it down on paper. Forty years later, whenever I hear a car backfiring or a similar explosive noise, I still have the urge to throw myself flat on the ground or jump into a ditch. I still suffer from nightmares that neither white doctors nor Indian medicine can cure, and to this day, I still cry when I think about the children.

After the truce was signed, I was posted to Okinawa for jungle training. I spent my days there in an alcoholic haze. I drank to forget, and I got rid of my anger by taking part in terrific barroom brawls. By then, I had made sergeant, but everybody called me Chief. I had a California Indian friend named Ruiz, and together we did some very serious drinking. I was drinking everything from rice wine to carrot beer to Purple Jesus to good Canadian whiskey. The whole town of Okinawa seemed to consist of nothing but bars and whorehouses. Everyone in our outfit had his own special girl, and I was no exception. I spent all my free time drinking, raising hell, and bedding down.

Okinawa was actually quite beautiful. We could rent old army horses left over from the war, complete with regulation saddles. I sometimes rode out to an old castle, where I would sit looking out over the sea toward the east, thinking about home. Often I would pray in my own Lakota language, thinking, "Here I am, thousands of miles from home, and nobody is missing me." Then I would ride back to town to get sickening drunk and pick another fight.

Later, I was posted to Honshu, where I did some more boozing and fighting. There I just about took on the whole Japanese nation. I spent a lot of time in Japanese jails and had some epic battles with MPs. I thought I was the toughest *hombre* in Honshu until I tangled with a sumo wrestler who threw me through the air as if I'd been a bag of feathers. After that, I stuck to fighting American GIs.

In January 1954, when I was nineteen, I got special orders to head for Hokkaido, the northernmost of the Japanese main islands, for some arctic weather training. This was quite a change from Okinawa's tropical heat. I somehow got myself an Ainu girlfriend, the next best thing to a Lakota *winchinchila*. My buddies made fun of me because my new love was tattooed on her upper lip, making her look as if she had a small, dark blue mustache. I didn't mind.

My girlfriend took me to her village and introduced me to the chief, who was also the head shaman. The Ainu had some strange beliefs—for example, that a woman should lie absolutely still during lovemaking, that even the slightest wiggle would bring bad luck to the man. I assured my girlfriend that I would take my chances. They also believed that a woman was especially powerful during her moon time and that menstrual blood was big medicine.

The Ainu's holy animal was the bear, and they let me take part in their bear dances and ceremonies. These people kept a live bear in all their villages, praying to the Bear Spirit and honoring it like a god, but at the end of the year the bear would be sacrificed.

On the day before this solemn ritual, there was a lot of wailing and lamenting for the bear on the part of the women. The head shaman would talk to the bear, saying, "We have cared for you well. We have fed you and bathed you in the river, but now comes the time when you must serve us as a messenger to the spirits." The next day came the great bear-killing ritual. Afterward, the bear's flesh would be eaten, and his ghost would bring to the spirits the wishes of the people. It reminded me a little of our own Lakota Dog Feast.

During the time I served in Japan, I found myself serving with a man named Eddie Custer, whose great-grandfather was a brother of General George Armstrong Custer. Our ancestors had fought each other at the Little Bighorn, and now we were serving side by side in the same outfit attached to the First Cavalry Division. When I think about a Custer and a Lame Deer serving amicably together as American soldiers in Japan, I wonder if the day will come when the human race can form such friendships *without* first fighting bloody wars.

In the fall of 1955, while out on the firing range, I suddenly realized that my discharge date had passed twelve days before. It wasn't long until I was back in the states. The first thing I did on my return to the reservation was to climb to the top of Cross Butte, where I prayed with my grandfather's buffalo horn. I looked out upon the valley. I knew every inch of that sacred land like the palm of my hand. It was the land of my ancestors, where the heart of our nation is buried.

For a short time, I was elated to be among my own people again, soaking in the sights and smells of the prairie, listening to the familiar bird calls and the distant powwow drums. I was happy in the thought that I would never wear black face paint or a uniform again.

But soon, disillusionment set in. Corn Creek Valley had become a valley of misery. The situation on the Res was much worse than when I had left it. Now the government was pursuing its so-called "relocation policy." As unemployment reached almost 90 percent, they tried to "relocate" as many of us as possible—to become soda jerks, gas station attendants, and manual laborers in various big cities. For the next two years, I bounced around from place to place, from one lousy job to another, and from bar to bar.

The year 1957 found me in Cincinnati, on Vine Street, a long alley lined on both sides by solid rows of bars. I stumbled from one bar to another, sampling the wet goods and raising hell until I passed out. When I regained consciousness the next morning, there was a black guy standing next to me. He asked me if I was all right. I asked him, "Where the hell am I?" He told me that we were in a recruiting station and that we had just been sworn in.

I said, "No way! Don't give me that shit!" A sergeant came over and asked me what was wrong. I said, "This crazy guy here is trying to fool me into thinking I've reenlisted."

"You sure have, Chief," said the sergeant. "You're now a member of the United States Army."

We had three hours to catch our bus to Fort Campbell in Kentucky. I spent the time sitting on a park bench with a big hangover, trying to figure out how this could have happened. At Fort Campbell, I was assigned to my old outfit, the 101st Airborne, which had been reactivated to jump status. There, I went to jump school and made one jump in order to reactivate my own status as a paratrooper. Afterward, I was made supply sergeant in charge of all the paint stores for the battle group. I spent my duty hours painting signs and jumping out of airplanes. My off-duty hours were spent hitting the bottle.

In November 1958, I got thirty days' leave and headed for South Dakota to visit my father in Winner. I traveled with a Sioux friend from Pine Ridge, and together we raised as much hell as we could between Kentucky and South Dakota.

In Omaha, we found an Indian bar, where we got acquainted with some girls who took us to a nearby hotel for a little partying and some heavy drinking. There were already a bunch of white people there, all on a crying drunk set off by a pathetic-looking girl who started bawling over a brother who had died. I had no great desire to sit around with a bunch of weeping, blubbering drunks, so I told my buddy that it was time for us to leave.

When we got up to go, a couple of bruisers near the door were blocking the exit, backed up by a few more such characters. Rather than getting rolled trying to fight our way out in our sorry state, I took a flying dive through the second-story window with my buddy right behind me. The ground was frozen hard, but at least there was a two-foot cushion of snow, and my paratrooper training helped a lot. Also, the more drunk you are, the easier and softer you fall.

As soon as I got to Winner, I bought a secondhand car so that I could come and go as I pleased. I drove forty miles to see some friends in Mission, a reservation town that was allowed to have bars because so many whites were living there. I took my friends to do some elbow bending in one of those whiskey mills, and we came out pretty well lit up.

When I got to my car, I had a lot of trouble getting the key into the lock, and when I finally did, it would not open the door. We climbed in through the window, but the key wouldn't work in the ignition, either. So I hot-wired the car and drove back to Winner.

The next morning my father woke me up, saying the police were at the door wanting to see me. They told me I had stolen the car I'd driven home from Mission. I produced the registration number, but it was different from the car standing before me, and I was taken off to jail. It turned out that in my drunken stupor I had confused the strange car with my own. My father went to Mission and brought my car back to show the sheriff that both cars were identical.

I was charged with grand theft all the same. At the trial, my court-appointed lawyer was dozing most of the time rather than defending me. I got two years' probation, meaning that I could get back into the army on condition that I would stay out of South Dakota for two years.

As soon as I reported back to Fort Campbell, I was given orders to fly to Mainz, Germany, where I was attached to the 504th Airborne as a physical training instructor for the paratroopers. Again, I had to live on white man's time—by the clock, in a mechanical, rigid routine: get up, wash, make your bed, eat, go to the bathroom—always on schedule. I wondered what an Indian like myself was doing in this white man's army.

Whenever I ran out of money, I would wander into the forest, spending my time there in blissful solitude. Yet, when I had money, I would head for town and spend it inside a bar, where I was beginning to acquire a taste for Rhine wine.

In January 1960, I was drinking in one of the enlisted men's clubs when the man next to me made a remark about "lousy, drunken Injuns." I knocked him off his perch and thereby started a big fight, which turned into a full-scale race riot. In no time, blacks and Chicanos were going at each other with chairs and beer steins. But when the whites got into the act, both blacks and Chicanos threw in together to have a go at Whitey.

All hell broke loose. The MPs arrived in force but couldn't handle the situation. They were reinforced by the air force APs, and all of them together waded in with their nightsticks, cracking skulls, which only made things worse. The place was a shambles. A lot of people got hurt. As the old saying goes, "Them ain't grapes on the barroom floor, them's eyeballs!" It took several detachments of MPs to get things under control.

They threw the book at me, and I was brought before a special court-martial. The captain asked me why I was causing them so much trouble. I told them that I just had my belly full of the army, that I wanted out, and that army life was destroying my mind. I told them I was a Sioux and just couldn't fit in, couldn't live by the clock. If I ever fought again, I said, it would only be for my own land and my own people. I repeated again and again that, having been brought up the Indian way, I could never become the automaton they wanted.

The captain looked at me for a long time and then said, "I will give you thirty days in the stockade and take away your stripes, but in view of what you said, and considering your personality, I recommend that you be discharged. You're just not worth the trouble."

I thanked him, saying that he had made me very happy. I stayed in the stockade only three weeks instead of a full month. The army was eager to get rid of me as quickly as possible. A sergeant of my company came for me, took me to a football game between the airborne and the air force, and then saw me off for Fort Dix, New Jersey, where I finally got my discharge. I was a soldier boy no longer.

Chief
Rattlesnake Catcher

rattlesnake Catcher

During the two years between my first and second hitch in the army, I had many jobs. For a while I was the official chief rattlesnake catcher of the state of South Dakota.

When I was at the Catholic boarding school, the priests had told me about the snake—that it was cursed by God and the enemy of humankind, condemned to crawl on its belly for making Eve eat the apple of knowledge. I could never understand why eating the fruit of knowledge was such a wicked thing. Native Americans look up to the snake—not as an evil creature but as a sacred being. To the ancient Maya and Aztecs, the image of a giant rattlesnake, the "Plumed Serpent," represented one of their chief gods—Kukulcan or Quetzalcoatl, the kind-hearted, compassionate law giver and civilizer.

The Hopi Indians dance with live rattlesnakes and bullsnakes, which are later released to bring rain to the people. In many Native American legends, humans marry snakes and look upon serpents as their tribal ancestors. My own Lakota people recount the Legend of the Four Snake Brothers, young hunters who disobeyed the voice of the Buffalo Spirit and were therefore transformed into giant rattlesnakes. Even in their new shape, these brothers continued to protect and do good for their human relatives.

Once, when my father and I were traveling, we found ourselves near Cedar Butte at an old, abandoned wreck of a house. The house had belonged to a long-dead German who had a shoe repair shop there. What such a shop was doing in the middle of nowhere, with no customers within miles, I never could figure out. My father said, "Some people told me that a gigantic, centuries-old rattler has his den somewhere around here. They never see him, but they can smell his powerful odor and, on moonless nights, hear him rattle like a rumbling express train."

"It's true," I said. "I have never seen this monster, but I've seen his huge track in the sand. And one time, over there where the grass is some five feet tall, I saw a long row of grass moving as that snake pushed his way through it. A few years ago," I continued, "a friend of mine was riding through here and saw the snake's tail lying across the road, moving slowly. My friend's horse shied and bucked him off, and he almost landed on the tail. So this monster snake lives here somewhere. Nobody from Corn Creek will go anywhere near that place."

I was appointed the state's head snake exterminator, which is odd, since I always respected and looked on snakes as brothers. There are four kinds of poisonous snakes that live in North America. One is the coral snake, a small but very deadly and pretty creature with red, black, yellow, and white stripes. It looks like a precious necklace that a beautiful woman might wear. It is a tiny relative of the cobra and occurs only in Florida and Arizona. The other three kinds are all pit vipers—the rattlesnake, the copperhead, and the cottonmouth, or water moccasin. These all have a pit, or opening, between the nostril and the eyes. This organ is sensitive to heat and guides the snakes (who have bad eyesight) to their warm-blooded prey.

Among the pit vipers is the rattler, which lets you know when you have come too close. It rattles the buttons on the end of its tail as if to say, "Brother, watch out, don't step on me." It also flicks its supersensitive, forked tongue to find its way around. The rattler gets a new button on its tail every time its skin gets too tight and has to be shed. The rattler's venom poisons the blood, while the cobra's attacks the nervous system.

I learned about snakes from Mr. Dick Jacobi, my boss in the extermination business. I got the job because nobody else wanted it. Some of the hungover applicants were shown a rattlesnake den with maybe a few hundred serpents writhing in it. They had one look at it and said, "Mister, I think I'll take that other job, slinging hash at the diner, or shoveling manure." A rattlesnake den doesn't smell like a bed of roses, and some of the boys caught a whiff and got sick to their stomachs.

Old Man Jacobi was a wizard at finding the rattlesnake dens in caves, under rock ledges, or in badger holes. The snakes always returned to the same den when it grew cold. They emerged in the spring again when it got warm, so you had to do your cleaning out during the winter. As long as the weather was cold, the snakes were very sluggish—almost comatose—and very easy to handle.

There were usually between two hundred and five hundred snakes in a den. Our record number was seventeen hundred. As the state paid us by the head, we made good money. My father told me that the snakes emerge from their dens in spring at the sound of the first thunder. When it thunders, the earth vibrates ever so slightly, and this is the signal for the rattlers to uncoil themselves from the huge ball they have formed during hibernation. One by one, they wriggle off, leaving their den and crawling off in all directions.

This is also true of nonvenomous snakes such as blue racers, bullsnakes, and gopher snakes. All of these usually stray no farther than a mile from their dens. Snakes mate during warm-weather periods, usually in July and August. Rattlesnakes also engage in a regular mating dance, their upper bodies swaying upright in rhythm as they twist themselves around each other.

This was a fascinating thing to watch. I used to go up to the top of Rattlesnake Butte to watch the snakes play. And I'm not kidding; they *did* play. Four or five of them would make themselves into a ball, roll down the slope for a hundred feet or so, unwind and separate, crawl up the hill again, and then do it a few times more. Possibly this was part of their mating dance. It made me wonder whether rattlesnakes could think or possibly even have a sense of humor. I also quickly realized that snakes had a part to play in nature's scheme: they kept the rodent population down.

One day, a rancher whose land lay along the Red River called Mr. Jacobi for help. "My place is overrun by rattlesnakes," he said. "Hundreds, thousands—they're all over. For God's sake, come over here! I can't run my cattle on that land. I raise saddle horses; I have people working for me; I have kids. They can't even go ten feet without stepping on a rattlesnake. They're coming out of their dens; they're everywhere. Hurry!"

So Old Man Jacobi and I jumped in a Jeep and drove to Red River, about thirty miles north of Rapid City. We found the situation out of control.

There were not one but several dens in cavelike cracks in an embankment near the river. Almost all of the snakes had already crawled out. They were everywhere, and the sound of their rattling filled the air. Our Jeep was actually running over a wriggling mass of snakes. I had never seen anything like it.

Jacobi said that we could not use our usual method of cleaning out dens because the snakes had already left them. "This is a dynamite job," he told me. So Jacobi got out a box of dynamite. He drove along the embankment while I took a whole lot of sticks, set the fuses for sixteen, twelve, and eight seconds, crimped them, and threw them as we were driving along.

The result was more spectacular than we had bargained for. The whole place exploded in a cloud of flying rattlesnakes. The sky was raining snake parts—bodies, heads, tails, rattles, tongues—and some of this stuff was falling into our Jeep.

Old Man Jacobi yelled at me, "Watch out for the heads! They've still got the fangs and venom sacks, so they can still bite and poison you!" And it's true that a rattlesnake head still has life for maybe an hour after it is separated from the rest of its body.

We had bits of snakes all over us. It was a real mess. The explosions had been so powerful that much of the embankment had caved in. Even so, hundreds of snakes had gotten away. Jacobi surveyed the havoc we had wrought, shook his head, scratched himself behind the ears, and finally concluded, "Maybe dynamite wasn't such a good idea."

Almost every day, we got a frantic call from some farmer saying that there was a den on his land and he wanted us to come and clean it out. The established procedure to get rid of the snakes was first to dig a hole six feet wide and six feet deep, pick up the rattlers with a snake hook, throw them in the hole together with one or two old tires, pour gasoline over them, and set them on fire. That way, the snakes would be burned alive. I had to do this a few times, and the whole thing made me sick. I kept trying to find a better solution.

Nowadays, our sacred Black Hills have become one huge tourist trap—a jumble of curio shops, doll museums, miniature railroad rides, cave tours, phony Western stockades, and melodrama theaters. One of the main attractions is a place called Reptile Gardens. It includes a Gator and Croc Pond, giant land turtles for children to ride on (for a fee, of course), an Iguana

Rock, and snakes from all over the world. It also has a lot of curio junk: baby rattlesnakes in plastic belt buckles, rattle key rings, rattlesnake ashtrays, and whatnot.

Around Easter, they even used to sell live baby rabbits in tiny boxes, ready to mail. Most of them were dead on arrival. Luckily, they don't do that anymore. They also sold live baby alligators ready for mailing. I was once told that New Yorkers flushed these unwanted, living souvenirs down the toilet and that, consequently, there are a few huge 'gators living in the sewers, bleached white for lack of daylight, existing on a diet of human waste. It sounded like a fairy tale to me.

At any rate, Reptile Gardens has huge displays of live rattlesnakes. Most of the snakes won't eat in captivity and consequently die. Therefore, the place is always in need of live replacements, not only for itself but also to supply other such outfits. So, instead of burning the snakes, Jacobi and I started catching them alive, selling them to Reptile Gardens and to snake farms where rattlers are "milked" to make antivenin serum.

I began making three-foot-long boxes to trap the snakes. These boxes had hinged lids on one side and wire screens on the other. I would put the traps at the entrance to a den. As the snakes came out, they worked their way into the traps by pushing in the lid. When we had enough for a load (generally five hundred to a thousand snakes), we'd load them in the truck and deliver them to Reptile Gardens.

We got paid $2.50 per "living pound," and I have to confess that I cheated. Snakes absorb water through their skins. Before delivery, I would throw the critters into a trough of water, letting them soak it up for a while. This would make them heavier, which meant more money for me.

After August, Reptile Gardens stopped buying rattlesnakes, but I kept right on catching them. The problem was where to put them until I could sell them again. My headquarters at the time were on a ranch owned by Mark Madson, Dick Jacobi's brother-in-law, a fine man and a good friend. There I had a large shed in which I kept my live snake supply. I put them in large, straw-lined boxes stacked up on shelves. Rattlers can go for over a year without food, so feeding them was no problem.

One time, in the middle of the night, I decided to check up on the snakes. As I went into the shed, I could hear the buzzing of fifteen hundred rattlers. It was pitch dark in there. I stumbled and knocked one of the boxes off the shelf, and it broke open. I shined my flashlight at it and saw that some thirty snakes had gotten out and were crawling around on the floor.

At that moment, the flashlight decided to go out. I sensed that there was a lot of excitement going on around my feet, not to mention my own. In my panic, I forgot where the door was, so I edged along the walls, feeling my way around the shed hoping to find the damn door. When I finally got to it, I remembered that it opened inward. So first I had to step back into the snake pit before I could pull the door open.

When I finally got the door open, I lunged out into the night, jumped five feet into the air, and ran like the Devil was after me. I was lucky not to run into some of the farm equipment that was lying around in the dark. I lost one of my shoes but didn't even notice it. I only wanted to get away from those snakes!

I ran about two hundred yards before I stopped. I must have screamed in my panic, because Old Man Madson came out onto his porch in his long johns, a lighted kerosene lamp in his hand, wanting to know what was going on. I told him, and he said, "Never mind. Just lock the door and go back to bed. We'll take care of it in the morning." The next day, we put all the snakes back inside their box again, and that was that.

One time, when I arrived at Reptile Gardens with a load of snakes, the owner paid me only $1.50 per pound instead of the usual $2.50. Naturally, I complained. "Chief," he told me, "this is where the law of supply and demand comes in. We are expecting a truck with some three thousand snakes from the great yearly Oklahoma roundup. And of course, with so many snakes, the price goes down."

I said nothing but decided to hang around. Sure enough, a little later, a huge semi with an Oklahoma license plate pulled up in front of Reptile Gardens. I waited until lunch break and made sure nobody was around. Then I opened the door of the truck and turned my competitor's snakes loose.

There were a lot of them! Some of those rattlers had scotch tape on their backs with the name of the fellow who had caught them. Some were even marked with their length and weight, because at the roundup they had prizes for the biggest, longest, heaviest, and fattest snakes. After I had gotten a good look at the snakes, I drove back to the ranch. I was lucky that nobody saw me turning them loose.

A day later, I got an urgent phone call from the owner of Reptile Gardens: "For Chrissake, Archie, get over here, and step on it! Those Oklahoma snakes got out. We can't figure out how it happened. There's three thousand of them crawling around, and we had to cordon the whole place off. We'll lose the whole weekend business. Get your ass over here and catch those snakes. We'll pay you by the hour."

Well, I didn't bust a gut to catch them all. I got maybe three hundred, just about a tenth of the lot, but the price for my own snakes jumped up to $2.50 a pound again.

On another occasion, I was drinking heavily and did not secure the boxes full of snakes on my pickup. They fell out, busted open, and some seven hundred rattlers were left wandering about in the streets of Rapid City. It was one of the town's more memorable days.

One sideline of this strange business was the selling of snake meat. This high-protein food was often canned and sold as a sandwich spread. It was very popular for a while in cowboy country, and many tourists bought a can or two to take home as conversation pieces. I even developed a taste for it. I would cut off the snakes' heads, extract the poison, slit the belly down one side, and strip the skin off the meat. Then I would put a little grease in the pan and throw in the snake, backbone and all. Once it's cooked, the meat just falls off. It tastes just like chicken.

A funny thing happened in 1973, just after the siege of Wounded Knee. I was visiting a friend in Wamblee, on the Pine Ridge Reservation. We caught a rattlesnake and were frying it up when Russell Means, one of the chief leaders of the American Indian Movement, came in.

"Hey, Lame Deer," he said, "that smells good. Can I have some?"

I handed him a big chunk on a plate, together with a fried egg.

"This is delicious," Russ said. "What kind of sausage is it?"

"No sausage," I told him. "It's rattlesnake."

He gagged and was about ready to puke. "Jesus Christ," he said, finally, "you're still a primitive savage at heart!"

"And you," I answered, "have lived too long among the fleshpots of the white man."

He didn't look too pleased but finally laughed and said, "The joke was on me."

Nowadays, I never kill a rattlesnake. I respect it as a friend, a gentleman, and a scholar. During my youth, when I was drinking, I just didn't know any better.

Another of my jobs was milking the snakes for their venom. Small quantities of venom are injected into horses. Their blood then builds up an immunity and is used to make snakebite serum. The price for an ounce of venom was around two hundred dollars at the time.

In order to milk a snake, I tied a lid of gauze over a glass jar, forced the snake's fangs into and through it, and squeezed the poison sacs until I saw the yellow drops of poison dribbling into the jar. Some people used to defang the snakes before they milked them, forcing the poison out through the openings where the fangs had been. That was a very unsatisfactory method that yielded little venom. Such people also often forgot that a snake grows new fangs in a short time, and the consequences were sometimes serious.

It is often said that rattlesnake venom is harmless if swallowed, as long as it does not get into the bloodstream, and therefore, if somebody is bitten, you should suck the venom out. The trouble is, if you've got a sore in your mouth, it could be curtains: you can't tie a tourniquet around your neck.

When struck by a rattlesnake, the thing to do is not to panic and run about, because that spreads the venom through the bloodstream. Usually, you have a few hours to get to a doctor and get a shot of antivenom. Most bites are not fatal—it depends on the size of the snake and the amount of poison and whether the rattler has struck prey a short time before. (If so, there is less poison in the gland.)

I was bitten twice. The first time, I was walking through a meadow to milk some cows. The grass was high, and I got stung on the outside of my right leg. It hurt like the dickens and made me kick. My leg swelled up and turned black. I was driven to a doctor for a serum shot. A few weeks later, I went to milk the same cows again and was hit at almost the same spot in the meadow on the other side of the same leg. I accepted it as my well-deserved punishment for having been a snake exterminator. After I was bitten, my leg turned black around the ankle, and it has stayed black to this day.

Much later, the snakes also got back at the owner of Reptile Gardens. His wife, who was fooling around with another man, sued him for divorce and tried to take Reptile Gardens away from him. At the trial, the poor fellow went crazy, shot the judge, the opposing attorney, and his two-timing wife. As far as I know, he is still in jail today.

Snakes were not the only things I sold to Reptile Gardens. One day, the owner asked me to bring him a load of horseshit.

"What for?" I wanted to know.

"Never mind," he said, "just get me the stuff—and some buffalo shit, too."

I went home to the ranch and filled up the pickup. Old Man Madson came over and asked, "What in hell are you doing with all that horseshit?"

I said, "They want it at Reptile Gardens, and a lot of buffalo chips, too. They're paying me fifty bucks for this load."

Madson grinned and waved his arms around. "Help yourself to all you want," he said. "There's tons of this stuff around."

Then I drove over to the buffalo range and picked up a load of *ta-chesli* (buffalo chips). At Reptile Gardens, they took the best-shaped horse apples and buffalo patties and put little white eyes and feet on them and sold this shit to the tourists, together with a little card that read, "The Real McCoy." Can you imagine, tourists buying horseshit for souvenirs? It strengthened my opinion that white society was going crazy.

I had the *zuzecha* power, the "power over snakes." I could control a rattlesnake by waving eagle feathers over it. Eagles, hawks, and even roadrunners eat rattlers. In a fight between bird and snake, the snake always loses. So when a rattler senses the movement of feathers, it does not coil to strike but stretches out, trying to get away. Then I could grab the snake and pick it up. The Hopi also use two large eagle feathers to control rattlers during their famous snake dance.

Sometimes I would impress people by holding up two rattlesnakes by their tails, one in each hand. The snake can only lift itself up about a third of its own length, so this stunt is quite safe, but it always made those who watched me shudder.

I was a foolish showoff in my youth. I could grab a large *sinte-hla* (rattlesnake) by the tail and crack it like a buggy whip, snapping the head clear off. I once wanted to surprise my father with this trick. When I snapped the snake, the head with its dripping fangs just missed him by a hair, and the tongue came off and got stuck on his cheek. My father did not say a word; he just brushed off the tongue, gave me a long look, then got up and walked away.

In 1970, I was preparing a Purification ceremony and found a coiled, white rattlesnake in the pit that had been prepared to receive the heated rocks inside the sweatlodge. I coaxed the snake out of the pit. It was about five feet long with a snow-white body, sparkling ruby eyes, and a pink tail. I showed it to my uncle, who said, "This snake is very sacred, as sacred as a white buffalo." I prayed for this white *sinte-hla* and thanked it for guarding the sweatlodge and the fire pit. Then I gently released it.

My strangest snake story has to do with my Granduncle Frank Sleeping Bear, a powerful *yuwipi* man, one who performs our sacred Yuwipi ceremony. A certain white man and his wife were homesteading near White River. These people had a problem with a very large rattlesnake that crawled into the house every day. They could not figure out how this snake was entering their home because they had stuffed up every opening through which it might come, and they were very much afraid.

The couple went to Jake Kills-on-Sight, the tribal-land-enterprise chairman at Rosebud at that time, and asked him, "Is there someone who could help us?" Jake told them to get ahold of a Sacred Pipe and to load it with traditional Indian tobacco. "Present this Pipe to Frank Sleeping Bear," he advised them. "He has the power to rid you of that snake." They did what he had told them.

Frank Sleeping Bear was our neighbor at Corn Creek. He grew blind in his old age, but at the time all this happened, he still had his eyesight. When the homesteader arrived with the pipe, explaining the problem he had with that big *sinte-hla*, Uncle Frank hitched up his team and, together with his son Paul, drove his buggy the thirty-five miles to White River. Many Lakota people also went along because Uncle Frank was a very powerful shaman, and they wanted to witness whatever ceremonies he was going to perform.

When Uncle Frank arrived at the homesteaders' place, he made them remove everything from their living room, including furniture, pictures, and rugs. They left the room completely bare except for a huge old iron stove bearing the cast image of a hunter on horseback chasing a stag. Frank then had all the windows covered with blankets because the Yuwipi ceremony had to be performed in total darkness. He also made an earth altar, complete with buffalo skull and deer antlers. Then he laid out a sacred square with a string of tobacco offerings and told all present to sit with their backs against the four bare walls. When all was ready, Uncle Frank blew out the kerosene lamp, and everything was engulfed in inky blackness.

Paul started pounding the drum, singing sacred songs with his powerful voice. All at once, little lights started flitting through the dark like fireflies. The door burst open, and through it came a large *wagmuha*, a ceremonial gourd rattle flying through the air. It was made from buffalo intestines and filled with tiny crystals taken from the ant people. It was making a noise like the rattling of a *sinte-hla*.

Then an eagle flew into the room, filling it with its high-pitched scream. You could not see it, but you could feel its presence and its feathers brushing your cheeks. Then there was a rumbling in the chimney. This was the rattle-snake entering the house. Uncle Frank cried out, "All you people, bend down. Put your heads on the ground, because this snake is going to fly through the room."

Everyone heard the whoosh of the snake circling and rattling overhead. Uncle Frank talked to the snake in Lakota, and with a tremendous noise it rushed out the chimney again. Uncle Frank lit the lamp again, and everyone saw that the iron stove lay broken in a hundred pieces. The chimney had been crushed, and there was a big hole in the roof. The old white woman started wailing that the stove was an heirloom that she and her husband had hauled all the way from Pennsylvania and that her own grandfather had brought it to America from Germany in a sailing ship.

Then Uncle Frank turned off the lamp for the second part of the ceremony. The snake came in again, and the glowworm-like lights flitted through the air in rhythm to the drumbeat. Spirit voices were whispering as Uncle Frank spoke with the *sinte-hla*. And once more, the snake went out through the hole in the roof amid the sound of metal striking metal. When Uncle Frank lit the lamp again, there stood the stove, all joined together again as if welded, and the hole in the roof was gone. Everything was as it had been before the ceremony.

Uncle Frank told the white couple, "You will never see that snake again. Iyan Wasichu has taken it away for good, but you will also never be able to use your stove. Its parts have melted into each other through the power of the Yuwipi."

The two white people thanked Uncle Frank for having rid them of the snake that had been such a nightmare to them. The husband asked, "Mr. Sleeping Bear, what do we owe you for your services?"

Uncle Frank told them, "We never want to be paid for doing our ceremonies. You have fed us, and that is enough."

Later, everyone was standing around the house, stretching and yawning. Uncle Frank noticed a white stallion in the corral next to the house. "That's a fine horse you have there," Uncle Frank told the homesteader, nodding toward the corral. When it was time for Uncle Frank and his son to go back to Corn Creek, they found the stallion tied to their wagon and the white couple smiling, waving their goodbyes.

"These folks have Indian hearts," was Uncle Frank Sleeping Bear's comment as he drove off.

CHAPTER 9

Hollywood Heyoka

A *heyoka* is a "contrary," an upside-down, cold-hot, backward-forward man, a tragicomical spiritual clown. He can make weeping people laugh. He has special, supernatural powers. A *heyoka* is a thunder dreamer. He becomes a sacred clown by dreaming of the Wakinyan, the Thunderbirds or Thunderbeings, or things spiritually connected with them, such as lightning, gray horses, snowbirds, or frogs.

There have always been *heyokas* in my family, on both my father's and my mother's side. Old John himself was a *heyoka* for a while. That's why he became a well-known rodeo clown in the guise of Alice Jitterbug. Maybe it was due to my own inherited *heyoka* nature that I was fated to become a Hollywood stuntman.

In the spring of 1949, when I was fourteen, some people came out from Hollywood to interview Indians for bit parts for a movie. I thought, "Here is my chance to make some money." I was then working at a sawmill earning starvation wages. I was always hungry and thin as a reed. The movie people had set up their office on the second floor of the old Alex Johnson Hotel, a nice art deco building with heavy overhead beams decorated with Indian designs. There were a lot of Sioux there already when I showed up.

The "interviewers" didn't bother to ask us any questions; they just hired us on the spot—two big busloads full of Indians. Of course, all the big speaking parts were played by white actors made to look like 'skins. The picture was called *Tomahawk*, and the big star was Ward Bond. I was supposed to be his youngest son. We spent the first day of shooting in the Black Hills, sacred to the Lakota people as the home of the Thunderbirds.

The whole heyoka business started with the makeup people trying to make us full-bloods look "more Indian." For a start, we were all sprayed with coffee-colored body paint to make us look "authentic" in Technicolor. It was like sheep dipping, and we Indians were the sheep. Then we got flesh-colored jockstraps, breechcloths, and leggings. They also gave us moccasins; however, when they ran out of these, some of the Pine Ridge boys were left in their striped socks and sneakers.

It hardly mattered. There was a lady designer on the set whose job was to make sure that we looked like "real" Indians. She was from New York and had never seen an Indian before, but she said that she was a costume expert. She was very friendly and thought that our jockstraps were just the right color.

We next had to have our faces painted. The makeup artists were told to make us look "real mean and savage, like olden-day braves." As a result, we looked more like circus clowns than Lakota warriors. The Hollywood folks did not know that face painting always had a spiritual meaning and was done according to a warrior's vision. Whenever Crazy Horse went into battle, he painted his horse with lightning and hailstone designs to make it fast and bulletproof. Our lady designer knew nothing of such things. The cubistic designs she had them put on our faces could have been thought up by Picasso.

Next, cheesecloth and wigs were put on our heads. Everybody was given a wig made out of what appeared to be old mattress stuffing. At this time, most Sioux men wore their hair short. Braids or long hair, the movie people told us, were signs of backwardness, of "going back to the blanket." Being a traditional full-blood, I wore my hair long, but they put cheesecloth and false braids on top of it, anyhow. The producer came, together with his hangers-on, to inspect us. He said we were a "colorful lot," and he was right. The lady designer told us, "Now you look like real Indians."

Finally, we got our "weapons"—including rubber tomahawks and African shields, which made us look even more colorful. We also got guns loaded with blanks. The blanks included both yellow and red shells, the red ones making a bigger bang. Then we were told to go and pick our horses.

There were no less than four hundred horses inside a huge corral, and some of them had never been ridden before. They gave us all short ropes, and one of the film crew told me, "Chief, you're on your own. Catch any horse you can!" I knew horses, and I looked for one with saddle marks on it, making sure the critter had been ridden before. Some of the boys didn't know about horses and got bucked off. A few of them quit then and there.

For the first scene, we were told to ride to the top of a hill and, on a given signal, to come thundering down upon a "fort" that had been put up for the occasion by the construction crew. We had to attack the fort four times before the director was satisfied. He was waiting for a cloud to cover part of the sun for "dramatic lighting," but the cloud always went where it was not wanted.

One scene was loused up by one of my uncles, Tom Jumping Elk, whose mouth was full of gold teeth. He came charging down the hill with a big grin, and the sun made his teeth flash like a truck's headlights. So they painted his teeth black, and we finally got the scene right on the fourth attempt.

During the following days, we had to attack a wagon train. The wagons were gathered in a circle for defense, and we were told to ride around and around those buggies, hollering and firing our guns. Every few seconds, one of us had to fall off his horse, pretending to be shot by the soldiers and settlers. They paid each of us twenty-five dollars for falling from a horse at a dead run; otherwise, we got only ten bucks for a full day's work. Of course, I fell off as often as I could and managed to get myself "killed" three times in one afternoon.

I could never figure out why, in all those Western movies, the Indians are always shown riding around and around these wagons to get themselves shot instead of charging in and counting coup. If we really had been that stupid in those times, there wouldn't be any Sioux left.

Soon a routine was established. Every evening we would be driven down from the hills back to Rapid City and the Alex Johnson Hotel to receive our ten bucks and the extra money for being "shot" off our ponies. The next morning, we would be loaded up into our buses again and driven to whatever location the director had picked for the day's shooting. It sure beat working for the sawmill.

A short time later, they made another film called *The Savage.* I had developed a taste for the movie industry's green frogskins and again got myself a job as an "extra." *The Savage,* too, was shot in the Black Hills. Most movies having to do with Indians are either filmed in the Black Hills or in

Monument Valley, whether it makes historical sense or not. In the movie *Cheyenne Autumn*, the Cheyennes are supposed to travel a thousand miles from southern Oklahoma to northern Montana; but somehow, they never make it out of Monument Valley.

During the making of *The Savage*, still years before I went in the army, I had my first chance to do a real stunt. Somebody said, "We need a kid who can swim." I immediately volunteered. I had to be way up in a tree with a river thirty feet or more below. A white soldier was supposed to shoot me down from the branch on which I was sitting. One of the bit players aimed a gun at me and fired, and I plopped down into the water, only to find myself entangled in some moss-covered roots. Some of the older guys had to jump in and rescue me.

"Sonny," said the director, "you've got to do it again." They dried me off, spray painted me again, and fixed me up with a new wig. I had to fall into the river three more times before they were satisfied.

"Sonny," the director told me, "you'd make a damn good stuntman. We need an Indian stuntman like you in Hollywood." It was fate speaking to me.

As early as the next day, I had to do another stunt. We were filming near Sylvan Lake. At that time, it was still unspoiled and beautiful with its spectacular rock wall. There were no stores, tourist cabins, or campgrounds. Three of us Sioux had to cross the lake hanging on to the tails of our horses. This looks easy, but it is actually hard to do. If you pull too much to one side or the other, you might flip the horse over, and it could drown.

I was happy. Here I was, doing what I thought was great fun and getting paid for it. I thought to myself: "It's the movies for me from now on!"

Eventually, after many other odd jobs and serving in the army, I went to Hollywood. There, I became a stuntman, bit player, horse wrangler, and trainer. After a number of years, I also became an advisor, trying to make sure that Native Americans were no longer depicted as mindless, tomahawk-wielding savages. I also saw to it that the films I was involved in were historically and visually correct. I was a stuntman or bit player in more than a dozen films, including *The Battlefield of Chief Pontiac, Stagecoach, Across the Wide Missouri,* and *Broken Arrow.*

Both my father and I were also hired as consultants for *Return of a Man Called Horse.* In typical Hollywood fashion, they did it all their way. When our recommendations didn't agree with their sensationalism, they ignored us. Then in the end, they used our names to promote their product, which made a mockery of Lakota religion and culture.

During the making of *Return of a Man Called Horse*, the script called for the Indians to kill a buffalo with bows and arrows. Of course, there was hardly anyone left alive who could kill a bull buffalo with an arrow; besides, it would have been too dangerous. If the bull turned and gored or killed a rider, the studio would have a million-dollar lawsuit on its hands. What was shown, then, was Indians shooting arrows and then a quick cut to a dead buffalo with some arrows sticking in its side.

A friend of mine from the reservation who was working on the film told me that one of the agreements between the film people and the reservation was that any buffalo killed for the film would be butchered and given to the poorer families on the reservation. But that evening, when when it was getting dark, the director said, "Hang that carcass up in a tree so the wolves and coyotes don't get at it. We'll get a freezer truck out here to take it to the meat locker after we're through with it tomorrow." There hadn't been any wolves in the Black Hills for years, but someone had told the director a cock-and-bull story that wolves were still roaming around in the sacred Paha Sapa.

Through my friend, word quickly got out around the nearby Pine Ridge reservation that there was a buffalo hanging from a tree and destined for a meat locker. During the night, several men from Pine Ridge drove over in a pickup and cut the buffalo down, and the next morning, many poor families found packages of buffalo meat at their doors.

That same morning, when the film crew arrived at the place where the buffalo was supposed to be, only parts of the hind legs were left hanging from the tree—just the first joints and the hooves. The director was having a fit, cussing and carrying on about how he still needed the buffalo for the next scene.

My friend put on his most innocent expression and said, "The wolves must have had a go at it." The director gave him a dirty look, mumbling something about a wolf with a knife or a hatchet. So they had to buy and kill another buffalo. This time, they made sure it wound up in a freezer instead of in a tree.

Another scene in *Return of a Man Called Horse* called for Indian women mourning the death of their men killed in battle. The director said,

"We've rounded up a lot of women, and we want you to teach them a sacred death song."

Of course, I had no intention of using a sacred song for a white man's movie. I got all these women together, some of them non-Indian made to look like Sioux, and taught them a funny little kids' song that every boy and girl on the Res knows by heart. To the whites, all native songs sound sad because they are in a minor key. So here came all these women singing this humorous song while tearing their hair and pretending to weep. Sioux, whenever they see this picture, always crack up at this scene. I guess it was my *heyoka* nature that made me do it.

Speaking of language, one of our all-time favorite movies is an oldie called (as far as I can remember) *The Great Sioux Uprising*. It has some real 'skins speaking real Lakota. Of course, no one but Sioux can understand what they are saying. The film has subtitles like, "This white man speaks the truth; he does not speak with a forked tongue," or "This soldier chief is a man we can trust." What our bit players were really saying were things like, "This white man does it in the ass," or "This *che-hinkta* can't get it up anymore." That, too, was *heyoka* business, making our people laugh.

When the original film in the series, *A Man Called Horse*, was filmed many years earlier, I was not yet a consultant and could not influence the script; I was not even allowed to read it. I therefore could not prevent the desecration of the Sundance, and the film portrayed a caricature of our most sacred ceremony. The movie scene was depicted as shown in paintings by George Catlin that were more than a hundred years old—paintings not of a Lakota Sundance but of a Mandan "Okipah." In that grotesque movie scene, Richard Harris is shown hanging from the beams of an earth lodge, his rubber or plastic "chest" pierced by skewers. He was supposedly undergoing this self-torture in order to show his bravery, to be accepted into the tribe, and, incidentally, to get himself a pretty wife.

All this is a gross misrepresentation. In the real Sundance, men make a vow to undergo the "piercing" in order to take pain away from a sick mother or father, or to get a son back from a war in one piece, or maybe to get a brother out of jail. The whole thing was not the fault of Harris, who is a nice guy and who at that time knew nothing about Lakota rituals.

Years later, they made *Return of a Man Called Horse*, with now white-haired Richard Harris in the lead. Richard and I worked well together. I spent nights trying to teach him Lakota, which was not an easy job. Richard is different from most actors in that he does his own stunts. He does them wrong all the time, but he is a very stubborn Englishman. He does things his way or not at all. It was fun watching him.

We were shooting in the Black Hills near Custer, South Dakota, which bills itself as "the town with the gunsmoke flavor." The American Indian Movement has called South Dakota the "most racist state in the union" and Custer the most racist town within it. The town is, of course, named after General George Armstrong Custer of Little Bighorn fame. Custer is a typical Western tourist town with motels and shops selling "Indian" curios made in Taiwan and Hong Kong. During the summer season, there are daily reenactments of famous shootouts and the hanging of "Flyspeck Billy," a local nineteenth-century bad man.

During the shooting of *Return of a Man Called Horse*, I walked into one of Custer's restaurants, wearing my braids and Indian outfit—and waited, and waited, and waited. No one would serve me. Twenty minutes went by, and I was just kept sitting there. Then Richard Harris came in and sat down at my table. In no time at all, the owner, a waiter, and a waitress were dancing attendance around us.

"Why wasn't my friend served?" Richard asked them. "He's been sitting here for a long time."

They answered, "Oh, we've been very busy."

Harris told them, "We are very busy, too—going to find a place where we are welcome." And we left. So I like that man.

I was one of thirty Indians who got a part in a movie called *The Battlefield of Chief Pontiac*. The leading actor was Lex Barker, who also used to play Tarzan. This movie, too, was done in the Black Hills, even though Pontiac had never been west of the Mississippi.

The director, whose name I forget, asked me and two friends of mine to ride our horses to the top of a hill and make smoke signals. So the three of us took a blanket, a jug of water, and rode up. We took dry leaves, wetted them down, and made some pretty good smoke signals. They told us they would flash us a sign from below with a mirror if our smoke signals were all right.

After five or six smoke signals, the mirror flashed that everything was OK. We did not have any other scenes to do that day, so we decided to have a race. I said, "Let's have a run down to the location. The first one gets all he can drink at the nearest bar, the last one pays."

The three of us came thundering down the hill in a huge cloud of dust. My big brown horse was running full speed, and I was riding it bareback with just a rope around its mouth. I pulled back on the rope, and it broke. My horse bolted, and we burst into the middle of a scene where Lex Barker was shooting it out with the Redcoats.

Everything went ass-over-teakettle. That horse was knocking down everything in its way—cameras, cameramen, microphone booms, and movie lights. I had no way of reining the critter in. Three cowboys chased after me, trying to stop my horse. They chased us for three miles, all the way from the grass-covered hills down into the timber. Everything was in a mess, and the director was flat on his backside, hollering, "Cut, cut, cut!" In the end, though, he took it philosophically: "What's one more day of shooting? Let's all go and have a drink."

The most ridiculous movie I was ever involved in was *Crazy Horse*, with Victor Mature, of all people, portraying the greatest of our Lakota warriors. The trouble with Victor was that he was deathly afraid of horses; he panicked at the mere smell of them. He wouldn't ride a horse if his whole movie career depended on it.

The script called for Crazy Horse riding into battle surrounded by his faithful band of warriors. Gorgeously attired with a huge feather bonnet on his head, "Crazy Horse Mature" galloped forth to fight the white man—riding on a stepladder. The ladder was carried by four burly guys who moved it around in such a way that Victor's head kept bobbing up and down above the surrounding crowd of warriors. The cameramen tried in vain to make this *heyoka* ride look natural. All of us, whites and Indians alike, had a hard time keeping straight faces. Though it was comical, to us Sioux, the whole thing was a travesty and a slap in the face.

In *Stay Away Joe*, a movie made in Sedona, Arizona (a spectacular place of red rocks shaped like battleships, clouds, and ghosts), I rode a Brahma bull for Elvis Presley, who was playing a no-good, Indian hell-raiser. First, from different angles, they took long shots of me actually riding the bull. Then, for closeups, they put Elvis on a bucking bronco machine and told him to hang on. Around him, they placed padded mats to land on in case he was thrown. So he was just sitting on that damn "mechanical bronc" with his head bobbing up and down while the cameramen did fillers and cut-ins, always with the same background.

As for me, trying to hold on for dear life while bucking all over the place on that ornery bull, I belatedly worked up a mighty respect for my father. I had many occasions to remember that he had ridden Brahma bulls as a steady routine in countless rodeos and that he had also been "sky fishing" atop genuine, wild buffalo bulls.

I was drinking heavily in those days. Elvis, Kathy Jurado, and the other actors in *Stay Away Joe* weren't exactly teetotalers, either. We demolished an average of two cases of beer a day, plus a few bottles of wine and Jim Beam on the side. Kathy is a fine and beautiful woman who played a barfly type, and Elvis played an incorrigible boozer, so it all fit together nicely.

When I was told, usually three days ahead, that I would have to do some difficult stunts, I always went on a drunk for the first two days and sobered up on the third with oceans of black coffee. Often, we had to delay shooting because one or the other actor had belted down one too many. A few times, Elvis threw tantrums, and we all got the whole day off. On such occasions, the director would say, "OK, let's do a scene Elvis has no part in," but by then everybody would be inside the big company tent swilling wine.

It took nine months to shoot *Stay Away Joe*; it was supposed to have been finished in three. Coincidentally, I had known Elvis before, when we were both serving in the army in Baden-Baden, Germany. He had the bed next to mine, but he was seldom in it.

After my first experiences with moviemaking and movie people, I went to Los Angeles. I lived there off and on for a good part of my life. Hollywood was about the only place an Indian could make a living. There, I became "Tinsel Town's" Native American stuntman. I did tricks with horses, worked as a wrangler at ranches that specialized in training horses for the movies, drove stagecoaches, did parachute jumps, and performed a lot of dangerous acts the white movie stars could not or would not do. In many movies, the face of the man on the bucking bronc was the actor's but the body was mine. In these films, they "chopped" my head off and replaced it with the one of the lead man.

Stunts paid a lot more than "walk-ons" such as saloon fistfights. You got more for falling off a cliff than for walking around in a blanket and Uncle Joe hat. Back then, stunting was not the scientific business it is now. Today, they teach beginners how to fall from a galloping horse without getting hurt; I had to figure that out for myself. In the old days, we lost a lot of horses. Today, they stage huge buffalo hunts with dead horses and buffalo all over the place, but in reality, not a single animal is killed or injured. In the old days, they used invisible wires to trip a horse as it ran, making it go down end over end. Sometimes the wire would break the horse's neck. Later, horses were taught how to fall. Today, each Western stuntman has his own personal horse. He trains it to rear, fall over backward, or tumble on its side. Rubber stirrups are also used so that when the horse falls on its side it doesn't fracture a rib, as sometimes happened with wooden or metal stirrups.

To prevent injuries, stuntmen also prefer saddles without horns. A horse is taught to fall while standing still with its rider beside it. The horse has to learn to know its rider and the signals to do its different tricks. It takes a good month for the horse to learn this. Some animals are trained to run at full speed on a hard surface but to go down the moment they hit sand. Hitting anything soft is their cue. This also gives confidence to the rider, who knows that he'll be landing on soft sand.

If a stuntman retires, he has to put his horse out to pasture or have it destroyed because it is no good to anyone else. It is so used to its rider that it would be dangerous for anyone else to try using it for stunts. The bond between man and horse is very strong. It is not just a bread-and-butter business. I have seen rough, grizzled stuntmen weep when they had to shoot their old, staggering, or ailing horses. There is a lot of heartache involved in this profession.

Some horses I knew were the equivalent of four-legged movie stars. Just as a famous actor had stuntmen to do the dangerous work for him, his famous horse also had its look-alike to do the falling down. Horses like John Wayne's Dollar or Roy Rogers' Trigger were too valuable to be exposed to the dangers of stunting. Thunderhead, Flicka, and Black Beauty all had their four-legged stand-ins, too.

I had a friend, Yakima Kinook, another full-blood Indian "fall guy," who trained John Wayne's horses and did the stunts for him. Old Yak had a body like Wayne's and from a distance looked exactly like him. He also trained Wayne's famous horse, Dollar. Dollar was a dark, sorrel horse. He was so tame you could put ten babies on his back and he would never buck. He was the gentlest critter I ever came across, but in the movies they made him look like a wild, ferocious, eye-rolling stallion.

Wayne had another famous horse named Cochise, a truly magnificent Appaloosa that he used in the movie *True Grit*. Like Trigger, Cochise was too valuable for rough work and had his own "double," another Appaloosa that was very similar if you didn't look too close.

One day I was currying Trigger, the horse of the "singing cowboy." (Actually, this was not the original Trigger, but Trigger VI or Trigger VII. Moviegoers had gotten so used to the obediently rearing horse that, when it died, it had to be replaced by another one that looked exactly like it. So there was a whole succession of "Triggers.") While I was currying Trigger, a man came into the stable and introduced himself. "My name is Leonard Sly, from Ohio," he said. "I see you're taking good care of my horse."

I told him, "This is Mr. Roy Rogers' horse."

"Roy Rogers is my stage name," he said.

I said, "Funny, you don't look a bit like Roy Rogers."

He grinned. "I never look like myself until I put on my fancy duds and white Stetson." That is how I first met the singing cowboy.

One of the old favorite stunts in "Oaters," or Westerns, was riding horses in and out of saloons, breaking windows and all the bottles on the bar. For this, they used some stuff called "breakaway." It looks like glass but is made out of a candylike substance. You can tap it lightly with your fingernail and it breaks without sharp edges. In saloon scenes, when you see guys hitting each other over the head with whiskey bottles, they're using breakaway.

Then there are the stagecoaches. You don't just jump in a stagecoach and drive away. You've got six horses in front and six reins to manipulate, meaning you've got to concentrate. The horses have to be trained to work as a team. It all takes skill. The old man from Czechoslovakia who used to make traditional stagecoaches for the movies passed away years ago. Now all the stagecoaches you see on the screen are made from fiberglass—the whole body. They are all made in Silmar, California.

Also, on stagecoaches, they don't use the old-fashioned wagon brakes anymore, but modern disc brakes. I was there when these were first demonstrated. The driver made the mistake of applying the front instead of the rear brakes, and the back of the coach came up in the air and fell over on him. Luckily, he wasn't hurt.

We have no wheelwrights anymore, either—men who could fashion a wheel with oaken spokes and iron rims. You can't find a place now where someone can shrink down a wagon wheel and fix it the old way. It's all make-believe now.

Movie animals get awards, just like human actors. I remember a horse named Blake who was supposed to get an award for some fancy jumping. It belonged to a millionaire who had put some of his money into a movie ranch and who had his son run the place. The young man was not sure he could handle the horse onstage, fearing that the lights and loudspeakers might spook it, so the job was given to me.

The "rancher" showed up in a glittering, brocaded cowboy outfit complete with a huge white Stetson. He was chomping on a huge cigar. As I led the horse out to get its award, it promptly pooped all over the red carpet that covered the stage.

I said to the millionaire, "This is not my job. You're the papa—*you* clean up." He gave me a dirty look.

Someone brought the man a shovel. Just as he was cleaning up the huge pile of horseshit, and just as the MC was reading the award citation, the horse pissed all over him. So they handed the poor fellow a mop while hanging a ribboned medal around the horse's neck. This goes to show that even when you're not doing stunts, working with horses has its dangers.

Of course, there are other animals in the movies besides horses—everything from elephants to insects. My friend Jim Arness was telling me about a scene in which a snarling wolf was supposed to attack him. For this scene, they got ahold of a very friendly collie and stuffed a ferocious-looking set of rubber teeth into its mouth, which made the dog look like a man-eater. Jim had to do the same scene almost a dozen times because that mutt kept losing its teeth and wagging its tail and licking his hands.

Arness also had a scene in which he was being attacked by a cougar. For this, they used a pet mountain lion that was forever jumping into Jim's arms, rubbing up against him, and purring loudly. It sounded like somebody's motor running. Jim finally managed to play-wrestle with the animal, which gave them fine shots that made it look as if the big cat was tearing him apart.

Another animal that sometimes visited the ranch was a large playful bear named Gentle Ben, who liked to wrestle and was the children's favorite. He had to wear a muzzle because bears are supposed to be unpredictable. The muzzle was painted the same color as Ben's fur to make it invisible. Countless actors in countless scenes have been "hugged to death" by this lovable mountain of fur.

I had a friend named Mo who specialized in training small animals for the movies—foxes, badgers, squirrels, anything smaller than a coyote. Once they were making a horror movie about rats, and Mo had to train the animals for it. He found that the rats were intelligent, cooperative, and fast learners. Mo's superstar, which he called "Jimmy Durante" on account of its long, twitching nose, had its own rat "stand-in," naturally. That's Hollywood for you.

During my stunting days, I fell not only from horses but also from trees, roofs, and cliffs. This was easy because down below there was always a big air balloon waiting to catch me. If the cameramen kept shooting a bit too long, they could later see me bouncing back up when they ran the "dailies" in the projection room.

Nowadays, stuntmen are specialists. The ones who do car crashes don't fall from horses, and the guy who dives head first out of a plane doesn't work with explosives. But I was "that crazy Injun all-around fellow." Almost every day, my agent would call: "Archie, you want to do a stunt with buffalos?" . . . "You want to do some parachuting?" . . . "You feel like jumping from a fifth-floor window?" I even had to do a car stunt once, flipping over. I was fully protected: there was a roll-bar in the car; I wore a helmet; and I had padding all around me. Today, car chases, crashes, and fiery explosions are staples in most crime movies, and specialists do incredible stunts that nobody in his right mind would have dared to perform in my day.

Jumping out of airplanes was a specialty of mine. I jumped for commercials, for TV series, and for World War II movies. In my day, parachute jumps seldom turned out perfectly because the cameraman would have to jump right alongside me in order to get an ideal shot, and none of them wanted to do that. Once, they put a camera in my hands so that I could film another jumper coming down. I did free-falls and every kind of stunt one can do with a parachute, and I was always scared. Altogether, I jumped out of airplanes about two hundred times. Sometimes, after I landed, I had to feel around to see whether I had wet my pants.

As I mentioned, I had learned jumping in the army, in the 504th Airborne Regiment of the 82d Airborne Division—the "Devils in Baggy Pants." My scariest experience was not doing parachute stunts for movies but during a routine jump near Wiesbaden, Germany. At the preselected altitude, everybody went out the door. I was last because I was the jump master.

According to standard procedure, if your chute doesn't open after you've counted slowly to four, you look up. If the chute is streamlining or doing what they call a "Roman candle," spiraling or all tangled up, then you open your spare chute. That time, after counting to four, I tried to pull the cord, but nothing happened. I felt myself bouncing against something. I looked and saw to my horror that I was dangling on the side of the plane, a C-132 Flying Hercules.

"Oh my God!" I said to myself. "How in hell am I going to get out of this mess?"

I saw the huge tail above me, and I was spinning around constantly, bumping into the plane's side again and again. In such a predicament, we had been trained to put our hands on our helmets to indicate that we were alive and conscious. I did this, hoping that somebody would cut me loose so that I could use the reserve chute.

As I was hanging up there, the plane was already making a second circle—a big one, coming back around. The crew wanted to cut me loose, but first they had to fly into the drop zone. It was like an eternity. One member of the crew was yelling, "Hang on! Hang on! Hang on! Just a few more minutes! Just another second!" I dangled there for the full circle, praying. I never prayed so hard in my life.

Finally, I heard somebody yell, "Are you ready?" I touched my helmet and felt myself falling. They had cut the cord from the plane. I felt a tremendous relief, but it was a little premature. I looked up to see the static line streaming after me when it should have been the parachute. The static line is what pulls out the chute. I pulled and pulled at the reserve, but with my luck the pilot chute didn't spring out like it was supposed to; it fell down. I picked it up and threw it until it caught the air, all the time falling, falling, falling. At last I saw the chute opening up. What a beautiful sight! When I felt the tug, I thanked Wakan Tanka, the Creator: "*Pilamaye!* Thank you, thank you!" I didn't care how I might hit the ground or whether I might break a leg or crack a rib—I was alive!

As it happened, I landed very easily and unhurt. I was just folding up my parachute when the captain came up to me and said, "Come on, Sergeant, time for you to go right back up."

I said, "Oh, my God, can't you wait a week or two?"

"No, this is a confidence jump. You've got to go right back up there."

The plane landed, and up we went, the captain and I. Even though I was a jump-school instructor, I didn't feel too confident, thinking, "What if it happens again?"

As a souvenir, the jump attendants gave me a piece of the cord they had cut loose. Then out the door I went, the captain alongside me.

Of course, my chute opened beautifully this time. As we floated down, the captain kept talking to me through the air: "What a beautiful sight! Isn't jumping great?" and all that shit. I freed one hand for a second to give him the finger.

Having related this story, telling about my jumps for the movies would be boring. They were all routine.

When a stuntman became too old, too heavy, or too slow to do stunts with horses, he often became a wrangler. A wrangler takes care of horses back at the movie ranch or on the set. In that way, an old bit player or stunt-man can continue working in the motion picture business. That's what happened to me.

When I was about thirty-eight, I became a foreman at the Randall ranch, which kept and trained movie horses and other animals. The ranch had been started by by Glenn Randall, an old cowboy from Nebraska, and he and his two sons were still training horses there. Randall was just about the best trainer of stunt horses I ever met, and I learned a lot from him. On the ranch, we kept 225 horses, as well as mules, donkeys, Brahma bulls, cows, and even camels—any kind of good-sized critter the movie people might want.

We had only a half dozen or so full-blooded Arabians on the place because real Arabians are too high strung and nervous to be used in movies. So we got common horses of different breeds, some of which looked like Arabians.

A movie horse must be able to stand very still and not get shy or jumpy when a rifle is being fired close to its head. It must also be able to stay calm when cameras are rolling and coming at it. Such horses are hard to find, and they have to be carefully trained. I was told that the French emperor Napoleon's horses had cannons fired off close to them and had live chickens thrown between their legs for weeks. Only when absolutely nothing could spook them anymore would Napoleon get on them. He was a lousy horseman, just like most of our movie stars.

The horses of famous Western actors all had doubles. The movie stars' horses were all very tame, while their doubles, to be ridden by the stunt-men, were always frisky. There were also two sets of look-alike saddles, bridles, boots, and spurs. We had to have two of everything.

The feet and hooves of our horses were the most important things to watch over, and we had three blacksmiths working all the time, doing nothing but making and fitting horseshoes. We never allowed a horse to stand longer than necessary in mud or water because the underfoot, called the "frog," starts to deteriorate and get sore. Therefore, you have to keep the foot dry—but not too dry, or you'll get cracks in the hoof, which in turn calls for corrective shoeing. For parades or riding on hard, smooth surfaces, we used rubber cleats so that the horses would not slip or fall. We even had horseshoes for special occasions made out of thick rubber. They were like galoshes, fitting completely over the horse's hooves. Each horse on the ranch got a new set of shoes every four to six weeks.

I was responsible for the whole ranch: the food, the water, the clean-liness—in a word, everything. I had to make sure that the horses going out for work were in top condition and that they were in top condition when they came back.

Once, I worked with cows—thirty-six young heifers and one Brahma bull from a ranch in Brawley. They had all been running wild, and we had to catch, tame, and train them for a Barbra Streisand movie to be filmed in, of all places, Manhattan. First we had to rope and transport them to Randall's place, and they didn't like it. They also didn't like being tied up. We had to scratch their sides with rakes and brush them down with curry combs to make them clean and pretty.

As with horses, we had to work very close to these wild cows in order to avoid being kicked. At six feet, a horse can kick your head right off. It doesn't know any better; all it sees is a shadow.

After two weeks, our cows were like kittens. They were so tame they would let us sit on top of them. They were more docile than pet poodles. We didn't even need tranquilizers to get them on the airplane.

Then, in New York, the movie people paraded them into the streets. Cars were honking, people were screaming, and the air was filled with the never-ending noise of the Big Apple. But the cows behaved beautifully, trotting in step down the avenue. The Brahma bull even had a rider, and he, too, did his part without a hitch.

Since this was a kind of Christmas parade, we also provided three camels for the Three Wise Men to ride—three very arrogant-looking critters, trained by "camel specialists." It was quite an experience.

When I started out in the movie business, the better Native American parts were all played by whites. Indians were played by Hungarians, Greeks, Italians, Hawaiians, and Hispanics, but never by Indians. There were some native actors, but they never got bit roles. Also at that time, the Indians portrayed in movies were usually ridiculous stereotypes—drunks, bloodthirsty "red devils," or romanticized "noble savages."

It was not until around 1970 that things began to change. Chief Dan George, in *Little Big Man*, and Will Sampson, in *One Flew Over the Cuckoo's Nest*, were among the first Native American actors who were given a chance to play memorable roles. However, fame came too late for these two. When they finally got the recognition they deserved, they were already in the twilight of their careers. About that time, I switched from running the Randall ranch to being an advisor on Indian movies, seeing to it that our people were depicted in a true light.

I loved doing motion picture work because the movie people never discriminated against me for being a full-blooded Indian and also because I could make a living at work I enjoyed—being outdoors, riding, and taking care of horses.

I had many friends in Tinsel Town. One of my drinking buddies was the actor Montgomery Clift. We hit the bars together, one after the other, raising hell. Clift was really hot after his great success in *From Here to Eternity*, and the agents were swarming around him with offers like bees around a pot of honey. But he just clapped me on the back and said, "To hell with this shit, Archie. I have more fun sitting with you and a couple of bottles down at the creek, singing and listening to your stories."

We drank anything with alcohol in it. That was the life we chose. It ruin-ed Montgomery, and he passed away like so many other of my drinking companions. That was the sad part of it. Nature created me more rugged than my friends, so I got through that part of my life without too much damage.

Once, when I was pretty well plastered and in a horn-tossing mood, I got into a fistfight with actor Jack Palance and broke his nose. Recently, during the filming of *Young Guns*, a friend of mine asked him whether he remembered the incident. He grinned and said, "It could have happened."

I also got to know Lon Chaney, Jr. when he was playing the faithful Indian sidekick of the white hero in the awful *Hawkeye* series, doing the part in modern bathing trunks. And, of course, as described before, I got drunk with Elvis Presley and the whole cast of *Stay Away Joe*. I also number Charlton Heston and Richard Harris among the top actors I worked with.

Naturally, I felt most at home among Native American actors. Some of them, such as Strong Bull, Yakima Kinook, and Tug Smith, live on in my memory. These actors are completely unknown to white moviegoers because they were never given a chance to show what they could do. I also fondly remember John Big Tree, who started his movie career in 1915. He was already an old man when I started out. Then there was Iron Eyes Cody, one of my father's close friends. He got many of the bigger Native American parts, even though he is only part Indian. He was seen in many posters and on TV with tears in his eyes—an Indian grieving over what the white man is doing to the environment. Iron Eyes is married to a Seneca lady, so his children are real, honest-to-goodness Indians.

One of my closest Native American actor friends was Will Sampson. He was a Cree from Canada and often came to the Rosebud Fair. We always gave him a warm welcome. He was a great actor, and now he has gone to the spirit world. Will was a big fellow like myself. While he was still alive, people often came up to me, saying, "Oh, Mr. Sampson, will you give me your autograph?" And I had to tell them, "No, I'm not Will Sampson. He's my good friend, but I'm getting tired of saying, 'I'm not Will Sampson.' It seems that to you whites, all Indians look alike."

I loved and admired Chief Dan George. He was a wonderful actor who could move an audience to tears. He was a chief of the Squamish tribe in Canada. Sadly, he, too, has gone south over the Milky Way Trail, like so many of my old friends. Another true pal was Eddie Little Sky, who had good parts in *The Way West* and *Run, Simon, Run*.

Possibly closest to me was Jay Silver Heels, who played Tonto in *The Lone Ranger* series. One time, we made a video together—*In Search of Reality*—and in it, Jay read some Indian poetry so beautifully that I burst into tears. He always told me, "When I die, you've got to do the ceremony for me," and I did see him on to the spirit world.

So many friends, and so many of them gone! It seems as though one moment they were on the set, and the next they had disappeared forever.

There came a time when I remembered that I was a Lame Deer and a Quick Bear, a descendant of medicine men and spiritual leaders. I remembered Grandfather Quick Bear's teaching and the old ceremonies. So I set up a sweatlodge at the place of a friend in Santa Monica, and there we did Inipi ceremonies. Indian stuntmen often came there before doing something dangerous, and so did Jay Silver Heels and Will Sampson before they were tested for big parts.

When my father died, he passed his power on to me. He laid upon me the burden to become a medicine man and healer, a spokesman for the Sacred Pipe. If it were not for this, I think I would go back to Hollywood, to a world of fantasy and make-believe. The world of lights was my life, and I loved it very much.

Archie Fire Lame Deer, 1992. *Veretta* © 1992.

My father, John Fire Lame Deer, in his bonnet in the Paha Sapa, the sacred Black Hills. *Richard Erdoes © 1992.*

Before my father died, he passed on his bonnet to me. I wear
it only during the Sundance in my role as intercessor, the
living link between the people and the Spirit above. *Veretta*
© *1992.*

These rock formations form the heart of the sacred Black Hills, the home of the Thunderbeings. *Richard Erdoes* © *1992.*

Near the place where I lived as a child rise the Badlands, strewn with the bones of long-extinct animals, including Unktehi, the Great Water Monster of our legends. *Richard Erdoes © 1992.*

The Buffalo is our brother who gave its flesh so that our people could survive. White Buffalo Woman, who brought the Sacred Pipe to our people, was the personification of this sacred animal. *Richard Erdoes © 1992.*

We look upon the rattlesnake as sacred. Our legends tell of brothers changed into rattlesnakes. In my youth, I was the chief rattlesnake catcher of South Dakota. *Richard Erdoes* © *1992.*

Bear Butte, at the edge of the Black Hills, is sacred to our Cheyenne brothers as well as to our people. It is a place where I often go to pray. *Veretta* © *1992.*

Before the American Indian Movement discouraged such things, "NO INDIANS ALLOWED" signs could be seen over the entrance to many saloons. *Richard Erdoes © 1990.*

I am a spiritual advisor for Leonard Peltier, the Sioux who is doing two lifetimes in prison for the killing of two FBI agents, something he never did. He is the innocent victim of the white man's hatred for those who speak up for their people. *Richard Erdoes* © *1992.*

Tobacco and cloth offerings are always tied to the branches
and trunk of the Sundance Tree. A buffalo skull serves as our
altar. *Richard Erdoes © 1992.*

In the old days the Plains tribes, including us Lakota, built a so-called "Sundance Lodge," roofed over with poles, like a tipi. Nowadays, we make do with the "Shade," a circle of poles roofed over with pine boughs. *E. Walt Hitts © 1992.*

This is one of our sundancers, his sage wreath around his head, wearing his medicine bag and blowing on his plumed eagle-bone whistle. *Richard Erdoes © 1990.*

It was my father who instructed me in the use of the Sacred Pipe—the "flesh and blood of our people"—whose smoke represents the breath of the Great Spirit. *Richard Erdoes* © *1972.*

I often end my lectures with teaching my listeners how to
purify themselves in a sweatlodge. *Veretta © 1992.*

Archie Fire Lame Deer; his wife, Sandy; their son, John (named after John Fire Lame Deer); their daughters, Josephine (l) and Sarah (r); and, at the far right, one of their nephews, Victor. *Veretta* © *1992.*

CHAPTER 10

Lila Itomni

Lila itomni, in our language, means being drunk. This is a chapter about drinking, especially my own battles with alcohol. In a way, after the army, I was in a continuous state of drunkenness for some twenty years. Much of the time, I couldn't walk straight. I had to walk spraddled, my legs spread way apart, in order to balance myself. My hands shook. I couldn't even hold a cup of coffee in the morning until I had a couple of shots inside my belly to steady me. It got so bad that close friends were afraid to come near me when I was boozed up for fear that I would get violent.

I had at least sense enough not to get married, knowing that I would starve a wife and children. All my money went for drink. I had plenty of girlfriends, though, whom I met in the bars. There were always lots of *winchinchilas* around who would love me truly if I had a bottle of wine or *suta*—the hard stuff—to share with them.

My body bears many scars to remind me of innumerable barroom brawls and policemen's night sticks. During my drinking years, I collected more than 130 stitches on my head and an arrest record as thick as a telephone book, with "cop fighter" stamped all over it in big, red letters. Altogether, I got myself arrested 184 times as the result of drunken sprees—four times during a single weekend.

I thank the Creator for having kept me sober for the last twenty years. I have even advanced to the stage where I can have a glass of wine with a meal without ever asking for a second one. That is almost unique for a full-blood like me.

The "drunken Injun" has become a stereotype in the minds of white

Americans. My father, who himself could hit the bottle hard, had the following to say on this subject in his book, *Lame Deer, Seeker of Visions*:

> Why do Indians drink? They drink to forget the great days when this land was ours and when it was beautiful, without billboards, fences, and factories. They try to forget the pitiful shacks and rusting trailers which are their homes. They drink to forget that there is nothing for a man to do, nothing that would bring honor or make him feel good inside. There are only a handful of jobs on the reservation, which go mostly to the *iyeska*, the better educated half-bloods. Unemployment runs to eighty percent. You have to be an Uncle Tomahawk, an "apple"—red outside and white inside—to land a government job. Then you have to behave like a middle-class white man to keep it. If you have such a job, you drink to forget what kind of person it has made you. If you don't have it, you drink because there's nothing to look forward to but a few weeks of spud-picking—if you're lucky. You drink because you don't live; you merely exist. That might be enough for a *wasichu*. It isn't enough for us.

Some Indian activists say that alcoholism is a white problem because whites invented the stuff, introduced it to our tribes, manufacture it, and sell it. That's too easy an answer. Alcohol is destroying our people and, in the end, only we ourselves can conquer it.

There is one legitimate excuse. Some scientists cite medical evidence of an enzyme that is important in the body's ability to absorb and break down alcohol. Apparently, this enzyme is missing in the systems of most Indian people—especially full-bloods. As a result, white people can tolerate a larger amount of alcohol than Native Americans. Also, most whites have the ability to stop after a few drinks while many Indian people cannot. Once they have one drink, they want another—and another, and another. There is also the fact that white people have had some five thousand years to get used to alcohol, while the Indian has had only about two hundred years. Some full-bloods run amok after just two beers. Even so, it is up to us to overcome this problem.

I have seen the inside of a thousand bars: the Idle Hour, the Horseshoe, the Longhorn Saloon, Arlo's, the Blarney Stone, the 921 Club, the Ritz Bar, the Green Door, the Crazy Horse Saloon, the Silver Dollar, and countless others whose names I have long ago forgotten. Immediately after hitting a big town—Chicago, for instance—I would head for the Indian bars. I never had any trouble finding them. There I met Indians on relocation, people from different tribes who brought their tribal animosities with them to the cities.

The Navajos hung out in one bar, the Chippewas in another, and, naturally, there were two bars for us Sioux. We not only had old tribal hostilities but new hatreds that were getting stronger than ever. No matter how drunk I was, I never forgot that the Cheyennes had fought side by side with us on the Rosebud and at the Little Bighorn and, especially, that the Crows and Arikaras had been scouts for Custer and the white soldiers.

I didn't spend half a lifetime without interruption in Hollywood. At certain times, I became itchy to roam around and have a change of scenery. Sometimes they didn't need an Indian stuntman for months at a time, and I had to look for other work to feed myself. All through those years, I was drinking. Periodically, I returned home to Rosebud, returned to my roots to get my bearings. But always, I found the reservation a place without hope.

In 1955, after my first stint in the army and before my movie career began in earnest, I was down and out and decided to go on relocation. As I mentioned earlier, "relocation" was the word for a government program intended to get us "surplus" Indians off the reservation and into the big cities. The idea was to solve the "Indian problem" by assimilation or "acculturation," making us part of a cheap labor pool. Of course, that was not how it was explained to us. The Bureau of Indian Affairs (BIA) people told us that if we would move to a city, we would get help finding housing and jobs, which were nonexistent on the Res. When I checked into it I found that I would have to pay back any money I got for having myself relocated, so I sold a piece of my reservation land back to the tribe and with that money went where I was told to go: Cincinnati, Ohio.

By the time I got to Cincinnati (by way of a dozen bars), I had managed to drink up most of my money. The moment of truth arrived when, at the relocation office, I was told that as far as jobs and housing were concerned, I was on my own. The watchword was, "Get assimilated! Become a red-white-and-blue American!"

The problem was that full-bloods like myself don't assimilate; we don't meld. I had a few friends in town, both red and white, and they gave me a big welcome, taking me to their favorite watering spot. The bartender got top-heavy himself, setting up drinks on the house. Everybody took turns buying drinks, and by the time it was over, nobody knew which way was up.

For a short period in his life, my father had been a sign painter, so I thought, "Why not become a sign painter?" and I promptly got myself a job. I also went to sign-painting school for two hours every night, learning lettering, how to mix paint, and making layouts. I got a cheap room in the cheapest part of town, treated myself to a couple of hamburgers a day, with huge amounts of French fries on the side, and drank up what was left of my pay.

I would walk into a bar, and everybody would want to buy the Indian a drink. Also, in many joints, the customers would look at me—six foot, two inches tall and 195 pounds—and listen to a couple of stories about my fighting and hell-raising, then keep filling me up with booze just to keep me happy. I made such a name for myself by flattening out several guys at a time that when the police picked me up, they would come in groups of six or seven and jump me from behind with billy clubs swinging.

I used to go to the clubs on Vine Street, Cincinnati's tenderloin district. For six miles, there was nothing but bars, nightclubs, pawn shops, and whorehouses. In about six months' time, I became known as the "Chief of Vine Street," and all the bardogs, barflies, winos, and hookers knew me. About that time, a mixed drink was fifty cents. At the rate I was going, my money went like shit through a goose.

Then I had a brilliant idea: why not get a job where you don't have to shell out for painting your nose? So I applied to become a bartender and enrolled in a mixology school. I learned how to mix drinks—Grasshoppers, Manhattans, Gibsons, Singapore Slings, Bloody Marys, and what have you.

I went to work at the 921 Club, a nightclub and bar with a hillbilly band. The place was always full of hillbilly gals, mostly from Kentucky, Georgia, and Tennessee. In every bar, there were always three or four of these girls. Being the Chief of Vine Street, I could have my pick. I had more of those country chicks than I can remember. As far as booze was was concerned, a funny thing happened: once I could pour myself a drink whenever I wanted, I lost interest in the hard stuff and switched to beer.

After Cincinnati, I went to Zanesville, Ohio, and worked as a bartender for the Horseshoe Club. For five hours during the day, I worked as a tree surgeon, and from 6 p.m. until 2:30 in the morning I tended bar. We had eleven go-go girls at the club who took turns singing and dancing all night, and the place was always full of businessmen, storekeepers, and factory workers making eyes at our "artistes." Then the winos started shooting rubber bands at the girls and groping for feels and pinching bottoms, so we had to put our dancers in cages to keep them from getting squeezed black and blue.

We also had two shifts of prostitutes at the Horseshoe. At eleven in the morning, the first shift of about ten to fifteen opened up for business, and somewhere around five in the afternoon, the second shift took over. Both married and single men dropped in, had a drink, picked up one of the hookers, and went out. After five o'clock, the blue-collar workers came out of the factories and made a beeline for our "wilted flowers of the prairie." Beginning around ten in the evening, we had both shifts on tap, which included about thirty whores.

After a while, it dawned on me that the nightclub was not the right kind of environment for me. One night, I went to a nearby park and stretched out on the ground. I had a sudden urge to feel earth and grass under me, to bury myself in leaves, to look up at the moonlit sky. When I woke up, it was daylight. The sun was shining. I tried to open my eyes, tried gradually to adjust to the brightness. I felt a faint, cool breeze on my face and sensed the presence of something alive close to me. I looked up and saw a white dove fluttering only three feet above me. It was hanging in one spot above my head as if suspended by a string. As I watched, it slowly began rising higher and higher and finally disappeared. There were many pigeons in the park, but this bird had been the only white one. It reminded me that I was part of nature and of my grandfather's teachings. I felt that it was a sign sent to me—a reminder that I did not belong in this big city where I couldn't truly relate to anyone. It was a sign that it was time for me to go home.

I worked at the club for two more weeks to get money enough for the bus fare to the Res, but the night I got paid, I went out, got liquored up, and didn't stop drinking until I was flat broke again. Early next morning, I put on my best clothes, left everything else behind, and started hitchhiking without a penny in my pocket.

I caught a ride with a master sergeant who took me as far as Indianapolis. I was pretty hungry by then, so I headed for the nearest Salvation Army lunch counter. Just when I finally got to the head of the line, they ran out of food and closed the door. My stomach was really rumbling by then. I came to a roadside stand that was selling fresh farm produce. There I got a sack, filled it with fruit, and walked away without paying. Someone saw me and began to shout. I took off running. I was starved; I had no intention of letting anybody catch me. I had arrived at a point where I would steal food and hide in a roadside ditch while eating it.

As soon as I got back to the highway, I got a ride with another master sergeant, a paratrooper who had just retired from the army. That evening he stopped, got us some supper, a case of beer, and two fifths of whiskey. We drank and talked until the sergeant turned the driving over to me and passed out.

By the time we got to Chicago, I was really boozed up. I thought neither of driving nor of parking by the roadside; all I could think about was getting more liquor. So I rolled my sleeping friend and split—just walked away without looking back. I took what must have been over a thousand dollars and left him with a hundred-dollar bill. That is how I repaid his kindness. I hate myself thinking of it now, and my conscience will bother me as long as I live. It didn't bother me then; a drunkard has no conscience.

I caught a few more rides and finally made it home sober for once. Ida, my stepmother, did what all Indian women do in such cases: she immediately took me into the kitchen for soup, bread, and coffee.

I was sitting outside in the yard that evening when my father got home. I told him how I had been living, that I wanted to stop drinking but wasn't able to walk away from it. He wanted to help me, but he knew he couldn't. I couldn't help *myself*.

The next day, the folks took me to a big powwow at Ponca Creek, where they had a big feast and give-away in honor of my return. It made me feel good but did nothing to solve my problem. I had gone home to Rosebud to get away from the booze but I found it waiting for me there, too. It was a case of jumping from the frying pan into the fire.

One of my drinking buddies on the Res was Gordon Grass, the son of John Grass, a chief who was famous for the part he played in making treaties with the U.S. government. Gordon was not only a sign painter but a real artist. He was also a happy drunk who never got into fights.

We celebrated the Fourth of July in Rapid City in the usual way, by getting plastered. We were painting a store sign. Gordon was drawing the outline of the letters while I filled in the colors. While doing this, Gordon kept lighting firecrackers with his cigar and throwing them out the open window in honor of the "national holiday." Finally, though, he got so boozed up that he clamped a firecracker between his teeth and threw the *cigar* out the window. The firecracker went off in his mouth, cutting it in several places and burning him badly. He was writhing on the floor, and we rushed him to the hospital, where they stitched him up.

Besides Gordon, there were three other Indian artists in Rapid City at that time who were old drinking pals of mine: Godfrey Broken Rope, Noah Jumping Elk, and Tommy Little. One day, these three set up their easels by the creek below the railroad bridge, and I went down to help them. They already had several finished paintings that they wanted me to sell for them. I took the paintings to a bar full of local characters and tourists and managed to sell all of them for a total of seventy dollars.

Each of my friends had specified a favorite brand of "poison" that I should bring back. So I returned to the creek with a sackful of jingling bottles, and we really got going on them. By the time the booze was gone, Godfrey had one more painting finished, and he sent me back to the bar to swap it for a couple of gallons of *mni-sha*, or "red water," meaning the cheapest California Tokay. He told me, "Also get us two pounds of raw kidney and some salt to go with the wine."

I did as I was told. So there we were, swilling down the *mni-sha* and chomping on the sweet kidneys (which my father always called "the Indian's candy bar"). By then, all four of us were so drunk that we had spilled wine and kidney blood all over us. But Noah and Tommy each had another picture to sell. "You're gonna be our secretary, our treasurer, and our agent," they said. "Go sell the pictures and bring back more wine."

I tottered off. When I got back, there were two policemen standing on the railroad bridge, looking down. One of the two was Sergeant Smitty, whose acquaintance I had already made on several occasions.

"Jesus," he said, "look at that. Three dead guys all covered with blood. My God, a triple murder case!"

My three buddies had passed out and were lying there, having slipped halfway into the creek. I started laughing. "They ain't dead," I said. "They're just sleeping off a drunk."

Smitty wouldn't believe me: "No, no, for Chrissake! Somebody musta' stabbed them or cut their throats! Holy Mother of God, look at all that blood!"

The two of them climbed down, and Smitty started to curse when he found out that I had been right. "Goddamn it, look at them rummies! Look at all them bottles! Jesus, don't tell me they drank all this up in one day! Shit, they had me fooled!"

He called for the paddy wagon and had us hauled over to the Pennington County Jail. We all pleaded not guilty and bailed ourselves out at ten bucks apiece.

Some of my binges were no laughing matter. Once, after I had bought a secondhand jalopy, I got stewed again. In my befuddled state, I thought it might do me good and clear my head to take a little drive up into the Black Hills. I was driving my four-wheeled pony up Skyline Drive, overlooking Rapid City, to the top of Dinosaur Hill, which gets its name from a large cement statue of a diplodocus, or a tyrannosaurus, or whatever. There is a really steep drop off that hill. I still don't know how I did it, but the car went over the side and flipped end-over-end, all the way down to the bottom.

The next thing I heard was a tremendous commotion and someone saying, "Don't burn his leg!" The car was so crumpled and twisted that they had to cut me out with a blowtorch. The longer they worked, the hotter it got—and the madder I became.

When they finally finished cutting, the chief of police grabbed my shoulder and jerked me out of there. He roughed me up without even bothering to make sure I wasn't hurt, in spite of the spectacular wreck I had been in. I spun around and hit him square on the nose. In no time there were cops all over me, raining blows on my head with their nightsticks and doing more damage than the accident.

I had so often been a victim of police brutality that whenever I was drunk and saw a policeman, I was ready to fight. I got six months in jail and a five-hundred-dollar fine. The only kick I got out of it was the newspaper headline, "Car Flips Off Skyline Drive." While in jail, I had to watch while every Indian who was brought in was welcomed with a beating. This fueled my hatred of the white system of "justice."

I got my bonus of $640 for having served in Korea and used that to bail myself out. I was so happy to get out of jail that I went downtown to celebrate, and I'll be damned if I didn't get thrown in jail again the same night for the same thing—another car accident. This time the headline was, "Archie Does It Again!" I was fast becoming the "most notorious dipsomaniac" in the annals of the *Rapid City Journal*.

That August I went to the Pine Ridge Sundance, which was rapidly becoming a degrading caricature of this sacred ceremony, a carnival show for tourists with hot-dog stands and kiddie rides. This was another cause for some serious drinking. I started a fight and knocked a guy through a big drum in the middle of a song. The Indian police hauled me off to the tribal jail.

As soon as they got me inside, they let go of my arms and I swung at the police chief, knocking him ass over teakettle down a flight of stairs. When his pals rushed to see if he was hurt, I ran into the drunk tank. It was overcrowded with winos sleeping all over the floor. I flipped a man out of his bunk and crawled in, pretending to be asleep. I guess there were so many of us in there that they didn't want to stir things up, so they left me alone.

They kept us in the "Heartbreak Hotel" for the four days of the powwow; then those of us who were not from Pine Ridge were invited to leave the reservation. I was from Rosebud, so I left.

I decided to go to my father's place in Winner. Nobody gave me a lift, so I started walking. I walked all the way to the town of Martin, got drunk, started a brawl, and wound up in jail. I got out and headed for Kadoka, where I spent a little time in their slammer, too. From there I walked to Murdo, discovering that the drunk tank there was nicer than the one in Pine Ridge. And from there it was on to Belvedere, where they have a pretty civilized cooler. I continued to White River, spent a day or two in the jug there, and wandered on to Mission, sampling their facilities as well. It took me a little over three months to travel the eighty-seven miles to my dad's place in Winner, and I didn't miss a single jail in all the towns along the way. I arrived one day before Thanksgiving and landed in the local hoosegow on my first evening in town.

Altogether, during the years 1956 and 1957, I spent some ten months in various jails. It got so bad that I would drink anything I could manage to swallow, and I would sell anything I could lay my hands on to get frogskins for booze. I even sold my stepmother's flock of geese and the wheels off my stepsister's car. All of my friends in Winner lived the same way.

I finally wound up in the "big house" at Sioux Falls, the largest and most "secure" joint I had ever been in. It was a sobering experience. At Sioux Falls, one quarter of all the prisoners were Indians, and we looked out for each other.

There is one problem common to all prisons. If a guy is in jail for the first time and he is young and nice looking, quiet and shy, he is usually approached by some of the stronger old-timers. The inmates who are there for life without parole want this boy for a "wife." The newcomer has no choice. All of a sudden, he gets a carton of cigarettes with a note: "My name is so-and-so, and I'm sending you these cigarettes to let you know that I am your friend. There's a lot of tough guys in here, and I'll protect you from them—if you'll let me." If the kid is too weak to take care of himself, he has to accept one of these "protectors," and eventually he gets used to being the "wife" of the stronger fellow. That's the way many inmates are educated by the system to become proper members of society again.

With a more-than-six-foot-tall Indian like myself, these "husbands" have a problem. Soon after my arrival at Sioux Falls, I was walking down the corridor when a young, white inmate made some obscene remarks and said, "Hey, why don't you come into my cell?"

I said, "OK, I'm coming." I walked in and started beating him up. One of the bulls came running and grabbed me from behind, trying to stop the fight. That was his mistake, because then I turned on him. Three or four more guards came to his rescue, and we had quite a free-for-all.

I got thirty days in the "hole," which is a prison within a prison. Everybody in the hole was put on a diet of bread, water, and soup. In my cell I had a blanket and a toilet, and that was all. There's nothing to do in the hole, nothing to keep you occupied—no TV, no radio, no books. Every day for an hour, they left the cells open so that we could go up and down the corridor and socialize. The only entertainment we could think up for ourselves was cockroach races, and the only things we had to wager were slices of bread. We would put a piece of bread at the end of the hall and tell our roaches, "Go get it!" The roach that got to the bread first was the winner. Sometimes I went two or three days without bread because my cockroach lost, and sometimes I wound up with six or seven extra slices because my little "racehorse" won.

After I got out of the hole, one of the bulls asked me, "Would you do it again? Are you prone to violence?" I told him, "Yes, under the same circumstances. That man had no right to make a pass at me and make obscene remarks. If he does it again, I'll flatten him out again."

Most of the Indians in our jails are there for some alcohol-related offense—usually for having hurt someone during a drunken brawl. Being imprisoned is especially hard for Native Americans, who are used to a free and easy outdoor life. They have a difficult time merely adjusting to white society, let alone the prison system. They have one advantage, though, over other inmates: they protect each other. As soon as word gets around that a young Indian has been brought in, all the 'skins in the joint form a sort of protective ring around him, making sure he is not molested.

In the late 1950s, I had returned to Rosebud to get away from the bars in Ohio. Later, I went to Los Angeles to get away from the general drunkenness on the reservation. But to kick the habit is one of the hardest things to do. I drank almost continuously throughout my movie career.

In 1971, not long after returning to Hollywood from another stay in Rosebud, I went on my biggest binge. I was arrested one Friday around noon for being intoxicated and was released the same evening. The liquor stores were still open, so I went right back to drinking with some of my buddies. About three o'clock in the morning, we got into a fight outside a joint called the Ritz Bar and were thrown in jail again. Early on Saturday, they fed us and around noon kicked us out. Saturday afternoon, we were hitting the bottle down near the railroad tracks. We got arrested that evening for making a ruckus at Fifth and Wall, in one of the hardest bars there is. The bartender turned us in. That was the third arrest, and I spent the night in jail.

The jail wasn't what you'd call a nice place. They took all our personal belongings, leaving us only our jackets for pillows. The floors were padded, so they didn't need mattresses. There were two open toilets at each end, and the place stank.

Sunday morning they released me, and I was doing all right until the afternoon, when I started working on a case of beer. I kept at it until nightfall, when I was arrested for the fourth time on a "drunk and disorderly." I was thrown into the drunk tank and taken to court on Monday morning. The judge said to me, "This is your fourth arrest over the weekend for being drunk and the sixth arrest this week. I give you three days to sober up."

I spent the time in the county jail. I had the "jim-jams." I couldn't eat, sleep, or walk straight. The bed seemed to keep turning over on me. Finally, on Thursday, I had breakfast and managed to keep it down.

At ten o'clock they let me out, and I said to myself, "Enough of this shit! No more booze!" Right then and there, I stopped drinking, went cold turkey.

I walked right over to the Harbor Lights, a place for alcoholics to dry out. Almost overnight, I became a counselor of Indian alcoholics. About six months later, at a powwow, I met a Chumash Indian woman named Sandy, who later became my wife. I started thinking of what it would be like to become a father, and that helped to keep me on the straight and narrow. Eventually, I became a spiritual advisor to Native Americans inside federal and state penitentiaries. As such, I was instrumental in bringing the Sacred Pipe and the Inipi into the jails and winning for Indian medicine men the same status and respect enjoyed by prison chaplains and rabbis. My drinking days were over at last.

C H A P T E R 1 1

Interludes

I was fated to be a medicine man, a healer, a Sundance director, and a teacher, but it took time for me to fully realize this. Between the time I stopped drinking and the moment I could truly call myself a *pejuta wichasha* (a medicine man), there was an interlude, or rather several interludes.

Helping Indians to stop drinking and counseling Native American prisoners were two of these interludes that helped to put me on the right path, though I didn't know it at the time. My life did not follow a straight line like that of a middle-class white who goes to college, gets a job, gets promoted every now and then, and retires at age sixty-five with a pension. My life followed a winding path that sometimes seemed to make backward loops. Periods and events tended to overlap.

I had put the booze away, but during my early days of sobriety I was afraid of going back to it. I asked the advice of a California Indian named Ed, who had been a tribal chairman at Santa Inez and who ran a halfway house for Native American winos in Los Angeles. He was a firm believer in Alcoholics Anonymous. "Brother, go to the AA," he told me. "There you'll find guys having the same problems you have. You compare your troubles and help each other to sober up. That's how it works."

I found out quickly that AA is not for most Indians—and especially not for me. At the meetings, there was always a white guy going on and on: "I had a beautiful hundred-dollar-a-day job, a beautiful house, a beautiful wife, beautiful children, a beautiful car, a beautiful TV, and a beautiful toy poodle, and then—sob, sob, sob—I lost it all to alcohol."

I couldn't relate to that because I had never had a beautiful house and all those other things he was moaning and groaning about. These guys were always weepy and pious and as sweet as artificial sugar, always talking about Jesus, the cross, and the Good Book. I couldn't relate to that, either. My Jesus was Wakan Tanka, my cross the Sacred Pipe, and my Bible the mountaintop. Other Indians felt just as I did about AA; they only came to get a free meal and a warm place to sober up.

One day at an AA meeting, while some guy went droning on about the "seven steps" and the "twelve steps," I noticed an old white man next to me looking me over. He was an alcoholic but also a doctor. He told me that he did a lot of counseling at the local hospital, even though he himself was an incorrigible drunk. He said, "Come upstairs to the roof with me. I want to talk to you in private."

Up on the roof he said, "You don't belong here. You don't belong in AA. You don't belong in this asphalt jungle. Your world is on the top of a mountain where the pine trees grow and the wind blows. I'll make you a deal: Here's a full bottle of bourbon, and here's a twenty-dollar bill to start you on a different road. Pick one or the other."

I took the twenty bucks. I am eternally grateful to this old white man whom I met only once and who talked like a father to me. He truly helped me, thereby obliging me to help others. This was in 1971.

After that, I went to a place in Los Angeles called Indian Lodge, a shelter for Native American alcoholics, and there I met Joe Seaboy, an old friend from the motion picture world who was running the place. He greeted me warmly. I said, "Joe, why are you here? Why are you not at the studio, on the set?"

He answered, "Arch, I'm human, too. I've got the same trouble you have: booze, the 'blue ruin.' I have a job for you." So that old white man and Joe Seaboy were my saviors.

Years before, I had buried my Pipe on a hilltop and promised myself not to dig it up until I was ready to start a new life. Now I went to that spot, dug my Pipe out of the earth, and took it down the hill with me.

At the lodge, my first job was driving the van. I already had a lot of experience in alcohol treatment. At two o'clock in the morning, the police would call: "Hey, we got a drunken Indian down here." I'd drive downtown to skid row, finding the drunk handcuffed to a lamp post. The police would get me to unlock him because he'd be in a fighting mood. Of course, he'd take a few swings at me, but I'd be sober and he'd be drunk, so I could handle him. I'd get him into the van, drive him to the Indian Lodge, and throw him into a cold shower. He'd fight me tooth and nail, but I always had the upper hand. Afterwards, he'd get some hot coffee, a good breakfast, and maybe some clean clothes.

Then the process of rehabilitation would begin—not like in AA, but in ways an Indian could understand and relate to. One of my Indian therapies was taking these guys out into nature, talking to them in the shadows of trees and later under a blue sky.

Soon I no longer waited for the police to call us to pick up drunken Indians. I patrolled the places where I was likely to find them, places I knew only too well, and took them to Indian Lodge before they got into trouble. Sometimes I found these poor alcoholics dead of exposure or drowned in their own vomit.

We also had the problem of attracting Indians to come to the center on their own. I volunteered to drive to the court where Indians got sentenced for alcohol-related offenses and bring them over to us. The director told me, "I don't think you can do it, but if you want to try, go ahead!"

I went to the judge and told him, "Instead of sentencing these guys to jail, why don't you turn them over to me? We'll cure them of their habit."

The judge said, "Mr. Lame Deer, I have your record here in front of me. It's as thick as a book, and now here you come to rehabilitate Indians. What kind of qualifications do you have for the job?"

I told him, "Sir, I have twenty years of on-the-job training."

He laughed and said, "I guess you're the man we need." As a result, many alcoholics were released to me. I am proud to say that, after their rehabilitation, some even finished college. One became a university professor, and another wound up as a doctor. Eventually, Channel 5 in Los Angeles made a movie about me called "In Search of Reality" documenting how I had fought my way out of skid row and helped Indian alcoholics get back on their feet.

Word of what I was doing got around. Eventually, I was offered a BIA-funded position as a counselor for Indian inmates in federal and state penitentiaries in California. Knowing what prison life was like for Indians and how they hungered for comfort and to learn about their traditions and beliefs, I accepted at once. At this time, the practice of Indian religion was not allowed inside the prison system, and the idea of having native medicine men ministering to Indians on the same level as Christian chaplains or Jewish rabbis was looked upon as preposterous. Indian beliefs, I was told, were not religion but savage superstition. I made up my mind to sensitize those who thought that way and to take the Sacred Pipe and the Inipi ceremony inside prison walls.

The first prison I went to was Lompoc, in California. As I parked my car in front of those high, forbidding brick walls, I panicked. It was totally illogical, but I felt as if icy hands had gotten ahold of me and were squeezing my heart. I could not get rid of my fear, thinking, "The white wardens in there know I have done time and that I am an Indian. Oh, shit, they'll keep me in there and never let me out!"

When I entered the prison and the steel bars clanged shut behind me, I jumped a foot into the air and broke out in a cold sweat. I had the jitters and couldn't figure out why. There was no reason for it, but my knees kept trembling.

At that time, some thirty Indians were in that prison, but only eight came to listen to me. I told them, "I came here to set up a group for you guys." I felt uncomfortable and awkward. All the odds were against me. The warden was against me, the inmates were against me, and even the Indians were against me. I ended by saying, "You guys are my brothers. I, too, have been in prison—many times."

The next time I came, they all showed up. I told them, "I'm neither a shrink nor an anthropologist. My only qualifications for this job are that I am an ex-con, that I have stopped drinking, and that I have never served time for doing hard drugs. I won't lie to you, and you won't lie to me. I'll make you no promises. I'm going to help you find your identity, help you become an Indian again. If you are not sure what tribe you belong to, I'll try to find out for you. I'll try to track down your tribal enrollment numbers."

That was the beginning. Soon I had eighteen prisons on my circuit. It wasn't easy. In one case, I had to sue and wait two years until the court ruled that Indians could have their Pipe to comfort them. But when I finally brought the Pipe in, they seized the sacred tobacco for fear it could be a "dangerous drug." Then they decided that Indians could smoke the Pipe but not hold Inipi ceremonies in the sweatlodge, because even in the yard the fire would be a hazard. Then it was OK to let them have an Inipi, but to let a man out for four days to participate in a Sundance—even under supervision—was unthinkable. "Archie," they said, "you must be crazy to think up a caper like that."

The system fought me all the way, and I fought back. I won many battles that gained *some* freedom of religion for *some* Indian prisoners, but the war is still going on.

Once, when I was working for the prison system, two tough drunks walked into our office building. We had a room where the children could play and watch television, and these characters were getting rough and scaring the kids badly. I heard their screams and ran down the hall. I grabbed those two men by their necks and slammed their heads together, knocking them both out at the same time. The story made the rounds via the "moccasin telegraph," and it grew taller and taller in the telling: I had knocked out five, ten, maybe even a dozen men all at once and singlehandedly. Thus, I gained a reputation that did me no harm as far as prison work was concerned.

At the beginning of my prison work, Warden Taylor at the Lompoc Penitentiary asked me, "Chief, what title shall we give you—priest, medicine man, reverend, shaman, or what?" I told him, "Why not 'spiritual advisor'?" Thus I invented this term, which is now widely used.

Years later, Taylor asked me, "Lame Deer, do you know Leonard Peltier?" I said that I had heard of him but had never met him in person. Peltier is the Indian who was convicted of killing two FBI agents during a firefight on the Pine Ridge reservation in 1975. The shoot-out, which occurred at the Jumping Bull place at the little settlement of Oglala, also cost the life of a young Indian named Stuntz. Peltier got two lifetimes on a first-degree murder conviction.

Today, I am absolutely convinced that Peltier is innocent. At the time of the shootout, there was a civil war going on at Pine Ridge. A group of men called the "goons" had been killing many people who sympathized with the American Indian Movement (AIM). Even children got shot. Homes were firebombed. People panicked whenever a car backfired. In this kind of atmosphere, the two agents went into the AIM camp near the Jumping Bull place, saying that they were looking for a young fellow who had stolen a pair of boots. With everybody in a state of near hysteria, a shot was fired and all hell broke loose.

Some young men were arrested on suspicion of having shot the agents. Later they were tried and acquitted. I think the government was determined that somebody—anybody—would pay for the death of the two agents, and they finally settled on Leonard Peltier. To convict him, they produced a poor, half-witted woman by the name of Myrtle Poor Bear, who swore that she had seen Peltier killing the FBI men. Later, the government admitted that the FBI had threatened the woman with death and browbeaten her to testify. The prosecution itself withdrew her as an "unbelievable witness." In the meantime, however, Peltier had been extradited from Canada on her false testimony.

Then the government claimed that they had found a rifle belonging to Peltier, which they identified as the murder weapon. It was found at the home of a Rosebud Indian who later turned out to have been an FBI informant. Subsequently, some of the so-called "ballistics experts" admitted that they had lied about certain matters at Peltier's trial.

At the Grass Mountain Sundance, in 1977, Myrtle Poor Bear stood under the Sacred Tree with the Pipe in her hands, tears streaming down her face, and described how she had been forced to give false testimony against Leonard. Our people firmly believe that if you lie at a Sundance, swearing on the Pipe, something devastating will happen to you. So all those present knew that Myrtle was telling the truth. Yet Peltier is still languishing in prison. He is a fine artist, but he is slowly going blind. All this is not only bad for Indians but for every American. When an American talks about civil rights, a German, Russian, or Frenchman will point a finger at him and ask, "What about Peltier?"

Well, when the warden asked me about Leonard, I knew next to nothing about his case. Taylor said, "It's within my power to have him transferred to Lompoc. Otherwise he's going to Leavenworth, Kansas. What do you think?"

I answered that an Indian doing two lifetimes was surely in need of being comforted by someone sharing his traditional beliefs and that the only place where native religion had gotten over prison walls was in California. So I was instrumental in having Leonard transferred to Lompoc. A few days after he arrived, I got rocks, willow sticks, sage, and a tarp and performed an Inipi ceremony for him.

One day when I visited Leonard, he told me, "There are two new 'skins coming in, and I believe they are coming for a purpose: to get rid of me—to kill me."

Warden Taylor was in the hospital at the time, recuperating from a motorcycle accident, so I mentioned Leonard's fears to the associate warden. He said, "If you want to, you can visit these two guys and check them out."

I went and talked with both of them. One was a sundancer from South Dakota, and he was OK, but the other was a shifty-eyed former goon, and there was something in his eyes that I didn't like. I told Leonard, "I don't think you are in any special danger, but look out for that one. He might be here to set you up. Tell your friends to keep an eye on him."

The following Wednesday, I put a man "up on the mountain" for a Vision Quest, intending to pick him up again four days later. On Saturday, however, I heard that Leonard had escaped, and I went back for the Vision Quest a few hours early. "I'm sorry to interrupt your fast," I said, "but you must come down right away. Our brother Leonard Peltier has escaped from prison, and his friend and cellmate, Dallas Thundershield, has been shot in the back and killed in the process. We think that the whole thing is a put-up job and that the man who killed Dallas did it because he mistook him for Leonard."

I went down to the Hollister Ranch, smoked the Sacred Pipe, and called the associate warden. He told me that Leonard had escaped and that Dallas had died shortly after being shot. He said, "You better come down here at once. You always take care of things when an Indian inmate dies. So hurry up and do your ceremony. Then try to find out whether Dallas had any relatives, because we have no information on that."

I had hardly hung up when there was a loud pounding at the door and two FBI agents barged in. "Which one of you fellows is Lame Deer?" one of them wanted to know.

"That's me," I said.

He asked, "Do you know that Peltier escaped last evening?" I said yes.

They thought they had me because I knew that Leonard had broken out and that therefore I had to be in on the escape plot.

"We'll have to question you closely," the same agent told me, and the two of them got out their notebooks and a tape recorder. They said, "OK, confess. How did you know what time he escaped and who was shot?"

"I phoned the warden," I said. "I work at the prison as a spiritual counselor. You can phone Lompoc and check it out."

They did. Then they put away their notebooks and threw away the cassette tape. They started cursing, "Damn it! Why did you waste our time?" and stormed out.

Leonard was captured a few days later. Somebody had set him up. A getaway car was supposed to be waiting for him outside but never showed up. I went to see Leonard and prayed with him. I asked him, "Why didn't you tell me that you would be trying to escape?"

He said, "Because I didn't want to implicate you. Spiritually, you are taking care of 'skins in eighteen different joints. Those guys depend on you. You've got a job to do and had no business being mixed up in this."

A new warden took over and said he suspected me of having helped Leonard escape and that he would no longer allow me inside Lompoc. That was, of course, unjustified and illegal. Leonard was given extra time, which was pretty insane, as he was already doing two consecutive lifetimes. He was transferred to Marion, a maximum security prison, then to Leavenworth, then to Springfield, then back to Marion again. At present, he is in Leavenworth. A man who was accused of helping Leonard escape later went out in a fishing boat on Puget Sound and was never seen alive again. His body was never found. There are many unsolved mysteries connected with this case.

I also had to give comfort and advice to Indian women prisoners. The first prison for female inmates in which I could set up a sweatlodge was Pleasanton Federal Penitentiary in Pleasanton, California. I don't know why they gave it that name, because there was nothing pleasant about it. Performing Inipi ceremonies for women is a problem. For the guys it is easy, because there are many medicine men, but there are no medicine women to run an Inipi in the joint.

Among the women I helped was Yvonne Wanrow, who was doing time for having shot and killed a white man who was about to rape her little daughter. It took quite some time until she was finally retried and acquitted.

Another victim of the system was Agnes White Rock, who is being held in the Oregon state prison in Salem. She has already been there for more than fifteen years and has never been given a chance, spending much of her time in the hole. Every time she gets out of prison, they promptly throw her back inside for "parole violations." Why? Because they don't want an innocent Native American woman outside, on the loose, telling people what she has been through.

One of the strangest things that happened to me was when two men approached me on behalf of a woman inmate at Pleasanton Federal Penitentiary. Both were white. One of them said, "My name is Randolph Hearst, and this is my bodyguard."

His name didn't register with me. I couldn't see why he needed a bodyguard, being a big, burly fellow. He went on, "I have heard good things about you—how you can relate to prisoners and help them psychologically. I have a daughter, Patricia, who was kidnapped by some madmen calling themselves the Symbionese Liberation Army. They brainwashed her, put a gun in her hand, and forced her to commit a bank robbery. That's how she landed in Pleasanton. Please try to help her."

So I went and spent a whole day with Patty Hearst. I prayed with and for her in Lakota, because I say all my prayers in the Indian language. I don't know how much good this did her, seeing that she couldn't understand a single word, but it seemed to have a calming effect. Of course, she was later released. When there is enough money and influence, prisoners get out quickly. I later found out that Randolph Hearst owned and operated a big gold mine at a place called Lead, right in the center of the Paha Sapa, our sacred Black Hills. Had I known this, I wouldn't have been so forthcoming.

The saddest of all things is when an Indian woman is incarcerated during her pregnancy so that she has to have her baby inside. They never allow her to keep it but take it away to an orphanage or infant's shelter. Whenever that happens, it always breaks my heart.

C H A P T E R   1 2

Mitakuye Oyasin

All Lakota ceremonies end with the words *Mitakuye Oyasin*, mean-ing "All My Relations." This signifies that we have prayed for *all* our relatives: every human being on this Earth and every living thing— every animal down to the tiniest bug, and every plant down to the tiniest wildflower.

We Lakota have a special relationship to animals, a relationship that springs from our religion and is part of our traditional beliefs. I always felt a close kinship to the four-leggeds, winged ones, and even the "six-legs" and "no-legs." From my earliest days, things happened to me in connec-tion with animals that cannot be explained by white man's science. These experiences formed a bridge between the thoughtless days of my youth and my later years as a medicine man. Knowing about and being close to animals prepared me for becoming a spiritual man, even though at first I was not aware of this.

The spirit of *Mitakuye Oyasin*, looking upon animals as our brothers, is ingrained in the minds of our people. Ptesan Win, White Buffalo Calf Woman, who long ago brought the Sacred Pipe to our people and taught us how to pray with it, was at the same time a human being and a white buffalo calf. The kinship between humans and deer is part of the old legend of how we Lame Deers got our name. My father was always conscious of how all living things are related to each other. He told me that during his first Vision Quest, he was talking with eagles and other winged brothers.

Once, my father was interviewed on TV, together with a white priest, a good man who supported Native American struggles for civil rights and who respected our religion. For years, he had his church on the Northern

Cheyenne Reservation, at Lame Deer, Montana. He could speak Cheyenne fluently.

This man told my father, "Chief, my church is built in the shape of a tipi. My vestments are beaded, and the Pipe hangs next to the cross. I purify myself in the sweatlodge, and every year go up to Bear Butte with my body painter to take part in the Sundance."

My dad asked him, "Father, does your bishop know about this?"

The priest laughed, "Of course he does. We are not the old-time missionaries who tried to suppress Indian religion. We support your old culture. But let me tell you, our religions are the same—God and the Great Spirit, Jesus and Sweet Medicine, Calvary and the Sundance, the cross and the Pipe, they are all the same. Only the names are different."

My dad looked at that man for what seemed to be a long time. Then he said, "Father, in your religion do animals have souls?"

"Chief, you got me there," answered the priest. He could not admit that animals have souls. For him, that would be heresy, and his bishop would be after him real fast. So there is a difference between the Christian and Lakota religions.

My father always told me, "All wild animals have power, because Wakan Tanka dwells in all of them, even in a tiny ant. The white man has built a wall between himself and that power. To understand what the animals are telling us needs time and patience, and the white man never has time. Yes, there is power in every *wild* animal, but none in those that are human-bred. There is great power in a Buffalo, but there is none in a Holstein or a Hereford. There is power in a Wolf or a Grouse, but not in a chicken or a poodle."

One early incident will always remain in my memory. It happened during my late teens. I was out with my Uncle Norris's .22 rifle one morning when I came upon a big buck and a doe lying in the grass at the bottom of a hill. I raised my rifle and aimed at the buck. He looked at me calmly without a muscle twitching. At that moment, ancient tales my grandfather had told me suddenly came back, and I suddenly burst into tears and put the gun down.

I remembered Grandpa telling me again and again, "When you are hungry, take only what you need to survive." I wasn't hungry then. I had eaten well that morning. I looked back at the buck and said, "You have a right to live." He jumped up, flicked his tail, and ran over the hill.

The doe was still lying there; she had not moved at all. She turned her head toward me. I smiled at her, sat down cross-legged, and offered her some herbs to acknowledge our relationship. She looked at me without fear, as if she understood that I would not hurt her. Suddenly it was *I* who was afraid. Of what? I didn't know. Maybe I was afraid that the killer instinct, hidden within every man, might rise to the surface and get the better of me.

I waved my arm, and the doe got up slowly and joined her mate. I had a last glimpse of the two deer standing on top of the hill, looking at me. They seemed to be saying, "Thank you," and it made me feel good.

When I got home I told a lie. Uncle Norris asked me, "Any luck hunting?" I was embarrassed to tell him that I had come across two deer and did not bag them, so I told him, "I shot and missed." He said I should learn to shoot better. I had to turn away and hide a smile.

Now I want to recount my grandfather's old tale, the one that I remembered just in time to prevent me from shooting the deer. Grandpa had told me, "Takoja, Grandson, go back to the pure ways of the Blacktailed Deer, an animal that has a lot of spiritual power and strength. This is an animal of mystery that can change itself into different forms—other animals, trees, even humans."

According to the story, many lifetimes ago, a man was cast out of his tribe. He wandered for many days and was lost in the wilderness. He was crying as he went, for he was without hope or understanding. He came upon an old, fallen tree trunk and sat down on it to rest. Suddenly, out of nowhere, a woman appeared to him—a woman more beautiful than he had ever seen before. As she stood before him, he became uneasy because he sensed that this woman was more than human. He pulled from his bag the bitter root of the sweet flag, a *heyoka* medicine, to protect himself from the power of this strange woman. As he did so, she turned herself into a Blacktailed Deer and walked away. The footprints she left behind were not human; they were deer tracks.

Grandpa explained to me, "This man made a mistake using sweet flag, which was not the right medicine to use. It spooked her. Had he looked down at this woman's shadow, it would not have had a human shape. It would have been a shadow with antlers, and he would have realized that a Spirit Deer had come to help him. Our religion was brought to us by a woman. This story is not just fantasy.

"Learn from this story to understand things not by what you perceive as everyday reality," Grandpa said, "but see them with the eye that is in your heart. Never kill a Blacktailed Deer, for only bad can come of it. Takoja, once in a lifetime you come across a blacktailed buck with a black line across his face like one of our old-time warriors in black face paint. Only one in a thousand Deer are so marked. Such a Deer is the most sacred of all. Every day at dawn, before the morning star rises, such a Deer comes down from the mountain and blesses the water and drinks. Should a man shoot such a Deer, his mind would become deranged, and he could never be cured. Let yours be the life of a Blacktailed Deer."

One time, when I was a young man in South Dakota, a rancher by the name of Burt Marks bonded me out of jail, where I was staying for the usual reason: drunk and disorderly. He needed a foreman for his ranch, which was someplace near Eagle Butte, and he had heard that I was the man for the job. I accepted. I had five Mexicans working for me. The outgoing foreman wanted me to stay at the main house, but I wanted a place for myself and moved into a little shack that was unoccupied.

One night, I had tied one on. I fell into my bed, which stood next to a window. My sleep was disturbed by nightmares. I woke up with a start and found myself in total darkness. The voices of several women in front of my window had awakened me. I was wide awake. I lit the lamp and looked out the window. I saw points of light moving in the darkness—eyes reflecting my lamp's light. I turned the lamp off and tried to fall asleep again. But then I heard the voices again, laughing and giggling.

Early in the morning, I got out of bed and went outside to investigate. There was no grass in front of my window, just soft, muddy earth with fresh deer tracks all over, but no sign of human footprints. I swept up these tracks to see what would happen next, and the following night I heard the voices again, laughing, talking, and chatting in a language I could not understand. In the morning, the ground was again covered with deer tracks. This happened night after night for about two weeks. Always I found the imprints of deer hooves, never the imprint of a human foot or boot.

One day Marks, who spent most of his time in Rapid City, came up to the place to see how I was doing. We were sitting on a bench in front of the main house. I asked him, "Was there ever an Indian working here for you?"

"Only one," he said, "a long time ago. You are the second one. This old fellow, he came here for a few years during August and September. He came out of nowhere in a horse and buggy, and he chopped wood for us for two months and always left toward the end of October. We paid him enough to last through the winter—not much, because he had few needs. We also gave him some food to take home."

"What was the name of that man?" I asked.

Marks said, "I think it was something like Quick Bear."

"Was his index finger a little bent, like it had been broken at some time?"

"Yes, come to think of it. He always took his meals with us, and I noticed it, watching him eating. That old man would go up that hill over there every day when the sun went down. Once I took my binoculars out to see what he was doing up there, and I found out that he was praying. He came and went, but we never found out where he was going."

I told the rancher, "That's my grandfather you're talking about, the man who raised me. He had a team of two buckskin horses to pull his wagon."

"That's him, all right. He used to sleep in the bunkhouse where you're staying, in the same bed you have there." Now Old Man Marks was staring at me. "As a matter of fact, you look a lot like him." Then I knew that my dead grandpa was sending me these laughing deer to remind me of his teachings.

Remembering these "talking deer" brings back to mind another strange and eerie happening. In 1964, I worked for another rancher, a man called Mart Madson. Mart was already in his late seventies when I began working for him. I really liked this old rancher. Living on his spread is among my happiest memories.

Mart was white, but he had the heart and mind of an Indian. He had grown up on his father's homestead among the Santee people, near the Missouri River, and he could speak the Dakota dialect. Mart bought a new car every six months. He used his brand-new vehicles to chase cattle clear across the roadless prairie, over rock-strewn hills and muddy river beds. Driving with him on these "roundups" was a hair-raising experience. After four months, the new car was a battered wreck. At the end of six months, it had gone to jalopy heaven.

On one of our mad rides, night overtook us on a hill, somewhere around Yankton, near the "Big Muddy." Old Mart stopped, turned off the ignition and the lights. So there we were, sitting in the pickup in total darkness, without even a single star anywhere in sight.

For a while we just sat there. Then Old Mart spoke to me: "Listen, Arch, let me tell you a story. Sometime around 1910 or 1912, there was a run-down outfit about ten miles from here. It was run by three brothers named Frazier—a mean bunch of horse thieves. They raided the Yankton Res and stole a herd of horses from those Indians. They had come all the way up here, to the little valley at the foot of the hill we're parked on. And here, three Yanktons caught up with the three rustlers. The Indians managed to get their horses back, including some the Fraziers had stolen from somebody else.

"So then the rustlers started chasing the Indians, and right down here they had a big shootout. All three Fraziers were killed, and two of the Indians. With the help of some neighbors, my father buried the bodies in a shallow grave on the spot where they had died. Later, they were supposed to be reburied someplace else, but somehow, those who were supposed to do it never got around to it. So they're still down there. Now I'll stop talking. I want you to keep quiet and listen."

We sat there for about ten minutes. Then, all of a sudden, I heard the sound of hoofbeats and guns firing. I heard screams and war whoops, curses in English, and Indians yelling to each other. It was a hell of a racket, lasting about fifteen minutes. Then it suddenly stopped, and all was quiet again.

Old Man Madson sighed and said, "That's what goes on here every night. You can't see anything—not even the gun flashes—but you sure can hear the shootout, just as if it was happening right now and not some fifty years ago. I'm the only one left to know that story and what this is all about. The souls of those guys are still here. I guess it's up to me to rebury them, the Indians as well as the rustlers. Maybe then what you witnessed here won't happen again."

Mart Madson was full of stories, a man who had grown up when life on the range was still raw and rough. He grew up learning ranching in the old way. He was a real cattleman with old-time cattle sense. The days I spent working for him and his wife were some of the happiest in my life.

To us, the most sacred of all animals are the Buffalo and the Eagle.

Grandpa used to say, "*Takoja, Tatanka lila wakan hecha*. Grandson, the Buffalo is most sacred. He is the friend of the sun. He loves those who are generous and hates the stingy ones. He is truly like a brother to us."

He also told me, "Tunka, the Grandfather Spirit, gave this holy animal to us—or, you might say, gave us to each other. The Buffalo people used to live deep inside the Earth, which was their tipi, but the Creator caused them to emerge and spread over the land. There was a time when humans could speak with the Buffalo, just as they could talk with other animals, trees, and stones. The Buffalo gave his flesh so that the people could survive. Never forget this."

Sometimes Grandpa would admonish me, "Takoja, let your life be that of a Buffalo, a Blacktailed Deer, or an Eagle." The Buffalo is one of the Four Direction animals. He represents the West. North is represented by Hehaka, the Elk; East by Tahcha, the Deer; and South by Hinhan, the Owl. In the old days, a hunter would say to a buffalo he had killed, "Forgive me, Brother, but my people have to live." He would leave the buffalo's skull facing south as an offering. When the first white men came to the plains, they found sacred circles made of buffalo skulls—the Indian's churches.

The buffalo skull is an altar. We use it as such in many of our ceremonies, including the Inipi, the Yuwipi, and, above all, the Sundance. This most sacred of our ceremonies celebrates, among other things, the special relationship between the human being and the buffalo. That is why the figures of a man and a buffalo, cut from buffalo hide, are always tied to the Sundance Tree. The *nagi*, the buffalo's spirit, resides in the skull. If the horns fall off, the spirit leaves. If you put the horns on again, then the spirit comes back. This my grandfather told me.

The buffalo gave to our people everything necessary to exist—shelter, fuel, clothing, and all the tools and utensils needed for our daily life. More than eighty different things could be made from the various parts of the buffalo's body, and nothing was wasted. And, of course, the tribes lived mostly on buffalo meat. It was not the U.S. Army that defeated us, but the methodical destruction of the buffalo, "the Indian's cattle." We were forced to surrender for lack of food.

Most Indians see animals differently than most white people. Things about an animal that may disgust or embarrass a white person may have spiritual significance to us. For example, "buffalo chips"—that is, dried buffalo dung—served as fuel on the treeless prairie. The French called it *bois de vache*. Even today, many medicine men and elders think that the Sacred Pipe should be lit with a glowing buffalo chip rather than a match. The only trouble is, we can't always get ahold of a buffalo chip nowadays.

Similarly, some of our ceremonial rattles are made from a buffalo bull's scrotum. And Grandfather told me that the animal's dried penis was used as a charm and fertility symbol during some of our ancient dances. The white man's attitude toward nature is also shown in the way he depicts his Devil: half animal, with horns, fur, tail, and hooves. This shows his disrespect toward our four-legged relatives.

History books say that the last tribal buffalo hunt was held in 1882 and that by 1887 all the bison, which had once covered the prairie by the millions, were gone. If it hadn't been for some people from the Museum of Natural History who found a handful of survivors in some Montana canyon, there would not be a single live American bison left—or so they say.

My grandfather told me that, in 1910, he and a few friends found the last wild buffalo bull right in our Corn Creek country. There must have been a small handful of buffalo that had simply been overlooked, and that ancient, stubborn, solitary bull had somehow managed to tough it out. He was standing on top of a hill, snorting and pawing the ground, turning his face to all the Four Directions. Suddenly he came tearing down that hill in a huge cloud of dust, heading west, trampling down everything in his way.

Grandpa and his friends followed his trail for forty miles, all the way to below Eagle's Nest, where he had dropped dead from sheer exhaustion. Running so hard for so long had proven too much for that old one. Grandpa took the skin and the skull but had to leave the meat. It was simply too tough, as hard as rock. That was Grandpa's last wild bison.

During my learning days, back in 1956 or '57, I was taught a lesson I'll never forget. I had gone to watch the annual Rapid City Rodeo and was sitting in the grandstand enjoying myself. I noticed a huge, ten-gallon hat being passed around and people throwing money into it. I saw the hat filling up with five- and ten-dollar bills. When it was about to overflow, the hat was handed up to the announcer in his booth at the top of the grandstand.

Then I heard the announcer's voice over the loudspeaker: "Folks, we got ourselves a live, wild buffalo bull from Custer State Park. This hat I'm holding up here has a few hundred dollars in it. That's for the man who can ride this bull and hang on for ten seconds. Step up, boys, and try your luck!"

There were no takers. Even the experienced bronco busters were holding back. I thought to myself, I can ride this bull; that money is mine. So I worked my way over to the chutes and told the announcer, "I'll ride him."

He asked me, "Are you sure you can do it? We won't be responsible for any damage."

I told him, "I've broken many horses, and I've ridden Brahma bulls. I can do it."

So they announced me over the loudspeaker: "Cowboys and cowgirls, we have Archie here, a Sioux rider from Rosebud. He'll take a whack at that buffalo. Let's have a big hand for our Sioux friend!"

I went down from the crow's nest to look that buffalo over. He was swishing his tail around and kept looking at me. He was big and fat. I thought, I'm glad he's not skinny. Skinny ones make trouble, but the fat ones are easy. I'm in top shape and have long legs, so I can ride him. He's my meat.

The boys at the chute told me, "There's two ways you can ride him— either with a bull rope or with the rig we use for bareback bronc busting." I took the bull rope.

I had ordinary street shoes on, so I borrowed some saddle-bronc rider's boots and spurs. I wear size nine, and he wore a size twelve, so the boots were kind of loose, even with the spurs. They wrapped horsehair around the rowels and gave me leather gloves with the fingers cut off. They put rosin on them for a better grip. One of the cowboys told me, "You're allowed to use both hands because it's a buffalo, not a Brahma."

"Dig your spurs as deep as you can into that bull's hair," one of those guys advised me, "and make sure they stay stuck in it."

Two men got ahold of my belt and eased me down onto the buffalo's back. Up to that moment, I had been very cocky on account of having half a pint of "bravemaker" in me, but once I was on top of that huge beast, I sobered up fast. I said, "Let 'er rip!" and the gate swung open. But nothing happened.

Brahma bulls generally get very riled up inside the chute, but that buffalo just stood there like a zombie. I dug my spurs in as deep as I could, and he walked out very slowly, like an old lady, and kept on like this for a few seconds longer. I thought, Damn it, I'm looking like a fool sitting here on an easy chair.

The buffalo took about ten more steps and then exploded. It was like coming out of the crater of an erupting volcano. Oh, God! All I could see was the grandstand whizzing by me every half second. I put my head down with my chin as close to my chest as possible, afraid that he might snap my head around and break my neck. I hung on for dear life, but I was off balance, hanging on to one side.

So it went for what seemed like an eternity. Finally, somewhere far off, I heard a whistle, meaning that I had been on that monster for ten seconds. But that was no help. Two riders were supposed to take me off, but they knew better than to come near that raging bull. It turned out that I didn't need them. I came off that bull like I had been shot from a cannon—but without my boots and spurs, which remained stuck on that damn bull. One of my gloves came off, too, together with a ripped-off thumbnail.

I was lying there, slammed into the ground as if by a sledgehammer, looking up at the buffalo looming over me. There was no rodeo clown around to divert him from me. The crowd was screaming, "Stay down, stay down!" But I was in a haze and got up. That was the last thing I remember. The bull picked me up between his horns and threw me clear over his back. He left me lying there while he ambled over to the catch pen.

I woke up in the hospital with a busted gut, caved-in ribs, and fourteen stitches in my hand. My prize money went for medical expenses. Out of the whole ride, I netted three dollars; that was all I got out of that bull buffalo. It was the beginning and end of my rodeo career. Looking back, I see now that I had it coming. That was my punishment for using Tatanka, our sacred animal, to amuse a crowd of yokels. But I was still young and ignorant then.

The buffalo and the Indian have been here on this Turtle Continent a long, long time—maybe fifty thousand years or more. The white anthropologists say that we came over on the Bering Strait, but I think that we and the buffalo have always been here, and this belief is shared by most Native Americans. Maybe we crossed the Bering Strait once, but if we did, it was in the opposite direction.

Thousands of years ago, the buffalo were bigger by half than they are now, with straight rather than curved horns. Our ancestors hunted these enormous animals—and the mammoth, too—with weapons made only of stone, bone, and wood. They matched their courage against the strength and ferocity of those mighty beasts. I have to admire those ancient people from whom we are descended.

Between Cedar Butte and Corn Creek is a place called Shoe Shop Hill. A man by the name of Shoemaker had his store up there. His name was fitting because he was a cobbler who repaired boots. Why he set himself up there in the Badlands in the middle of nowhere, I don't know. He could not have had many customers. In the old days, a wagon road passed by this hill, but I doubt that many people stopped there to have holes in their boots mended.

According to my grandfather, Shoe Shop Hill was the scene of a shootout between a posse and a band of robbers who held up a bank in Nebraska, way back in 1911. There is a rumor that the bandits buried their loot up there, but nobody tries to dig there because the hill is believed to be haunted by the ghosts of those who were killed in the shootout.

Right near there, some thirty years ago, my father came upon the whole skeleton of an Ice Age buffalo. Its size was awe inspiring. The bones are still there, except for the skull, which had turned to stone and was so heavy that it seemed to be made out of lead. I don't know how my father managed to carry it all the way home, but he did. He painted the skull in a sacred manner and used it for many years as a Sundance altar.

In 1885, my grandfather came up against his last grizzly bear. That bear was so huge that, standing up, it was taller than a man on horseback. The first young buck who got near him learned the hard way how strong Mato Hota could be, because Old Griz broke his horse's head with one swipe. They roped the bear and pumped arrows into it for half a day, finally managing to kill it late in the afternoon. They skinned it and took some of the meat, which is good eating. Grandpa made himself a necklace from its claws and was proud to wear it.

Mato, the Bear, is a most powerful and sacred animal. "Takoja, the Bear is *wakan, lila wakan*," Grandpa told me. "Mato Nonpa, meaning 'Two Bear,' is one of the supernaturals. The white man would call him a god. He is a manifestation of Wakan Tanka, the Creator, who is Many Into One. The

Spirit Bear is called Mato Nonpa because he can stand and walk on two legs, like a man.

"The Bear is wise and very powerful," Grandpa went on. "He is the chief of all the animals as far as curing the sick and wounded is concerned. A Bear dreamer or Bear medicine man knows all the herbs to use in doctoring. Many medicine men have only one medicine; the Bear healer knows them all. He has many different kinds of herbs to cure a human. Mato is both positive and negative. He is ferocious and can kill you, but mostly he is compassionate and has pity on those who are sick."

Grandpa added, "Takoja, if a man should dream of a white Bear, he may never eat the liver or heart of any animal. And if a woman tans a bear hide while she is on her moon, her skin will grow dark and hair will grow on her upper lip."

He also told me, "Grandson, in the old days, Bear medicine men, when curing the sick, painted their bodies red, wore a bearskin, and carried a red forked stick and a knife, or flint. They also sang special Bear medicine songs." He sang one for me:

Pezi huta wan, yatinkte.	A medicine you will eat.
Kahantu nazinye.	Over there it stands.
Mato hemakiye.	A bear told me this.

Sad to say, while most other kinds of medicine have been preserved, I think there is hardly a Bear healer left among the Plains tribes. Much of the Bear medicine knowledge was lost as a result of the suppression of Indian tradition and wisdom by the government and the missionaries before 1940.

Grandfather also taught me, "Hehaka, the Elk, is powerful. He rules the relationship between men and women. Hehaka is strong but gentle. He is a protector, always placing himself between his females and any danger that might threaten them. He loves beauty and speaks softly. Even though he is big and his antlers are wide, he moves through the woods without any effort. His steps are as light as a feather.

"An Elk dreamer, a Hehaka medicine man, has the love charm," my grandfather said. "If a young man is in love and goes to the Elk man for help, he gives him a *siyotanka*, a flute, and a special song. When the girl that young man is courting hears the flute, she cannot resist but must go to him. *Hehaka tapejuta*, the Elk medicine (horsemint), when placed over a man's eyes, will heal their soreness. This medicine, chewed up and placed on a wound, will stop the blood from flowing and hasten the healing."

And then there is the Great Winged One—Wanbli, the Eagle, the embodiment of power. The Eagle is the Creator's messenger, the living bridge between Wakan Tanka above and the humans below. My father used to call him the sun's *akicita*—the sun's "warrior."

If you look at pictures of our old chiefs from days gone by, you see that they wear one eagle feather on their heads. This represents the Lakota nation. The eagle's plume, the fluff, is called "Grandfather's Breath." The white, hot steam that comes out of the sweatlodge we also call Grandfather's Breath. The fluff is very important to us in a ritualistic way. Eagle plumes are always used in name-giving ceremonies for children. A chief's daughter always wears a fluff in the middle of her head, while the second daughter wears one on her left. Those we want to honor wear eagle plumes on the right side of their heads.

Eagle wings are used to "fan people off," as we call it, or to "cedar them"—that is, to waft the smoke from smoldering cedar, sage, sweetgrass, or other incense toward a person's body during a solemn ceremony. An eagle wing is looked upon as a medicine man's hand, an extension of himself. It is very sacred.

The tail feathers of the eagle are highly prized for their power and ceremonial use. In the old days, a set of twelve of these feathers was worth a fine horse. A chief's bonnet was made of such feathers. A *wanbli-huhu-siyotanka*, a whistle made of an eagle's wing bone, was given to every sundancer. As all the dancers blew on their eagle-bone whistles, they made the sound of many eagles screaming. Eagle-bone whistles were also used in many other Lakota ceremonies. At the beginning of a Sundance, a medicine man who was "in the power" would blow on his whistle and raise his eagle wing high, praying for an eagle to come in and circle over the dance ground to bless this most sacred ritual. Most times, an eagle would promptly appear and obey the holy man's bidding. Hundreds of people have witnessed this.

The eagle's talons are a powerful charm, to be worn on the body or as part of a medicine bundle's contents. The majestic, mysterious "war eagle" also plays a major role in our rituals and legends.

Once, when I was a young boy, Grandpa took me way out into the Badlands, to a place where eagles were roosting. He had a length of rawhide and a day-old rabbit that already had begun to smell. Grandpa set out a loop of rawhide and put the rabbit in the middle. Then we waited. I couldn't see the eagles because they were too high, on top of a ledge where they had their roost. Suddenly, I saw a big eagle circling, coming down in spirals lower and lower. Then it circled upward again until it was just a little dot in the sky. Then it dove straight down, like a stone dropping from the clouds.

The moment the eagle plunged its talons into the rabbit, Grandpa pulled the rawhide and caught the eagle by both feet. Grandpa fought the eagle, which gave him a hard time until he pinned it down. Then he wrapped a piece of burlap around it so that the big bird could not use its claws or beak on him. He hollered for me to pull out four tail feathers. I did as told, and every time I pulled, the eagle let out a squawk.

"Forgive me, Brother," Grandpa told him, "but I have to borrow these feathers to do my doctoring."

I pulled two "power feathers" in the center and two others. Then we let the eagle go. It was not hurt and its flying was in no way affected, but let me tell you, that bird was mighty angry. Grandpa used the power feathers, together with his sacred buffalo horn, for an important healing ceremony. The two other feathers he put on a head "roach" as part of his dance regalia. I have always stood in awe of the power of the great eagle, the symbol of our Lakota nation.

About fifteen years ago, a Sioux woman named Nylak came to me and said, "A friend of mine, Annie Mae Aquash, has disappeared. She is a strong woman, a great fighter for Indian rights, and I am afraid that something bad might have happened to her. Take me on a Vision Quest. Maybe a dream will tell me what happened to her."

So I took Nylak up to the mountain, and four days later I went to bring her back to the valley. Nylak had not dreamed of Annie Mae. On the way down from the mountain, we stopped four times. The second time we halted at an old, hollow oak tree. In it sat Hinhan Sha, the Great Horned Owl. As I looked at it, the owl hopped down, spread its wings, and started walking in a circle. Male horned owls do that when they perform their mating dance—they put one wing up and the other down and shuffle round and round.

Nylak asked, "What is the meaning of this?"

I said, "Be very quiet and listen."

Far off, toward the east, we heard women crying. We stood there in silence, listening to the cries. They sounded so sad that a shiver went down my spine.

Nylak asked again, "What does this mean?"

I said, "Death. Someone we love is going to die. We don't know who, but it will come to pass."

The owl flew up to the treetop, and the crying stopped. I told Nylak, "Be very careful. There is great danger, for the owl represents death."

One or two days later, my friend Annie Mae Aquash was found dead at the foot of a cliff at the edge of the Badlands, inside the Pine Ridge Reservation. Tears were frozen on her cheeks. The FBI said she had died of exposure, and they lost no time burying her. They told members of Annie Mae's family that they had performed an autopsy and that her death had been due to natural causes.

Her friends and relatives suspected foul play and had the body exhumed. They found that Annie Mae's hands had been cut off. The FBI said that the hands had been sent to Washington for fingerprints. It was also discovered that she had been exposed, not to the cold, but to a .38-caliber slug that they found lodged in her head. The owl had told the truth.

Yes, the Owl stands for death, but that does not mean that this bird is feared or despised or looked upon as evil. On the contrary, death is part of the unending circle of life. According to Lakota belief, when a person dies, his or her *nagi*, or soul, starts its journey to the Spirit Land, the Land of Many Lodges. It walks along the Wanagi Tachanku, the "Spirit Trail," which whites call the Milky Way. Traditional Sioux always have some tattoo marks on their wrists—a kind of passport to the Spirit Land—because at some spot along the trail sits Hinhan Nagi, the Owl Spirit. It examines every soul and lets only those with tattoos pass on to their destination. Those who have no tattoos, Hinhan Nagi hurls back down to Earth, where they become wandering ghosts.

Hinhan also represents wisdom and healing. It moves silently by night, and it is at night that spiritual people receive their dreams and visions. Hinhan moves softly and gently, and its call is also soft and melodious. Owl dreamers therefore have great healing powers, and they do their doctoring gently, never causing pain.

An animal does not have to be big to have power. Essentially, all animals, even the smallest, are sacred and have special powers. Even the little Ant is powerful. It collects tiny crystals with which it covers its anthills, and these we pick to put in our gourd rattles, which we use in the Yuwipi and other ceremonies. Kimimila, the Butterfly, also has power. My father always said, "Kimimila, that's a good name for a pretty girl. Sometimes a Butterfly settles on a woman's shoulder, and if she is spiritually inclined, the Butterfly will whisper sacred secrets in her ear."

Lizards and turtles stand for long life because they are hard to kill. Some turtles live much longer than humans. A turtle heart keeps on beating long after the animal is dead.

One day, when I was a boy, Grandpa brought a turtle into our little log cabin. He killed it, cut out the heart, and handed it to me, saying, "Here, Takoja, swallow it." I could not do it because the heart was too big. Grandpa cut it in half, and even then the two pieces kept beating and beating. Again Grandpa urged me, "Swallow this, Takoja, so that one day you will be brave and have a long life like the turtle."

So I tried to swallow the first half but couldn't get it down. It was stuck in my throat and scared me, because it kept pounding and pounding. Finally, I made a big gulp and felt it drumming in my stomach. It felt as if I had two hearts, a human and a turtle heart. The second piece was easier, but now I had three hearts pounding away in my little body. Grandpa told me, "Keha, the Turtle, is big medicine. Now you'll have a long life and become a very old man.

Among traditional people, when a child is born the mother or grandmother makes two fetishes out of deerskin, each about four or five inches long, in the shape of a turtle or a certain kind of sand lizard called *telanuwe*. They decorate these little amulets with beadwork or quillwork. They take the baby's dried-up umbilical cord and wrap it in sage, buffalo hair, and eagle down and put it in one of these little fetishes and pin it on the cradleboard. This acts as a powerful protective charm against evil forces and is also thought to give the child health and long life. Later, when the toddler begins to walk, they fasten this fetish to his or her clothes. Eventually, the mother takes it off and keeps it. I had such a charm in the shape of a lizard.

The second charm is just a decoy. It is hung up someplace, maybe in a tree, for the evil spirits to vent their fury on, because they think the navel cord is in there and that through it they can gain power over the child. But they are fools; they always fall for this little trick.

Sometimes when a child is born, the parents ask me to come and do a ceremony. Immediately I tell them to make a beaded or quilled turtle or lizard charm. I come when the baby is about two weeks old, and I take that child and its parents into the sweatlodge and perform the long-life ritual for them. I pray for the family, put the umbilical cord into the fetish, sew it up, and bless it. I also have a forked stick painted red with a tiny tobacco offering tied to it and fluffy eagle plumes fastened to its tips. With this sacred wand and its beaded fetish, the child enters into the world of the tribe, physically and spiritually.

The Indian respects the power and spirit of his four-legged or winged brothers and sisters, The Indian kills to eat, taking game only in order to survive, and is always aware that taking a life is a serious deed that asks for forgiveness. The white "sportsman" kills for pleasure, for killing's sake.

This fact was forcefully brought home to me when I was in Holland on a lecture tour. A friend was driving me through the countryside on the road to Nijmegen. We saw two Mercedes stopped by the wayside. My friend stopped, too. "I know these people," he said. "You must watch this, our glorious hunters at their sport."

Five men had emerged from the fancy cars. They all had the green outfits customarily worn by gentlemen hunters in Europe. Four of these fellows carried guns. The fifth opened the trunk and took out a little box. He carried it into the field for about fifty yards and then put it down. He opened the box, and out popped a little tame rabbit. He shooed it across the field, and the other four heroic sportsmen blasted away at it, shooting the rabbit to pieces. Then the hunters all lined up with their guns, holding up the little animal's mangled body, to pose for a photograph. I would not have believed this had I not seen it with my own eyes.

My grandfather used to say, "The white man has eyes, but he does not see. He has ears, but he does not listen. He touches, but feels nothing. But you, Takoja, listen! If you listen close at night, you will hear the creatures of the dark, all of them sacred—the owls, the crickets, the frogs, the night birds—and you will hear beautiful songs, songs you have never heard before. Listen with your heart. Never stop listening!"

The Unexplainable

When I received my father's powers, I went into another dimension. I turned my mind to spiritual things. I became a medicine man. Right here I have a problem. The English language is useless for talking about sacred things. It lacks subtlety. One cannot express the different shades of concepts with it. *Power* and *medicine man*, for example, are empty words that, in their raw clumsiness, give only a vague idea of the thoughts behind them. *Medicine man* might be a good way to describe a pharmacist, and *power* might be an acceptable term in the sense of "turn the power on" or "America is a superpower." These words are of no use to me, but what can I put in their place?

I am a *wichasha wakan*. You call me a medicine man, but that won't do. *Wichasha wakan* literally means "holy man," but *wakan* can be translated in many different ways. It can mean "holy," "sacred," "mysterious," "otherworldly," or "supernatural." *Wakan Tanka*, the Creator, literally means "the Great Mystery." *Shunka wakan*—that is, "holy dog" or "spirit dog"— is our term for "horse." In the old days, dogs were our only domestic animals. They were used for burden-bearing, dragging small bundles behind them on two sticks called a "travois." Then the white man introduced the horse. What to call this wondrous animal, which could carry burdens much larger and faster than those carried by a dog? *Shunka wakan*, of course. You see the many shades in which this word *wakan* can be used.

I am most comfortable thinking of myself as a *spiritual man*, but even this is inadequate. Your dry-as-dust English has basically only one term, *medicine man*, to describe a number of different spiritual men. For this reason, I want to make some distinctions.

First there is the *wichasha wakan*, the all-around shaman. (*Shaman* is not the right word, either, but I can think of nothing better.) Then there is the *pejuta wichasha*, who uses the power of herbs to cure the sick. Then there is the *yuwipi*, the "man who finds out," the "tied-up one" who works with the power of Inyan, the rock. We also have the *waayatan*, the prophet, who can see into the future and who predicts what will come to pass. Powerful also is the *heyoka*, the sacred clown or thunder dreamer, who laughs through his tears and does everything backwards.

Feared as well as admired is the *wapiya*, the conjurer and magician. With his positive nature he heals the sick, while in his negative aspect he is the "bone keeper," the evil witch doctor who puts a sickness into you. One could even include here the "roadman" of the Native American Church, who uses peyote as a sacrament. For all these you have only this one term: "medicine man." Your language is poor, indeed.

The Indian medicine man is nothing like a Christian priest or a Jewish rabbi. My father used to say, "They respect me, not because I am good in the Christian sense, but because I have the *power*." He also said, "A *wichasha wakan* must be higher than an eagle and lower than a worm. He must be down to earth—human and, at the same time, something more than human."

My father always thought that in order to become a healer and a teacher, a man must experience life to the fullest, spending nights in the drunk tank and feeling a policeman's nightstick crunch his cheekbone. He must also have known the love of women and the happiness and heartbreak that comes from it.

In *Lame Deer, Seeker of Visions*, my father described the spiritual man at his highest stage as follows:

> The *wichasha wakan*, when he is old, has done everything. Such a one can cure, prophesy, talk to herbs, command the stones, run a Sundance, or even change the weather. But all this is of no great importance to him. These are merely stage she has passed through. He has gone beyond all this. He has the Wakanya Wowanyanke, the "Great Vision."
>
> The *wichasha wakan* wants to be by himself—away from the crowd, away from everyday matters. He likes to meditate, leaning against a tree

or rock, feeling the Earth under him, feeling the weight of the big flaming sky upon him. Closing his eyes, he sees things clearly. What you see with the eye in your heart is what counts.

The *wichasha wakan* loves silence, wrapping it around himself like a blanket—a silence louder than thunder. He likes to be in a place where there is no sound but the humming of insects. He sits facing the West, asking for help. He talks to the plants, and they answer him. He listens to the voices of the *wama kashkan*—all those who move upon the Earth—the animals. Something from every living being flows into him, and something flows from him.

This kind of man is neither good nor bad. He exists, and that's enough. He is as free as a tree or a bird. That freedom can be beautiful or ugly. It doesn't matter. His life is a teaching.

I have not reached this stage yet and maybe never will. For me, the essence of a medicine man's life is to be humble, to have great patience, to be close to the Earth, to live as simply as possible, and to never stop learning.

What we would truly call a "medicine woman" is extremely rare—so very rare that one might come along only once every hundred years. There are women who become healers—for instance, with herbs—as well as women who are seers and dream interpreters. Our people understand that in bringing forth and nurturing new life, women are giving the people the Creator's greatest gift: the children, the future of the nation, the renewal of the Sacred Hoop. A woman can become a *winyan wakan* (a medicine woman) only after menopause, because her power when she is "on her moon" nullifies her medicine power.

A man can become a *wichasha wakan* in a number of ways. A grandfather watches a young boy grow up. He notices that he is not like other boys. He is a dreamer, and he tells of what he has seen in his dreams. He is not interested in the silly things other boys do. He spends a lot of time being by himself. His eyes seem to look inward. The grandfather marks him out as a future *wichasha wakan*. He takes him to ceremonies, tells him about our people's beliefs and traditions. He keeps him out of school, because the white man's learning might spoil his spirituality. At the right time, he takes the boy on a Vision Quest and has a holy man instruct him in the ways of the spirits. Such a boy is likely to become a *yuwipi* or a *pejuta wichasha*. That is one way.

A man can receive power from an animal, either through a dream or as the result of a Vision Quest. This is a spiritual seed that grows slowly and eventually will bear fruit. I know of an old man who passed away who had the power of Hehaka, the Elk. The old man had a son who was childless, but his daughter had a boy who early on showed signs of his grandfather's power. No one told him because he was still too young to understand, but everyone knew that someday he would walk the sacred path. The seed was already planted within him. Later, when he was in his teens, he went up to the mountaintop and received his vision. He had a holy man interpret it for him, and he was told, "Tunkashila planted that seed in you, the seed of Elk power. So you will walk in your grandfather's footsteps." The boy went to his grandmother and told her, "The power has been passed on to me. It did not die." She was so happy that she burst into tears.

Power often skips a generation to reappear in a grandchild. I know the grandson of one of the greatest *yuwipis* who ever lived. He was already running ceremonies when still in his mid-teens. But later in life he started drinking and abusing his power in a number of ways, so it was taken from him and given to someone else. So one can become a medicine man by inheriting power from a grandfather.

A man becomes a *heyoka* by dreaming of the Wakinyan, the Thunderbeings, of lightning, and of things connected with the Wakinyan—for example, a certain gray horse, a snowbird, a frog, or a dragonfly. He instantly becomes a sacred clown, whether he wants to or not. He can free himself from this burden only by undergoing a long and complicated ceremony.

Finally, a *wichasha wakan* can simply give part or all of his power to a successor. In my case, I was given the knowledge and power from my father, but I also had the seed planted in me by some of my Quick Bear ancestors.

A medicine man has power, or a number of powers. The Indian concept of "power" is hard to explain. It is easier felt than put into words. Two things are important to know: *ton* and *sichun*. *Ton*, literally translated, can mean "to give birth to," "to possess," or "to acquire," but when used in connection with a *wichasha wakan*, it represents a spiritual power, a force that makes a person or thing *wakan*. It is the power to do something supernatural, which cannot be explained by the white man's science and which can manifest itself in many different ways. Not only humans can have *ton*; animals, plants, and stones can possess it, too.

Sichun is again one of those hard-to-explain concepts. It is a good power—the spirit of, or the spirit inside, a person or thing. It is a power that guards a person from birth against evil forces. It can be a protective charm or the power to forewarn against danger. It can also be a number of such powers, or *sichunpi*, derived from the *tons* of animals. It is the mystery inside the *wasichu*, the *wichasha wakan's* medicine bundle. It is the power of the universe pervading everything. And here is a big puzzle: *wasichu*, the word for "mystery power" and "medicine bundle," is almost the same as the disparaging word for a white man.

A person can obtain power not only through dreams or as a gift, but also through suffering, such as undergoing the "piercing" at the Sundance. I have been trying to explain the Indian concept of "power," but I fear that I have been able to give only a faint hint of its true meaning.

The typical medicine man is a *pejuta wichasha*, an "herb man" who has the power to heal the sick. He must speak the Lakota language, because language and healing are closely connected. He must have power to communicate with the spirits and be able to speak the shaman's secret language—Hambloglaka. He must know the right songs to go with every medicine he uses and those that belong to the ceremonies he performs. If he does not know them, or uses the wrong ones, whatever he does will be in vain.

The *pejuta wichasha* must have been instructed in his work by an older holy man. He must be honest. He must know when he is in the power. Power comes and goes. It can vanish in the twinkling of an eye, like smoke dissolving in thin air. He might use one medicine or several. No man can know and use all. He must have a few basic things to use in his healing ceremonies: a buffalo skull, an eagle wing, a pipe bag, and a red stone pipe. He must have a ceremonial rattle and drum, which are pleasing to the spirits and invoke their help. He must always have cedar, sage, and sweetgrass handy, herbs that are used in almost all of our rituals. He should have his *wozuha pejuta*, the bag containing his herbal medicines, and his *wasichun* or *wopiye*, his sacred mystery bundle. I have all of these, as well as my grandfather's buffalo horn.

A healer learns about herbs from an expert, or from dreams and visions. Badger wisdom is particularly welcome because this animal, like the Bear, is always digging up roots that have healing power. He is a four-legged *pejuta wichasha*. There are several Badger medicines, such as horseweed and wild columbine. They are mostly used against internal and digestive troubles. When a man receives herb wisdom from an animal, he gives thanks, says a prayer, and makes a tobacco offering. He might also carry something from his particular animal—a claw or feather—on his body or in his medicine bundle.

A *pejuta wichasha* knows when and from what direction to approach an herb and whether it is effective during the day or at night. He can put himself in the mind of a sick person and feel his pain.

I will not bore you with a long list of the names of herbs and roots and what they are for. You can find them in books dealing with what the white man calls "ethnobotany." You can also find some in my father's book. I will only mention that he treasured his "little black seeds" that, as he said, "make an old man's thing stand up at night." "This, medicine is very, very sacred," was his comment.

I will, however, mention one thing my father never talked about: the plants used by women. When Ptesan Win, White Buffalo Calf Woman, brought the Sacred Pipe to the people, she taught women to stay away from ceremonies and not to use certain curative herbs during their periods. The reason is that during a woman's period, the female power is so strong that it renders the medicine man's rituals ineffective.

Ptesan Win taught the women to use sage during their moon time. This is why sage is Ptesan Win's special gift to women. It can be used to make a tea, or it can be burned as incense. It takes away the pain women have during their moon. The female plant has the healing power; the male sage has none. Sage and anise grow wild on the prairie. In California, sage can reach the height of a tall man. The root of the anise plant is used at the end of a woman's period to purify her body and also to make her sleep well.

Two types of mint exist, one feminine and the other masculine. The male plant is small, the female plant very big. The latter is used for healing and purging, the former to relax the mind and body. Women also have a plant they can use as a contraceptive. The male plant prevents conception, while the female plants increases fertility. Those who use plants must know how to pick them. They must be able to distinguish the male from the female plant; otherwise, there might be some unpleasant surprises.

Some plants play a major part in our ceremonies, particularly those that are used as incense: sweetgrass, sage, and cedar. To utilize sweetgrass, it must be plaited into a braid of seventy-two strands. It must also be dried in the sun. The drier it becomes, the stronger it will be. Before the arrival of a woman's moon time, a braid of sweetgrass should be hung on the outside of the house.

There are many herbs for women only—to conceive, to abort, to ease childbirth, and to make the milk flow.

The Elk dreamer is good at treating sick women because the Elk is a gentle, loving protector of his females. A medicine man who got his power from the Elk uses *hehaka tapejuta*, horsemint, in his doctoring. It is good for many diseases.

In *Lame Deer, Seeker of Visions*, my father said:

> There's one thing a medicine man shouldn't do—treat a woman while she is *ishnati*—on her moon. Her power is so strong at that time, if she spits at a rattlesnake, that snake dies. It is no good if a woman in this state goes to a ceremony. Her power will clash with the power of the *pejuta wichasha*. It might harm him, or her. We have herbs which have to do with childbearing, baby care, and sex. *Hupe stola*—that's soapweed—is truly a strong medicine. Mixed with a certain cactus, *unkchela blaska*, it helps a woman in labor when the baby doesn't want to come out. Used in a different way, it becomes *hoksi yuhapi sni*—a medicine which aborts. You give this to a woman when there is a very good reason not to bear a child. One uses it carefully after thinking about it for a long time.

Generally speaking, one should always take the whole plant, together with the root, and never pick a plant with seeds. A plant picked unceremoniously will not heal. A *pejuta wichasha* does not wear a three-piece suit and does not walk around with a beeper, but he knows some things that the white doctor with a dozen diplomas on his wall doesn't even dream of.

If you ask an Indian medicine man for help, you should do it properly, by sending him a red stone pipe, which he will later return. I once had a pipe sent to me from a man in France who wanted my help. I myself will not come unless a pipe is sent first.

Some healings are done spiritually through ceremonies, prayers, "fanning off" with an eagle wing, and smoking the Sacred Pipe. In such cases, no special medicines are given. Other doctorings are done simply by giving the sick person a certain tea, an infusion, or a poultice made from a special plant. Sometimes this is combined with a Purification ceremony inside a sweatlodge. I favor a combination of ways.

Just as some white doctors are surgeons while others are psychiatrists, we also have specialists among our *pejuta wichashas*. In the old days, Bear or Badger dreamers often specialized in setting broken bones. They had a special medicine called *huhuwe hanhan pejuta*, which, when warmed up and mixed with fat, was put on a fractured leg or arm to keep the muscles from stiffening. Then rawhide, cut from a parfleche, was moistened and wrapped around the broken limb. As it dried, it shrank and tightened, keeping the set bones in place. Soft hair from a deer's belly was put between the flesh and hide for cushioning. Special songs were sung when fractures were treated. I knew a Shoshone Bear dreamer called Red Horse who made the sound of a growling bear while treating a fracture.

A medicine man named Black Moon was a snake doctor. In 1919, my father watched him treating a snakebite for a man who had been stung twice, both at the ankle and a little farther up. The leg was swollen and discolored. The man was in pain and vomiting.

"Black Moon could move his body like a snake," my father told me. "His tongue was like a snake's tongue, darting in and out of his mouth, flickering-like. He could make his eyes look hard and flinty, like a rattler's. He told the snake-bit man, "The snakes are my friends. It doesn't make any difference what kind of snakes. I got the power. If you believe me, you'll be cured in four days. I don't even have to use my medicine on you. I have it here—*zuzeka tapejuta* (beard tongue)—but I don't need it."

My father went on: "Black Moon then performed the Kankakpa, the snake-curing ceremony. He looked at the punctures made by the rattler's fangs where the blood was oozing out. He took a sharp stick, forked like a snake's tongue, put a dime in the fork, tied a string made of gut tightly around the leg and the stick, then snapped it hard, hitting the big vein. I saw dark, greenish stuff spurting out. As soon as the blood turns red again, you can tell that snake to go to hell. Four days later, the man was as good as new."

Kankakpa (hitting a vein to bleed a person) was often the job of a *wapiya*, a conjurer. The *wapiya* uses a stick of ancient wood to pierce a vein and let the bad blood out together with the sickness. That is, he does this when he is a good *wapiya*. Conjurers or magicians, like anything else, are positive and negative. If positive, they use their secret knowledge to heal the sick. If negative, they use their evil powers to do harm.

Chest, the medicine man who took my father on his Vision Quest, was an honest, upright *wapiya* who did only good. He could heal a person by inhaling, drawing the sickness out with his breath, and then spitting it out. This ceremony is called "Wakiyapa." He also had a powerful rattle, made from a white buffalo's scrotum, and a special feather. When Chest was singing his curing songs, the rattle would often jump up, fly through the air, and hit the one who was supposed to be healed. The feather was always placed on a square of black cloth. Sometimes it, too, would suddenly fly off like an arrow, seemingly disappear into the sick person's body, and then return to the square of cloth. Afterwards, there was always a tiny bit of blood or mucus sticking to the feather. This was the disease it had taken away.

Chest was a very strong healer, but he took his knowledge with him to the grave. My own uncle, Good Fox, was also a *wapiya* who helped people, and he also had a mysterious feather. When he made it hit an ailing person, the sickness attached itself to the feather. Good Fox, too, like many *wapiyas*, did not pass on his healing knowledge. Maybe he was afraid that it might be misused.

The negative *wapiya*, in the old days called *wakan skan wichasha*, is a sort of witch doctor. He works with the *wichahmunge*, the "wizard medicine," to shoot quills or tiny rocks into a person without their being aware of it. In this way, he can send a sickness into a person's body, a sickness that only he can cure. And he will take all your money—everything you own—for taking the ailment away.

Such a conjurer works on people's minds. He has the power to confuse. He can destroy you spiritually, physically, mentally, and emotionally. He can cure blood and nerve diseases, and he can give them to you. He can use parts of people's bodies—hair, fingernails, and so on—to bewitch them. He can take a person's soul away or change a person's mind. He can make love charms that induce a man to leave his wife and go to another woman.

A spiritual person senses it when he or she meets such an evil magician. When I was young, I took part in a ceremony at which a half dozen old medicine men were present. A certain man came in. (I won't mention his name, because his surviving relatives could bring back his evil medicine

THE UNEXPLAINABLE ☼ 159

and hurt people.) When this *wapiya* came in, all the medicine men got up and left, letting him sit there by himself.

Outside, one of the elders gave a certain herb to each of us, saying, "Keep this in your mouth. With this herb, you could be in the midst of twenty conjurers all trying to bewitch you, but their evil powers would be turned against them. So we went in again, where we had started our ceremony, and that *wapiya* looked at us, got up, walked backward out of that place, got on his horse, and left. Then we took the herb out of our mouths and finished the ceremony.

When traditional people meet a conjurer, they give him a wide berth. They scramble to get out of his way because they fear him. Now and then, one meets a *wapiya winyan*, a female conjurer, but not often. Bad conjurers usually come to bad ends. They make a lot of money by scaring people, but they always lose it. They see their children killed in car accidents or in a drunken fight. They are shunned by everyone and die a lonely death.

There is one conjurer who is even worse than our Indian *wapiya*. This is the white physician-scientist who, for riches and fame, mixes the genes of humans and animals, or mixes Native American herbs with chemicals, or makes a whole deadly goulash out of several different viruses. Such a scientific witches' brew could give rise to completely new diseases, plagues for which there would be no cure and that could bring an end to all humanity.

We have a special medicine man whom white people would call a psychic. He is the *waayatan*—the "dream man" who can foretell the future of a single person or a whole continent. He uses the powers from within himself. He needs no other medicine. His powers might work one day and be gone the next. He knows when they are not there, and he will tell you.

The *waayatan* will interpret your dreams, which, like everything else, are positive or negative and come to you from either a good or a bad source. A *waayatan* could take you up the mountain for a Vision Quest because he could explain to you the meaning of whatever vision you might have received. (In order to avoid misinterpretation, there should always be more than one medicine man to do this.) There are still those who are called *heyoka* or *yuwipi* men, but these are in a class by themselves and deserve a chapter of their own.

A healing can be a shattering experience—in the best and the worst

senses. When I am supposed to do a curing ceremony, I am always afraid—
scared to death. Once, I was running a Sundance at Big Mountain, in
Arizona. There were some sixteen or eighteen elderly Navajo ladies who
hold high positions among their own people. I guess one could call them
clan mothers. One of them had had a stroke. She was partially paralyzed,
and her face was contorted. The people turned to me for help, but who
could I turn to?

I immediately thought of my father and grandfather. I thought, "Where
are you guys? I need your help. I have been asked to heal this grandmother.
What am I going to do? And how am I going to do it?"

The Sundance was going on without interruption, and I myself was
already purified. Luckily, I had already set up a sweatlodge for the dancers,
and the rocks were ready. My son helped me load the Pipe. I took all my
sacred things, including my grandfather's buffalo horn. I also took whatever herbs I thought—or rather, hoped—would work.

After I had set everything up, the Sundance stopped for an hour to give
me a chance to do my healing ceremony. They brought the old lady in, and
I sat her down on a chair in the center of the dance circle. I covered her as
she would have been covered in her own sweatlodge. I used water, sage,
herbs, and my buffalo horn, and I sang the healing songs.

Around me, I also gathered two circles of sundancers who stood
shoulder to shoulder, making a living fence so that curious outsiders could
not watch the ceremony. The sundancers prayed and sang as I did, and the
ceremony I used was the Ritual of the Buffalo Horn.

As I finished, the woman got up. Her face had taken on its normal expression again. I led her to the Sundance Tree. We put our hands on the
sacred cottonwood, leaning against it, and the woman smiled at me.

To me, the woman's healing was like a new sun rising, and I thanked
Tunkashila, the Grandfather Spirit, for giving my hands the healing power
of the ancients. Everybody thought that I had done a great thing, but deep
down I knew that the healing power had come from within the woman
herself and from the power generated by the circle of dancers.

On the "Day of Piercing," a sundancer has the power of a *pejuta
wichasha*. When this most sacred ritual is over, sick people often go to the
sundancers, who give them medicine and lay their hands on them to make
them well. Sundancers have this power while their wounds are still fresh.

The healing also came from my father and grandfather, from the power of the buffalo horn, and from the mystery force within the old songs and the red, glowing rocks. Finally, I think, there was also power flowing from all those who had come to witness the Sundance and to help the Dineh people, the Navajos, whom we call the "Spotted Blanket Nation," in the fight for their land. These included Indian people from many tribes, plus many whites, blacks, and Orientals. So it was many powers uniting into one that effected this cure, not just my own. But at one moment, I felt my grandfather's *ton*, his *sichun*, hitting me like two lightning bolts fusing to form a healing rock.

Why am I telling of this? Because when a young man learning to be a *pejuta wichasha* asks my advice, I tell him, "Be humble. Accept failure. This is part of being a medicine man. Be aware of the negative and the positive in everything. Don't trust in your own little power, but try to unite many powers into one. And have patience. When you pick one herb among a clump of its own kind, don't be hasty. Feel. Listen. Then pick the herb that responds to you and gives you a good feeling. If you don't have the sixth sense to communicate with that one herb, stop right there. Stop trying to be a healer. Become a car salesman or a lawyer."

Thunder Dreamers

The *heyoka* is at the same time less and more than a medicine man. He is the "contrary," the man who does everything backward. People fear the *heyoka*, and he is even a little afraid of himself and of his strange powers. He is sorrow and laughter rolled into one, sacred and ridiculous at the same time.

Heyokas are powerful. They can cure certain illnesses, and they can also change the weather. They they can change a blizzard into a clear day and a summer breeze into a hailstorm. They can part the clouds to let the sun shine through, and they can protect people from being hit by lightning. There is quite a bit of this *heyoka* power in my family. One of my great-grandfathers was a *heyoka*. There is a little bit of *heyoka* in me.

A *heyoka* is a "thunder dreamer." The moment you dream of thunder or lightning or of the Wakinyan, the Thunderbirds, you become a *heyoka* whether you want to or not. Even if you merely dream of one of the many symbols of lightning—a gray horse, for instance—you are turned into one of these contraries. You become a sacred clown, an icy-hot, forward-backward, upside-down creature.

A *heyoka* puts his clothes on backward. He says, "I hate you" when he means, "I love you." He says yes when he means no. He sees a pretty girl "putting on her face," admiring herself in the mirror, and tells her, "How come you're so ugly?" He rides a horse with his face toward the tail. When the weather is hot, he covers himself with blankets, shivers, and pretends he is freezing. At ten degrees below zero, he runs around in his bathing suit, moaning, "Oh, I can't stand this heat!" I knew a man like this. We called him Heyoka Osni, the "Cold Fool."

A contrary's sweatlodge faces East instead of West like those of other men. When he calls the colors of the wind to him, he calls red for South; white for North; black for East; and yellow for West—just the opposite of what these colors stand for. Of course, he makes people laugh, because a man doing everything backward looks funny. But being a *heyoka* is no joking matter. The *heyoka* has strange and enormous powers.

My father always told me, "A *heyoka* has more power than an atom bomb. With his thunder medicine, sitting alone in his home on the reservation, he could blow the dome off the Capitol in Washington. His power is that great. That's why people are afraid of him."

Heyokas do much good for the people. For the Sundance, you need a clear, blue sky. If there is rain, a *heyoka* might be able to make the sun shine on the Sundance circle with no clouds overhead, while the storm continues to rage just a few miles beyond. But he could also turn fine weather into a blizzard. So he is respected and also feared, because there could be a bad side to him—or rather, a good-bad side. Just as with lightning, you are never quite sure of what a *heyoka* might do.

We symbolize lightning with a zigzag line that ends in a fork. At the end of each tine, there are tufted feathers to remind us that lightning gets its power from the Thunderbirds. One tine of the fork is positive, the other one negative. It is said that the positive tine brought the warming flame to the people—the light-giving fire, the power of the atom, the sun power, all of which can be used for both good and bad. But the other fork—watch out! That is the negative one that could strike and kill you.

The *heyoka* gets his power from the Wakinyan, the Great Winged Ones, which the whites call the Thunderbirds. The Chief Thunderbird, Wakinyan Tanka, lives in the West where the sun goes down. He is wrapped in clouds, as in a buffalo robe. He has his tipi on top of the highest mountain.

The Lakota once believed that Wakinyan Tanka had his home in the Paha Sapa, our sacred Black Hills, stolen from us for the sake of gold, silver, and uranium (a *heyoka* mineral). It was said that his nest, made of dry bones and containing an enormous egg from which the little Wakinyan keep hatching, was atop Harney Peak. But there are no Wakinyan now on Harney Peak, as you can find out for yourself if you climb up there. Some of our old people used to say that the Wakinyan went to some other place because they could not tolerate the white gold-seekers and tourists who defiled their sacred land, but I rather believe that they dwell upon an invisible, spiritual mountain.

Our elders say that Inyan, or "Rock," created Wakinyan Tanka to be his companion. In Inyan, or Tunka, our earliest sacred immortal, dwells the spirit and power of Rock, who lives forever and who will still be here when everything else is gone. But, of course, both Inyan and Wakinyan Tanka are parts of Wakan Tanka, the Creator, who is one but also many.

No human eye has ever seen the Thunderbeings, though in a vision a holy man might get a glimpse of them—not a whole Thunderbeing, but just a little part of him. As the old people used to say, it would probably mean death to see all of a Thunderbeing, even if only in a dream. My father always told me, "Son, the mountains are holy. It is good to go to the mountain to pray for a vision, but never go above the tree line. Further up, where there are no trees, that is the Wakinyan's place. Do not trespass on it."

When I was a boy, this is what some of the elders told me: "The Thunderbirds are like no other supernaturals. They have no body, but mighty claws. They have no eyes, but one of the eyes that are not there shoots lightning. They have no head, but huge beaks. They have no mouth, but out of that missing mouth comes the Great Wakinyan's voice—the big thunderclap—followed by the rumbling lesser thunders of the little Wakinyan." All this is hard to imagine, even for an Indian.

[handwritten margin note: description of Thunderbeings]

A man might be doing something quite ordinary, like eating fry bread, when lightning strikes somewhere near. He might hear human voices talking in the clouds. That night he might dream of lightning, or maybe of a rider on a gray horse with a grass belt and grass in his hair, which is one of several symbols of the Wakinyan. The next day, he will wake up as a *heyoka*. He will smoke himself with burning cedar as an offering to the Great Winged Ones who are fond of cedar incense. In the old days, a freshly made contrary might paint zigzag lightning designs on his forehead, shoulders, and arms, so that all might see that he had become a thunder dreamer.

In a *heyoka's* dream, there will often be something embarrassing—something he does not want people to know about—but he has to act this out in public. If in his dream he sees himself wearing women's clothes or tattered, shabby clothing, that is what he has to put on. He wishes he did not have to do this. But if he refused, there would be thunder and lightning. He knows that if he does not act out his dream, he might get killed.

A *heyoka* is a sacred fool, a clown whose task is to make people laugh. Life involves a lot of sadness and weeping, particularly for an Indian, so the Wakinyan sends a man a dream that there might be laughter among the tears.

My father was a *heyoka*. Years later, he became a *wapiya*, a conjurer and magician, and then a *pejuta wichasha*, an herbal healer. Later still, he became a *waayatan*, a seer into the future and an interpreter of dreams. Then he became a *yuwipi* man, who uses rocks and listens to the spirits while tied up in a star blanket. He had to go through all this in order to become, finally, a *wichasha wakan*, a holy man. But first he was a sacred fool. For four years, he had to be a *heyoka*, acting out his dream as a rodeo clown.

There was also an element of *winkte* in my father's dream, a vision of the hermaphrodite and the transvestite. Now, there wasn't the smallest bit of *winkte* in my father. But in obedience to his dream, he was forced to do his clowning under the name of Alice Jitterbug, dressed in a red wig, silk stockings, and high-heeled shoes.

As I said, it was a dangerous job; it was his task to divert an enraged Brahma bull from a fallen rider. In his high heels, he had to run like hell with the bull chasing after him. Many times, he had to jump into a big barrel to save himself, and then the bull would toss it around, making it roll from one end of the rodeo arena to the other with my father inside. People laughed at his antics, not knowing that he was acting in obedience to his thunder vision.

Once I went with my father to a big, four-day powwow. A long *heyoka* dance was part of it. Every day, about twenty clowns performed. Only three or four were real *heyokas*; the others were just ordinary powwow clowns. Suddenly, one day, it started to rain. I turned to my father to talk to him, but he had disappeared.

Then a new clown came in, wearing a fantastic outfit that hid most of his face. His antics were so funny that people couldn't stop laughing. He directed all the other clowns, hitting them with a stick if they didn't obey his orders. He dragged girls from among the spectators and pretended to make love to them. There was no end of screaming, laughter, and giggling.

When he had finished, the clouds parted, the sun came out, and the rain stopped. Then, without my having noticed his arrival, my father was once again sitting beside me. Later, my mother told me that *he* had been the funny clown who had made the sun shine—the clown who, by making himself ridiculous, had done something sacred.

Even in my father's old age, when more than eighty tribes looked up to him as a great medicine man, his *heyoka* nature still asserted itself. One time during the early seventies, an outfit called something like "Prince Albert's Own Hair Restorer" got ahold of him. "Chief," they said, "we'll do up your hair, which has a little gray in it, and photograph you for an ad and pay you three hundred dollars on top of it. You know, an ad like 'You don't have to be British to use Prince Albert's famous hair tonic.'"

Well, that damn hair restorer didn't work on Indians. It turned my father's hair carrot red. Imagine his dark, full-blood face framed by red braids. But my father just grinned, thinking it was a typical *heyoka* trick played on him and that he should accept it as such.

Afterward, he went on a tour, speaking to a number of tribes about spiritual things, but the elders and leaders couldn't stand it. They kept after my father, saying, "John, this won't do. Here you are, talking about sacred matters while people keep laughing at your ridiculous braids."

"Well," he told them, "maybe that was meant to be. It's in my *heyoka* nature. I'm supposed to make people laugh at themselves and the craziness of human life."

They said, "We have laughed enough. It has got to stop." So my father went to a beauty salon and had his hair dyed black. The ladies there made quite a fuss over him.

Before he died, my father taught me a *heyoka* song:

> From far away a cloud appears.
> It shows itself.
> You have shown yourself
> As a thunderhead cloud in the far distance.
> You are sending a voice to me,
> For I have been given a blanket;

A blanket to cover myself, made of clouds.
The clouds are my blanket, the Earth my bed.
And the power of the clouds and the Thunderbeings
Are coming in my direction.

This is a very strong song.

My grandfather always told me, "Takoja, I hope that you never turn into a *heyoka* because theirs is a hard life. They've got the power, but they suffer for it."

Well, I never became a contrary, but having so many of them in my family, I did many *heyoka* things. My ancestors' clown nature is strong within me, so it was only natural that, off and on, I would work for the Siebrand Traveling Circus and Carnival. That was a *heyoka* business, for sure.

This circus, whose headquarters was in Phoenix, Arizona, did performances in many Southwestern cities, including Tucson, Flagstaff, Holbrook, El Paso, Truth or Consequences, Silver City, and Socorro. I started out as a driver and was promoted to trapeze artist when one of the circus's Hungarian aerialists quit.

Old Man Siebrand told me, "Arch, you're young, slim, nimble, and single. Up you go!" So there I was, hanging upside down by my knees, swinging back and forth, catching those Hungarians somersaulting through the air on their flying trapezes. Everything went well as long as I was sober. The trouble was that most of the time I was drunk and failed to catch them. Luckily, there was a safety net.

Old Man Siebrand finally admitted that I was not cut out to be an aerialist, and he put me in charge of the carnival. That meant overseeing all its main attractions—the Fat Lady, the Bearded Lady, the Tall Man, and the Short Man.

The Fat Lady weighed about 740 pounds. She traveled in an old, battered Buick that had been specially customized to accommodate her titanic bulk. Instead of seats, it had just one double-thick mattress inside. And instead of doors, the whole right side of the car swung open to let her slide out. And she couldn't even do that by herself. I had to pull like hell on her arms and legs in order to extricate her from that vehicle. Then I had to put her on a dolly and roll her into the exhibition tent. The more weight the Fat Lady put on, the more she ate. I had to go twice a day to buy her huge loads of groceries—"to keep me from starving," as she put it. There was always enough left over for me.

The Bearded Lady had a luxurious red humdinger of a beard, which she always shaved off during the two-and-a-half-month off season. At that time, she looked almost normal, though she was not exactly a ravishing beauty.

The Tall Man towered way above me (I am six foot two), while the Short Man was just two feet high but very well proportioned. These two did all sorts of funny acts together, the Short Man riding on the Tall Man's shoulders. Sometimes they pretended to fight; of course, the tiny fellow always won.

All four of our "freaks" were very sad, lonely people. They had no love life, and the only way they could earn a living was to have themselves gawked at by a bunch of grinning yokels.

I was also the "ride boss." The circus had more than thirty rides, including the Ferris Wheel, the Octopus, the Spider, the Rocko Plane, the Parachute, the Zipper, the Hellfire, the Whip, and the Cyclone. The most popular ride was called the "Hammer." It was something like a giant seesaw with two cages at each end, each cage holding two people. The cages made it look like a huge hammer. The contraption went up and down at a dizzying speed, and to make it more interesting, the cages kept spinning throughout the ride.

Once, the carnival went farther north than usual, which gave my father a chance to visit me. Thinking I was doing him a favor, I treated him to a free ride on the Hammer. After the sixth or seventh up-and-down, though, he let out a piercing scream: "Let me out! Let me out! Let me out!" I got him down, unlocked the cage, and helped him out. He staggered a few feet and threw up all over the place. Then he gave me a long, hard look and said, "Never do that to me again!"

One time, during a big county fair, our carnival was only one among many other attractions. There was also a freak show whose star was the "Wild Man," billed as the nearest thing to a human werewolf. The creature was kept in a cage, naked except for a breechcloth of fur. Matted hair hid most of his face. The Wild Man howled and growled fearfully and was covered with blood. He also rattled the bars of his cage, bared his teeth at spectators, and devoured a chicken raw.

Once, as I happened to pass by, the Wild Man stopped his howling and called out, "*Hau, kola*—Archie, how are you?" The nearest thing to a werewolf turned out to be my good friend, Godfrey Broken Rope, a talented artist and drinking companion.

"Jesus, Godfrey," I said, "why are you doing this?"

"Art isn't selling right now," he said, "and eating chicken raw pays real well." Godfrey, of course, was a real *heyoka*.

Generally, there is a prejudice against *heyokas* participating in the Sundance. Somehow, their presence makes the dancers uneasy. They don't understand why the contraries do everything backward, different from everyone else. They think the *heyokas* don't show respect for the ceremony. Mainly, though, they are afraid of the thunder dreamers' powers.

In this they are dead wrong, because they forget the traditional ways and the history of the Sundance. For example, there are very ancient *heyoka* Sundance songs—even a special one for the piercing—which indicate that *heyokas* used to participate in our most sacred ceremony. But there are only a few people left who remember these songs.

When Stanley Walking Crow, a *heyoka* and my father's old friend, complained about not being made welcome at the Sundance, I told him, "I will make you welcome. I invite you to come." And he came.

That first year, he was the only thunder dreamer. The next year there were four. The third year, we had seven *heyokas*. They came in from the West Door and asked all the sundancers to sit in the arbor, under the shade, and watch the thunder dreamers perform their healing ceremonies and also the piercing. They came in backward, going counterclockwise, doing the whole ritual in exactly the opposite way from the other dancers. Stanley came to me and said, "Pierce me in the front." That meant that he wanted to be pierced in the back so that he could drag buffalo skulls from thongs embedded in his shoulders.

The 1991 Sundance was a very strong one for us. A *heyoka* came in, and we stopped the ceremony so that he could perform. He had painted one side of his body black and the other side white. He had yellow polka dots on his legs and arms, from the ankles up and the shoulders down. His cheeks were painted with a zigzag lightning design, and his head above the nose was covered by a black cloth with owl feathers dangling from it.

When I went to bring him in, all the other dancers sat down in the shade.

They did not want to be near him, being afraid that his "contrariness" might rub off on them. I asked the drummers to sing the *heyoka* songs. They did a good job, because I had taught them well. At the end, they sang the ancient *heyoka* piercing song.

While this *heyoka* was dancing, I went to him clockwise, and he jumped to the side like a horse, snorting and nickering. I realized that I had approached him in the usual way, not backward in the *heyoka* manner. I walked toward him again, this time counterclockwise, and he stood still and let me come close. I prayed with him and led him to the sacred Sundance Tree that represents the Tree of Life. He leaned his hands against the pole and cried like a baby, yet there were no tears. I took him and brought him around the circle. I was about to pierce him when a young kid, about fourteen years old, came running and told me, "I must do it."

I directed this teenage boy to piece the *heyoka* on the arms. After this was done, somebody brought a white horse, to which we attached the thongs. The horse was then "fanned off," and as it galloped away, it tore the thongs from the *heyoka's* flesh. But there was no blood on his wounds. As soon as I put sacred tobacco on his arms, they began to bleed.

I then took this *heyoka* to the Sundance Tree in the center, and he prayed. There was no one with him except myself and the young boy who had pierced him, because none of the other dancers wanted to be at the Tree with a *heyoka* man.

After he had finished praying, the *heyoka* shook my hand and said to me in Lakota, "I'll make sure I never pray for you." Of course, what he meant was exactly the opposite—that he would always remember me in his prayers. Then he smiled and left the circle.

Next, he walked toward the sweatlodge and crawled inside the little beehive-shaped hut. I asked the three fire tenders to keep an eye on him. We watched and waited for that *heyoka* to come out, but he never did. We waited for a long time, then finally opened the flap and looked in. But there was nobody inside; the sweatlodge was empty.

The kid who had pierced him said, "I happened to be beside the sweatlodge when this *heyoka* appeared out of the lodge. Nobody saw him go in. He grabbed me by the arm and told me that I must pierce him. I know nothing about the Sundance, yet I pierced him. He came from out of nowhere in a mysterious way, and in the same manner he has disappeared."

In 1990, during the preparations for a Sundance at Crow Dog's place, a *heyoka* appeared in the middle of the night near a campfire, followed by a big white owl, half flying and half walking. This *heyoka* was a big fellow in his forties, but he was whimpering for his mother like a little boy who is afraid of owls and the dark. The owl chased him right into his tipi. So these are the strange ways of the thunder dreamers.

A young man goes to the mountain, crying for a dream and he receives a vision of the Wakinyan, or of the horse, or lightning strikes nearby. And he hears voices that talk to him, the hoofbeats and snorting of horses, and the shrill cries of birds. He comes back down to walk in the ways of the *heyoka*. He says that he must do the Sundance four years in a row, after the manner of the contraries, in obedience to his dream. How can we deny such a man the right to take part in our holiest ceremony?

The sacred fool exposes himself to ridicule. He makes people laugh at him. That is one of his main jobs. But he also teaches us to laugh at ourselves, not to take ourselves too seriously. There is laughter hidden inside a sacred ceremony. There is laughter in death. That is as it should be. Otherwise, life would be unendurable.

There are no *heyokas* outside the borders of North and South Dakota, but most Indian tribes have their own kinds of sacred clowns and tricksters. Among the Pueblo people of the Southwest, they are called *koyemshi*, "mudheads," or *koshare*. The Zuni mudheads do their antics right in between the solemn, masked kachina dances—because there, too, the clown is sacred. Some of these *koshare* and mudheads put on very funny, erotic performances that make the missionaries wince. The missionaries don't know that these antics are holy, having to do with the renewal of all life.

And then there are the tricksters: Coyote; Veeho of the Cheyenne; and our very own Iktomi, the smart-ass Spiderman, who is powerful and powerless, wise and foolish, sad and merry, good and bad, all at the same time. There are also the trickster spirits, little supernatural imps who teach us to be humble: You lock your car doors and then find out that you left the keys inside. You have to go to the bathroom, but some son of a bitch has put the lid down, and in your hurry, you poop on the lid. You say, "God, what have I done?" And somebody laughs. Inside you, somebody laughs. That's good. It's better to laugh *with* the spirits than to have them laugh *at* you while you pout.

There are *heyoka* women as well as men, but never more than one or two at any given time. Doing everything backward in the contrary's way is hard and becomes a burden. If a man wishes to stop being a *heyoka*, there is a special ceremony to free himself of this burden. It is called Heyoka-Kaga or Woze, which means "ladling out." This is a dog feast. The man goes to the *heyoka* society and asks its members to perform this ritual for him. There will be a huge, bubbling kettle full of dog meat and, down at the bottom, the dog's head. The man wanting to "unheyoka" himself has to plunge his bare arm into that boiling water and fish the head out. The strange thing is that the chief of the clowns will so prepare him with a certain medicine that he feels no pain and that his arm is not even red or burned after he has done what he must do.

Some thirty years ago, I went to one such dog feast. The participants were singing *heyoka* songs, and the man for whom the ceremony was being performed attacked the dog's head four times, like counting coup upon an enemy in the old days. The fourth time, the head came up by itself, and he scooped it out. Of course, you do not just cook and eat any dog that's running down the street. You raise the dog, from the time it is born, in a sacred manner—as a sacrifice—and you take its life with a prayer.

At this particular ceremony, they were passing the dog meat around, and everybody got a piece. It was then that something very embarrassing happened to my stepmother, Ida—something that made her blush and everybody else laugh—a real *heyoka* occurrence. She somehow got the dog's penis but didn't recognize it as such. She told those sitting next to her, "I got the tail, and it was very good."

Grinning from ear to ear, her brother-in-law, Isaac Bear Shield, told her, "Auntie, this dog had no tail."

CHAPTER 15

Song of the Earth

I have talked about the various kinds of spiritual men in our Lakota tribes. Now I will speak about the sacred ceremonies they perform. The first of these is the Inipi, or Purification ritual done inside the sweatlodge. This is a cleansing, a healing, a prayer, an opening of the mind. It is an Earth song, a celebration of Tunka, the Rock, who is immovable and our oldest god. It is the breath of Wakan Tanka rising in a cloud of white steam. It is also our most ancient ceremony, going far back into a past hidden by the veil of time. I love this ceremony above all others. It is also the one I teach.

When I was a young boy, my grandfather told me a story as old as the Lakota nation. It sprang from the hearts and minds of our people who lived hundreds of years ago. Once, when humanity was young, goes the story, there lived in a hidden valley a maiden and her five brothers. They had no parents, and they did not know how they came to be.

Every day, one of the brothers went out hunting. Their weapons were made of wood and bone. They had not yet learned how to make weapons out of stone. Their sister did the cooking.

One day, the oldest brother went out after game. Night came, but the hunter did not return. The next morning, the second brother said, "I will go and find him." But he, too, did not return. On the third day, the third brother went out and also vanished. On the fourth day, the fourth brother left, and he also did not come back.

On the fifth day, the fifth brother got ready to go. "Don't leave me," pleaded his sister, weeping. "If you go, you will disappear like your older brothers. What will then become of me?"

"I must go," answered her brother. "Our food is gone. I must get meat. And I must find out what happened to the others." So he went, never to return.

The maiden wept bitterly. "I cannot fend for myself," she thought. "I do not wish to live alone. It seems I am now the only human being left in the world."

On an impulse, she picked up a round, shining pebble and swallowed it. This will kill me, she thought. Then she went to the brook, let water flow into her cupped hands, and drank. Instantly, the round stone inside her body began to move. Four days later, she felt a strange pain welling up inside her. So this is what dying feels like, she thought.

Instead of dying, though, she gave birth to a little boy. Where did he come from? she wondered. It must be the pebble I swallowed. Therefore I will name him Inyan Hokshi, "Stone Boy."

The maiden saw that this boy was not like her brothers. He possessed strange powers. In one day, he grew as much as other boys grow in a year. After four times four days, Inyan Hokshi had grown to be a handsome, strapping youngster. He made himself a bow and arrow. He made himself arrowheads and spear points out of flint. Who taught him this? his mother wondered.

Then she told him of her five brothers who had left, one by one, and never returned.

"I will go out to hunt," Inyan Hokshi told his mother. "I will find my five uncles. I want to meet them."

His mother wept. "Don't go," she pleaded. "You won't come back, either. Something terrible will happen to you. I can't bear to lose you."

"I must go," said Inyan Hokshi. And he went. After four days, he came upon a filthy, ragged tipi. An ugly old woman was sitting before it. She motioned to him, cackling, "Come over here, handsome one. Come inside my tipi. I have good meat roasting there."

Inyan Hokshi crawled after the old hag inside her lodge. In its center was a fire, and heaped upon it were red-hot, glowing rocks. Upon them meat was roasting.

The rocks were whispering, "This old woman is a witch. She wants to poison you. We give you this warning because you are Stone Boy, one of us." Inyan Hokshi could understand what the talking stones said.

When the meat was done, the old hag picked the pieces up with a sharpened stick and filled two wooden bowls with meat, handing him one of the bowls. When the witch was looking away, Inyan Hokshi quickly switched the bowls. The witch ate the poisoned meat and fell over dead.

Inyan Hokshi looked around. He saw five large bundles leaning upright against the side of the tipi. These must be my uncles' medicine bundles; they are very big, he thought.

He opened one of the bundles. Inside was the shriveled, dried-up body of a man. He opened the other bundles. Each contained the shrunken remains of a human being. He thought, These must be my uncles, whom the old woman has poisoned.

Again the rocks spoke to him. "Stone Boy," they said, "take willow wands and form them into a little lodge. Cover it with the witch's buffalo hides. Dig a pit in the center of the floor. Put us hot rocks into it. Put your uncles in the little lodge also. Likewise, take the witch's water bag. Make sure that the lodge is well covered and the entrance flap closed. Then pour water over us."

Thus, the rocks taught Inyan Hokshi how to perform the Inipi, the Purification ceremony. When Inyan Hokshi poured water over the glowing rocks for the first time, the five dead bodies seemed to come to life again. When he poured water for the second time, they began to move. When he poured water for the third time, they began to sing sacred songs. When he poured water for the fourth time, they crawled out of the little lodge, stood up, and laughed with joy.

Together with Inyan Hokshi, they all went back home. When Inyan Hokshi's mother saw them coming, she wept with happiness. By the power of Tunka, the Rock, and Tunkashila, the Grandfather Spirit, Inyan Hokshi had conducted the first Purification ceremony ever. A nation was born.

Some of our elders taught us that the Inipi came to us through the power of a woman, maybe Ptesan Win, White Buffalo Calf Woman, who taught us so many things. Both legends complement each other. Inyan Hokshi performed the first crude Inipi, while Ptesan Win showed us how to conduct this ritual, step by step, in a sacred manner.

Whenever a Lakota is about to do something important, such as participating in the Sundance, or going on a Vision Quest or on a journey, he first purifies himself in the sweatlodge. An Inipi can be a ceremony all by itself, or it can be a purification in preparation for another ritual—for instance, a Yuwipi.

To perform the Inipi, you must first construct the *initi*, the sweatlodge. You make it out of supple willow sticks cut from the white willow that grows along streams. In the summer, you can remove the bark in long strips. It comes off easily because of the sap. In the winter there is little sap, and the bark won't come off. So in summer, the willow wands you use to construct the lodge are peeled. In winter, they are not. In this way, you can always tell when a sweatlodge was built. The willows of a winter lodge can grow again because the bark is still on. We have a winter sweatlodge in California, built seven years ago, that grew its leaves back and is now a natural shelter.

Before beginning the construction of a sweatlodge, the medicine man makes tobacco offerings to the sacred Four Directions, to the sky, and to Unchi, our Grandmother the Earth. He then lays out a circle about eight feet in diameter and scoops out sixteen small holes around it. Into these will be planted the willow wands that form the framework of the sweatlodge.

The medicine man, or whoever else is running the ceremony, puts sacred tobacco into each hole for a blessing, going from west to east, praying all the time. He cuts the first willow. Then sixteen saplings are planted and bent inward to form a beehive-shaped dome a little higher than a man's waist. This is the framework, the skeleton of the *initi*, symbolically the bones and ribs of our people. The number *sixteen* stands for the Sixteen Mysteries, the Sixteen Great Supernaturals. For lack of a better word, these are sometimes called "gods," but they are all manifestations of Wakan Tanka, the Creator.

The first uprights are always planted on the left and right sides of what will be the door, which always faces west. If you see a sweatlodge facing east, you can be sure that it belongs to a *heyoka* who does everything backward. Never have a sweatlodge facing north. On top of the lodge, we put a string of 104 tobacco ties. These tiny bundles, which contain our prayers, stand for all the sacred herbs a medicine man uses.

Next, we clean, sweep, and carefully smooth the ground on which the sweatlodge will be built, making everything holy, permitting nothing to remain that is not needed for the Purification.

In the center of the sweatlodge circle, we make a hole two feet across to receive the heated rocks. The earth taken out of it we don't just throw someplace; we save it to make the sacred mound outside the lodge. We cover the ground on which the participants will sit with big-leaf sage. The ground, *maka*, represents Mother Earth, and the hearth stands for the womb of the universe, the pit of emergence. In the old days, the *initi* was covered with buffalo hides. Today, blankets or tarps must do. Once the framework is covered, we burn sweetgrass as incense, filling the lodge with its fragrance, sanctifying it, making it worthy to receive the spirits.

Outside, to the right of the entrance flap, we build Unchi the sacred mound, using the soil taken from the "Earth womb" in the center of the lodge. The little mound is round and flattened at the top. Around it, we plant twenty-four small sticks. These represent the twelve months of the year—two for each month, symbolizing the positive and negative that dwell in all things.

On the mound we place the Canunpa, the Sacred Pipe, resting it on a rack made of forked sticks, the bowl of red stone facing to the North. On the mound we also place the skull of a buffalo facing to the South. South represents the spirit world, the "Owl Nation." Sometimes we also plant a staff there, its upper half painted red to represent the day, its lower half painted black to symbolize night. At the top we tie an eagle feather; and to the center, where day and night meet, the tail of a stag or blacktailed deer. This is to remind us of our ancient sacred song:

> My life is that of the herbs and plants.
> My life is of the eagle and the deer.
> The buffalo is my brother.

These four sacred things—the mound, the skull, the eagle feather, and the tail of the deer—make up our altar, the Indian's church.

The earth that is left over from making the mound we use to lay out the sacred path that leads to the fire pit in which the rocks are heated. Unchi, the earth mound, our Grandmother, is at the end of the path, eight steps from the entrance. Once the sacred path is drawn, it should never be crossed or stepped over. It is the Road of Life, the way of the Indian.

Then there is the place where the sacred fire is kindled. This is the place of Peta Owihankeshni, the "Fire Without End," the flame that is passed

178 of GIFT OF POWER

on from generation to generation. This fire is pure. The fire pit represents Wi, the Sun, which gives warmth and light and without which nothing can live. It is formed like a horseshoe—a circle with an opening toward the lodge entrance.

To make the fire, we first arrange four sticks going east and west, and on top of these we place four more running north and south. We add to these more logs leaning toward each other, forming a shape like a tipi. Always we use the sacred number *four*, or combinations of four: eight, sixteen, thirty-two, and so on.

Upon and within the logs, we place the rocks. You must know the right rocks to pick for a sweat—the kind that won't crack in the fire or explode in your face inside the sweatlodge. We use as many rocks as the man who runs the sweat thinks are necessary, usually depending on the purpose of the Purification and how many people will be participating. As we light the fire, we pray to the sacred rocks and the Creator.

When the rocks are red hot, it is time for the Inipi to begin. Before we enter the lodge, we leave *all* jewelry behind. Metal will conduct the extreme heat that is created inside the lodge and burn the skin. You won't need your wristwatch, either, for there is no time in the world of the spirits.

As we enter the lodge, we must stoop—even crawl—to remind ourselves that we must be humble and that we are like our animal brothers; that we were the last animal to be created. I insist that men wear swimming trunks or large towels in my Purification ceremonies. Women must wear dresses that cover them modestly.

Men and women sweat separately. The *pejuta wichasha*, or the one who runs the Inipi, enters first. He goes clockwise around the fire pit and takes his place at the opening on the right side. The others follow, forming a circle within the circle of the lodge, which is part of a larger circle—the Earth. Thus, all within the *initi* become part of the Sacred Hoop, the Mystery that has no beginning and no end.

Outside the lodge we have a helper, the firekeeper, who brings in the heated rocks on a pitchfork, one by one. Inside the lodge, the leader receives the rocks, using a pair of elk antlers to lower them into the pit in the center of the *initi*.

To start with, we use six rocks. The first rock represents Wakinyan, the Thunder Spirit, who plays his part in the ceremony. It also represents Maka, the Earth, whose color is green. The firekeeper makes four complete turns to the left while bringing this first rock into the sweatlodge. The medicine man inside guides it with his elk horns to its place in the center.

As the second stone is carried toward the lodge, the firekeeper turns four times to the right. This rock is placed in the pit to the West, whose sacred color is black. The third rock is brought in the same manner, the firekeeper turning four times to the left. It is placed to the North, whose sacred color is red. As the fourth rock is brought in, the firekeeper turns four times to the right. It is deposited to the East, whose sacred color is yellow. The firekeeper does his "spiraling" to remind us of the movements of such heavenly bodies as the Morning Star. Spirits enter the sweatlodge while the first four rocks are brought in.

The fifth rock is placed to the South, whose sacred color is white. It represents the spirit world and brings to mind friends and relatives who have passed on to another world—who have "gone south," as we say. The sixth rock is put on top of the first. Its color is blue, because it represents the sky, which is a symbol for Wakan Tanka, the Creator. A ceremony can often start with six or seven rocks, but after the one representing the sky, any number of rocks may be brought into the lodge, depending on the person who is running the Inipi.

After the first set of rocks has been placed, the firekeeper closes the entrance flap, and all in the lodge are wrapped in darkness. We are not afraid of the dark. On the contrary, darkness stands for the night, or "spirit time." In darkness you have to see with the eye in your heart instead of the eyes in your head. This new kind of seeing reveals to us a reality that is very different from the so-called "realities" of the material, technological world.

After the flap is closed, the inky darkness reminds us that we are all one people, for we cannot see the colors or the looks of each other's faces. Now we must forget everything—all our day-to-day, worldly cares. We must concentrate our minds on the spiritual side, the right half of the brain.

There is warmth now, a dry heat rising from the glowing rocks. The reddish glow sheds a tiny bit of light. This light is pure, representing the purity of spiritual enlightenment. Now the leader sprinkles cedar on the rocks, and as its fragrance fills the little hut, we cup our hands and rub this wonderful, breathing scent over our faces and chests.

We use three different kinds of herbs during the Inipi: *wachanga*, or "sweetgrass," for bringing in the negative and the positive; sage to chase away negative spirits; and cedar for blessing the rocks and loading the Pipe. These sacred herbs are pleasing to the various powers we call the "Supernaturals." We ask them to be with us according to the teachings of Ptesan Win, the holy woman who brought us the Pipe. This is a time for prayer. We pray for all that is positive and negative and for the balance of these forces. For those sitting inside the Inipi circle, the sweatlodge becomes the universe, the whole world concentrated in a tiny hut.

Now we load the Pipe with *chanshasha*, our sacred red tobacco, and seal it with sage, tamping the sage down on top of the tobacco. Sage is an enemy to all that is negative, so we seal the Pipe and send it outside with the sweetgrass to be put against the buffalo-skull altar. The Pipe will come in again later to end the ceremony.

Finally, using a gourd, we splash cold water from a pail over the red-hot, hissing rocks. We also dip a whole bundle of sage into the water and sprinkle it over the stones. We do not use tap water, but water fresh from a spring or nearby brook. So we use all the four sacred, life-bringing elements in our ritual: earth, air, fire, and water.

As soon as the fire and water come together, the whole lodge is filled with white, hot steam—Tunkashila's Breath. And for those who are experiencing their first Inipi, there is a moment of panic. To them, the heat seems great, and they have an urge to cry out, "Let me out of here!" But then we sing the first song:

Kate wioch peyata	With the sacred cedar
Kate wazi ta	I come to the West,
Kate wio hjapata	To make an offering to the West,
Kate ito kachata.	Where the Thunderbeings live.

With the soothing words of the song, the first-timers relax. Heat fills their lungs, opens their pores, makes them light-headed and receptive to what the spirits want to teach them. After the initial shock, they discover that the heat feels good; that it works its magic on them, making them giddy with exaltation. Grandfather's White Breath unites us, makes us one. It fills every vein, every cell in our body, and every cranny of our little hut.

That breath, that hot steam, is recycled. It might have been inhaled and exhaled by a dinosaur, a plant, a mouse, or a famous chief of yore. It might be the breath of a dead grandparent of yours. Because of this breath, those who have come into the lodge as enemies will leave as friends.

The ceremony is divided into four parts. Four times, the entrance flap is opened, and four times, hot rocks are brought in. Four times, the "door" is closed as water is poured, and four different songs are sung.

During a good Inipi, the Supernaturals will come in. They are usually invisible, but their presence is felt. Sometimes they make the sweatlodge shake violently. On rare occasions, medicine men who walk in balance with the Earth can see and identify the spirits and understand their words. There are sixteen Supernaturals—eight positive ones and eight negative. To the *wichasha wakan*, the spiritual man who can see them, some of these spirits are nice to look at, and some are ugly.

Among the negative ones, first comes Anung-Ite, the Two-Faced Woman. One half of her face is beautiful beyond words, and the other half is hideous. The second negative Supernatural is Iktomi, the Spider Man, a smart-ass trickster and troublemaker. The third is Kanka, the Old Witch, who sometimes does someone a good turn. The fourth is Wazi, the Old Wizard, a conjurer who comes like a cold wind from the north. The fifth is Ksa, sometimes called a wise spirit and sometimes referred to as a water goddess—a cunning Supernatural. The sixth is Tob Tob, the friendly Four-Times-Four Spirit, a Four-Directions wind and godlike messenger. The seventh is Kate, another wind spirit. The eighth is Yumni, the Whirlwind, who taught the people the Hunka, or Brother-Making ceremony.

When we mention these Supernaturals to missionaries, they cry, "Devils! Imps from hell!" But these spirits are nothing like that. On the whole, they are mostly harmless troublemakers and tricksters. They are a pain in the neck, but often they are helpful to us humans. They are a little bit like the trolls and leprechauns of the white man's fairy tales. There is a lot of *heyoka* in them.

The main job of the Supernaturals is to make us laugh at ourselves—even during hours of sadness and trouble. They teach us not to take ourselves and our problems too seriously. They make us trip over our own shoelaces. Maybe you want to sit down, thinking there is a chair behind you, but there is no chair, and you land on your backside. They do things like that, but they never really hurt you.

Once, when I was going to drive my son someplace, I absentmindedly sat down next to him on the back seat. He asked, "Is Mom driving us?" I laughed, "Oh, well, I just wanted to see what it looks like back here." I knew that one of these little beings had played a trick on me, and it made me smile. Better to laugh than get angry, because then they let you make more mistakes. One guy I knew stubbed his toe. He got angry and cursed something awful. Next thing, he forgot to put the toilet seat up and shit on the lid.

The smoldering sweetgrass attracts these Supernaturals. They like its smell. But when you load the Pipe, or when you burn sage on the rocks, they leave in a hurry. They cannot stand sage. Then only the positive powers are left inside the sweatlodge.

These positive powers are our star brothers, the planets, the eight Superiors. They represent Wi, the life-giving Sun; Skan, the great Quickening Power that causes everything to move; Maka, the Earth; Inyan, the Rock, that which is everlasting; Hanwi, the Moon, our Night Sun; Tate, the Wind, which brings with it the sound of prayers; Unk, the spirit of Contention, a water goddess and the Earth's companion; and, finally, Wakinyan, the Winged One or Thunderbird.

All these are present in the sweatlodge, whether you know it or not. Also, somewhere, there is Niya, the Spirit or Soul; and Nagi, the Ghost. The Spirit is eternal, the Ghost only temporal, the shadow of a man.

We may be seven or more people inside the sweatlodge, but we are of one body and one mind. If one among us is not with us in spirit, if he is just participating out of curiosity "to see what those superstitious Indians are up to," we feel it immediately. We sense the negative energy coming from him. So we let the enveloping cloud of steam make us one.

Those who have never taken part in an Inipi sometimes think they cannot stand the heat. All they have to do is cry out loud, "Mitakuye Oyasin— All My Relations!" and the firekeeper outside will open the flap so that cool air can come in. There are some men running sweats who make it unbearably hot. They are showoffs, trying to impress us with their ability to endure. I run my sweats not in order to "cook" people. That's not my purpose. I conduct my Inipi as a prayer, a purification, and as a curing ceremony, because Grandfather's Breath has healing powers. You sweat all the poisons out of your system, and after the ritual, everyone feels wonderful—purified, as if reborn.

Once, on a farm in Europe just after I had run an Inipi, a deaf-mute came to me. He could neither hear nor speak. He came with his wife, indicating in a kind of sign language that he wanted to be helped. The man gesticulated and pointed to the sweatlodge as if he wanted to say, "I, too, want to go in there to be cured."

I took him inside the lodge. The rocks were still hot. There was enough water left, so I improvised a ceremony. It was not very hot, at least not for me, but it seemed that for him the heat was unbearable. He made frantic signs, imploring me to open the flap and let him out. I signed back to him, "I want to hear you cry out loud. I want to hear a scream. I won't let you out until you fill this lodge with the sound of your voice."

It took him a while to comprehend what I wanted. I poured all the rest of the water on the rocks in one motion, making it real hot. Then out of the deaf-mute came a mighty scream—like the first cry of a newborn, only much, much louder. It was the first cry that man had ever uttered in his life, and it was so piercing that it penetrated his deafness.

I opened the flap and let the man out. He was so happy that he burst into tears. He was dancing all over the place. People were staring at him, but he didn't even notice. He was dancing on a manure pile, turning somersaults in cow shit and cow piss. It didn't matter: he could yell; he could scream; and he knew that he could learn to speak. I had nothing to do with this. It was due to the power of Inyan, the Rock, and the power of the Inipi.

A Purification can be a very emotional experience. Many times I have witnessed men weeping during this ritual. We must relearn how to cry. A strong man cries; it is the weak man who holds back his tears. He thinks, "People will discover my weakness if they hear or see me cry." But when you keep your tears inside, it can destroy you emotionally. So make your feelings come out inside the sweatlodge. Cry out. This will also teach you to breathe correctly.

Inipi is a prayer. You can pray for whatever you want, but it is always best to pray for others, not for yourself. We pray for the living, green things—the trees, the grasses, the sage. We pray for the rock people who give us their heat. We pray for the animals—the four-leggeds, the winged ones, and the creatures of the sea. We pray for friends and relatives who are sick or struggling. We pray alike for the strong and the weak and for those yet unborn. We pray for brothers and sisters languishing in prison. We pray for the survival of humanity. And we pray especially for the revival of Indian spirituality. We keep our prayers short, because everyone inside the sweatlodge wants to say something. What we do inside the little dome-shaped hut makes a difference; it radiates far beyond the sweatlodge.

There is laughter and tragedy in the sweatlodge, as in all things. I remember two funny things that happened during Inipi ceremonies. The first occurred during a big, intertribal powwow. There were a lot of dancers from various parts of the country. They were 'skins, all right, but most of them had never taken part in an Indian ceremony. I had just run an Inipi. The lodge was still there, and the fire was still going. A group of 'skins asked me, "Can we do a sweat here?"

I said, "Sure, go ahead."

These dancers wanted to run the Inipi by themselves, even though they had only a very hazy notion of how to do it, and they wanted me to be the firekeeper. They wanted to use sixty rocks in all. I said, "OK, if that's the way you do it in your tribe."

So everyone went inside, and I brought in a heap of rocks and five gallons of water. The first round went all right. At the beginning of the second round, I asked them if the rocks were still very hot. They said, "Yes, very hot."

I asked if they wanted more rocks, and they said they did. So I sent in sixteen more rocks. And again, things went well. But when the third door came around, they asked me to bring all the rest of the rocks, which resulted in a big pile-up of red-hot stones inside the lodge. They thought they might need more water, so I sent in five more gallons to replenish the big pail they had in there.

Now, the trouble arose because they had used very little water up to that point. It is the pouring of water on the heated rocks that causes the intense heat in the lodge. They had only sprinkled a little here and there because they were not used to a Sioux-style, hot sweat. As soon as I closed the flap for the third round, one of those fancy dancers kicked over the pail and splashed all that water in one great swoop over those rocks—no less than forty-eight of them—and at once the whole sweatlodge exploded into a huge cloud of scalding, white steam. The heat was fierce. It scorched the guys inside. They were screaming and shouting. I never heard so much profanity in my life.

Somebody had the sense to yell the magic words, "Mitakuye Oyasin," and I opened the flap for them. They burst out of there like they were being fired from a cannon. Their leader tried to get out first, but he was not fast enough for the others, who flattened and stepped on him in their rush to get out the door. Screaming and yelling, they ran off in all directions.

Later I found out that they were all OK. Some of them had a little bit of blistered skin here and there, but no serious injuries. It was sad, but also very funny. And while I felt sorry for them, I also had to laugh, seeing them scramble around like crazy, using every four-letter word in the English language and a few more in their own lingo.

Another funny Inipi I witnessed took place in Europe. It was a Purification for white people run by my old friend, Wallace Black Elk, a Rosebud Sioux like myself. Again I was the firekeeper.

The way Wallace runs an Inipi, he wants to hear some animal sounds in there, as all our rituals are connected with our four-legged and winged brothers. Of course, Wallace thought in Indian terms: he wanted to hear the cry of the eagle, the scream of the cougar, the howl of the wolf and the coyote, the whistle of the antelope, and the deep bellow of our brother the buffalo. But he had white Europeans in his sweat, so when he asked, "I want everyone in here to make the sound of an animal," he didn't get exactly what he expected. As he started to sing an Inipi song, suddenly there was the cackling of chickens, the crowing of a rooster, the mooing of cows, the baa-ing of sheep, and the oink-oink of pigs. It sounded like a whole barnyard running amok.

Wallace came out of the lodge all bent over. I thought, What's wrong with him? He was doubled over with laughter. I, too, was laughing, tears rolling down my cheeks.

"I can't go on with this," Wallace sputtered.

Then all these people came out of the hut, wanting to know what was wrong. I explained it to them. They persuaded Wallace to start all over again. Then they had a good sweat.

And then there was tragedy. In 1978, when I was living in California near the Pacific Ocean, a friend named Ron came to see me. He wanted me to put him up on a Vision Quest. He said, "Brother, for four years you have taught me all I need to know. You showed me the Indian way. Tell me, what happens to those who put an end to their lives? The Christian priests teach that suicide is a sin. Indians think otherwise. What happens to those who kill themselves?"

I answered, "I cannot tell you because I do not know."

He said, "Maybe we'll find out."

We had a ceremonial Purification, just the two of us. We prayed in the darkness, illuminated only by the faint, red glow of the heat-giving rocks. Suddenly I had a vision. I saw myself standing in a hot desert, and the sand was burning. From far away, a man came toward me. As he approached, I saw that he had my face, but at the same time, the face of my friend Ron.

The man said, "Welcome to the land of solitude. There is no hunger or thirst here, only solitude and an endless road. Here we are many. All of us have walked the same path. Why have you come?"

I answered, "I came in order to understand."

The man carried a bag on his shoulders. He said, "This bag is full of riches. It would make you a big man in the white man's world. With what is in this bag, you would never lack anything. I will give this bag to you if you want it. I ask for only one thing in return—that when your days on Earth are over, you take my place and walk on this road that has no end."

I told him, "I do not want that bag of yours."

The stranger said, "Then you must pray for us. You must pray that our road will have an end, that it will bring us to the spirit world."

Suddenly, I found myself back in the sweatlodge. I had no idea how much time had passed. Whether it had been an hour or a second, I did not know. Then I heard my friend's voice coming out of the darkness. "I know that you are looking at me," he said. "You don't have to say anything. There is only one thing I have always wanted to do but have never done. After this sweat is ended, you must take me on a Vision Quest."

I knew that Ron was very sick. He was suffering from a very serious case of diabetes and was getting worse. "Impossible," I told him. "A Vision Quest lasts for four days and nights without eating or drinking. You are in too bad a condition to do this."

He answered, "Brother, I am going to do this whether you like it or not. But I wish that you would take me."

We left the sweatlodge. He had made himself a string of tobacco ties as an offering. He had already prepared himself. I led Ron to the mountain-top, taking my three-year-old son along with us. I felt that Ron would never come back. I felt that he wanted to die during his Vision Quest. But who was I to put myself between him and the Creator? It is not our way to pre-vent a man from following his chosen path. He wanted to carry my little boy to the top of the mountain along with the Sacred Pipe and the buffalo robe, but it was too heavy a load for him.

Up on the mountain, Ron dug his vision pit. From time to time, he stop-ped to rest. He said, "Isn't it funny that I'm digging my own grave?" I pre-tended to smile and helped him dig. I handed him the insulin, without which I knew he could not live. He said, "Must I take it?"

"You must," I told him.

I took my son by the hand and left. I did not want to leave my friend. Halfway down the mountain, I had a strong urge to go back up again, but some unknown power prevented me.

I returned to the mountaintop after four days, as is the custom on a Vision Quest. I thought that I saw Ron standing in a thicket, his hair fly-ing around his head in the wind. I thought that he should have stayed in the vision pit until I came to bring him down. But as I looked again, I saw him no more. I had brought a basket for him with fruit and water, but I had a strong feeling that he would not be needing it.

I found my friend stretched out in the vision pit, the buffalo robe around his shoulders. There was a smile on his face. He had not touched his in-sulin. I said, "Ron, Ron, don't tell me you are gone." His eyes were open and still moist. I closed them. He was dead, gone south to the Spirit World.

I called the sheriff's office, and they came to bring him back down. One lieutenant, when he saw the smile on Ron's face and the peacefulness of his death, made the remark, "What a beautiful way to die—in the process of praying."

That night, we had a ceremony in the sweatlodge. As we prepared to pray, an owl landed on top of the *initi* and hooted four times. Then it flew away on silent wings.

Again, I fell into a reverie. The sweatlodge turned into a forest, and I heard faraway voices. Many people were dancing toward me, and among them I recognized many friends and relatives who had passed on. They looked so happy dancing that I experienced an irresistible urge to join them, but they motioned me away.

I saw Ron coming at the tail end. He was the only one looking at me. He smiled and waved at me as if saying goodbye. Then he joined the others in their ghostly dance.

After I came back to reality, I told those present, "Ron is at peace. Don't mourn for him. He has chosen his own way to leave us. And what better way to end your life than during a Vision Quest, after an Inipi ceremony to send you to walk the Milky Way Road?" The owl was his messenger.

As always, we ended the Inipi by smoking the Pipe, everybody taking four puffs. As we opened the door for the fourth and last time, the white steam, Grandfather's Breath, followed us out of the sweatlodge. Water, air, the fire's warmth, and our prayers all combined in this cloud. And, as in all Inipis, particles of this cloud, released into the sky, traveled to the farthest reaches of the Earth, floating and circling in the wind and touching every living thing.

Although Ron was Indian, he had been raised as a Catholic. I heard that he had once said he would not live to be thirty-six. The Saturday after his death would have been his thirty-sixth birthday.

Later, Ron's autopsy showed that, besides diabetes, he had been suffering from three other deadly conditions. He had already been in the process of dying when he went to the mountain to leave this world in prayer. At the coroner's inquest, the judge remarked that if a Catholic received Communion and died of a heart attack, it would not be the fault of the priest.

I have talked about the Inipi, the song of the Earth, but I have not mentioned women's Purifications. Women do their Inipis separately. As a matter of fact, from the moment of puberty to the onset of menopause, our very traditional women do not go into the sweatlodge at all. One reason for this is that we Lakota see menstruation as a natural form of purification in its own right.

Perhaps in some tribes, men and women sweat together, but not Lakotas. Many young white people want to strip naked and go in together, but I won't let them do it, for many reasons. Some women might call me a male chauvinist, but my religion is not for everyone, and I will not change it or modernize it to suit other people. The Inipi is a religious purification ceremony. Women during their moon time do not take part in rituals because during menstruation their power is so great that it overcomes the medicine power and renders all ceremonies ineffective.

Another reason is what you might call "lost innocence." In the Bible, Adam and Eve are naked in their innocence. Then they eat that damn apple of knowledge, and suddenly they are ashamed of their nakedness and cover themselves up. Similarly, the white man brought with him certain things that made some Indians lose their innocence. There was one fake medicine man who ran mixed sweats, and I overheard two girls saying to each other, "Don't go in the sweat with him, because the spirit will come in, feel you up, and touch your breasts."

I want to avoid such things. I want to avoid even the suspicion of them, which could give our rituals a bad name. I do run special Inipis for women when they are not on their moon. During these ceremonies, they must be covered up, wrapped in a sheet cloth or a cotton gown similar to a nightshirt. My grandmother went into the sweatlodge fully dressed in buckskin. She had her little Pipe, used only one rock, and was out of the hut in less than one minute. She told me, "That is the traditional way for us to do it."

The Inipi was brought to our tribes by Ptesan Win. She brought this ceremony mostly for the men. Maybe men need purification more than women do. There is also a belief among us that women carry a special purification mechanism in their own systems that makes the intensely hot, male-type Inipi unnecessary. Instead of the Inipi, women have been given special powers having to do with herbs, and many become highly respected medicine women and healers, generally after menopause when their moon power no longer clashes with the ritual power. So I do run women's sweats, but I do them strictly according to our Lakota traditions.

Crying for a Vision

Hanblecheya means "crying for a vision." It means going on a Vision Quest, up to the hilltop, maybe crawling into a vision pit, and staying there without eating or drinking for four days and nights, praying for an answer from the Supernaturals. That's a hard thing to do.

A man going to the hilltop for Hanblecheya gives his flesh and bones to Wakan Tanka, the Grandfather Spirit. And if he is accepted, he goes on living, but his spirit somehow works apart from his body. He has been given a power. In order to have a vision, you have to give yourself up completely. It is almost like dying, only you come back. Hanblecheya is one of the toughest things a man can experience.

"Crying for a vision," my father once told me, "that's the beginning of our religion. It is the thirst for a dream from above—a vision which, while it lasts, will make you more than just a man. If you never had a vision, you are nothing. This is what I believe.

"It is like the prophets in the Christian Bible, like Jesus fasting in the desert, or Jacob wrestling with the angel, wrestling for a dream. It means hearing soundless voices, seeing things with your heart and mind, not with your eyes. It means shutting your eyes in order to see.

"White men have forgotten this. Their God no longer talks to them out of a burning bush. If he did, they wouldn't believe it. They'd call it hallucination or science fiction. They'd say, 'A voice from a burning bush? That guy had too much LSD!' Those old Hebrew prophets went into the desert praying for a vision, but the white men of today have made a desert of their beliefs. Inside themselves, they have made a desert where nothing grows, a dead place without dreams. But the spirit water is always there to make the desert bloom again." That my father told me.

Usually, Lakota girls do not go on Vision Quests. My daughter Josephine went on a Vision Quest because my father told me that she would one day become a medicine woman. For her, Hanblecheya was necessary; for most women it is not. In the old days, the staying alone for four days during the moon time was in itself a Vision Quest for the women.

A young boy goes on a Vision Quest searching for his own path, which he will travel to the end of his life. He comes back from the hill a man. But the crying for a dream does not stop there. Men do not go up to the mountaintop just one time. I know of men who have undergone this four-day trial more than a dozen times—even very old men who keep crying for visions until the end of their days.

Usually you need the help of a *wichasha wakan*, a spiritual man, to go on Hanblecheya. A man might come to me and say, "Uncle, my mother is sick. Perform a ceremony for her. Pray that she will get well, and a year from now I will go on a Vision Quest for four days and nights." So this man makes a vow to do this. It is a solemn commitment. And when the year is over, I prepare him for his ordeal.

Or someone might say, "Lame Deer, I need help. I have these dreams that don't reveal their meanings. I need understanding. I have to find out. Prepare me for a Vision Quest."

To tell the truth, a man should go to the hilltop whenever he is about to do something of great importance, or whenever there is a great crisis in his life, in order to seek guidance from above.

Before your Hanblecheya, you have a medicine man perform an Inipi with you, and you get instructions on how to conduct your long vigil. You go to the mountain naked, just as you were born, except for your loincloth and a buffalo robe or star blanket around your shoulders. You go up with your Pipe and sacred tobacco; you will need it. If you have a medicine bundle, wear it. Maybe your mother or sister will have made a flesh offering for you by cutting forty small pieces of skin from their arms. Put them into a gourd; they will help you endure your Hanblecheya, your long, lonely watch amid the hooting of owls and the mournful call of the coyotes.

Up on the hill, make yourself a small, holy place in which to settle down. Maybe lean against a rock or tree while praying for your vision. Do not

192 ☆ GIFT OF POWER

go to dream at a place where nothing grows, where there are no plants or trees. Such a place of no dreams could harm you mentally.

Those who pray for dreams inside a vision pit do it the hardest way. Sometimes a tarp is spread over the pit and strewn with earth and grass. *Canli*—that is, tobacco ties—mark out the space, and Four-Direction flags are planted at the four corners. The one left down in the pit is then truly buried alive. He sees, feels, and hears nothing. To stay like this in a vision pit is a brave thing to do. It demands fearlessness and a complete giving of yourself to the spirits.

When you are up there alone, you should pray as hard as you can. Do not think of anything tying you to the everyday world. Do not think of your joys, your sorrows, your problems, or your pains. Think only about what is holy. Empty your mind. Make it into a receptacle for visions. Listen to the spirits of the winds and the clouds.

You will suffer up there, fasting, praying, wrapped in loneliness. And even this is no guarantee that you will receive a vision. It is easy to fool yourself. I know an old traditional man who went on Hanblecheya twenty-seven times and never had a vision. He prayed and prayed but never got his dream.

And then there is a young man, twenty-two years old, with a beautiful buffalo robe, a gorgeous Pipe with a quill-decorated stem, and fully beaded, sparkling moccasins who goes up to the mountain and comes down with seven visions. He goes into the sweatlodge and says, "Lame Deer, let me tell you about these terrific visions." Then he tells me about his heroic, elaborate dreams, and his imagination runs away with him.

He sits up there, and his mind is full of ideas. He thinks up visions, and he comes down and tells of the wonderful things he has thought up—not what he really received on the mountaintop. This young man should have saved himself the trouble and stayed home. He could have more comfortably fantasized while sitting in an easy chair eating a hot dog. He had received no true vision.

I get that way, too. Sometimes when I'm mentally fatigued, I see psychedelic images. I see a tree jumping over another tree. Was that a vision? No! You're tired, sucker. You haven't slept for three days, so your brain is playing tricks on you. A vision is hard to explain. You receive it consciously, when you are wide awake. You see it in front of you, like turning on the TV. You pray hard, and all of a sudden, you see yourself doing something specific, or you see an eagle fly into your vision pit, as happened to my father. These are visions, and they come to you while you're conscious, or at least half awake.

There are also images or scenes you see while you are semiconscious or asleep. These are dreams rather than visions, but they are also important. But both must come *to you*, not *out of you*. We have to weigh what is real and what is just fantasy. That is not always easy.

You could also *hear* a vision rather than see it. Up on the hill, you might hear someone speaking Hanbloglaka, a dream language that only a medicine man could understand. During a Vision Quest, birds spoke to my father, and he could understand what they were saying.

Some medicine men are afraid of going on Hanblecheya. They are afraid their visions might tell them something that would make them come back as a *heyoka* or a *winkte*. A vision could put you on a path you don't want to follow. Those who have a vision receive a great gift that could change their lives. Those who experience this come down singing. The ones who have had no dream descend silently.

After the Quest, the dreamer goes into the sweatlodge again and describes his vision to the medicine man, who will interpret it and lay out a path for him to follow. So there is always an Inipi at the beginning and the end.

You cannot force the spirits to give you a vision; you have to approach them humbly. This my father taught me. He once told me the story of a big chief—my father called him the "Super Indian." Before going to the mountain, this chief boasted that he would receive the greatest vision ever given to a human being. Well, he was up there, singing and lamenting, praying up a storm, imploring the spirits for a most terrific vision. Suddenly he heard a voice shout, "*Shut up!* You keep me from sleeping, carrying on like that. *Shut up!*"

The chief was scared and stopped his chanting, but after a while he started up again. And once more the voice shouted, "*Shut up!* You're keeping me awake. You're disturbing the trees, the plants, and the animals with that awful racket."

The chief noticed that this voice came from within a great boulder above him. He said, "No lousy rock is telling me what to do. It won't prevent me from getting my vision."

The Super Indian went on chanting and lamenting with such force that his helpers, waiting far below, could hear him. Then the boulder got really angry and rolled down with full force upon the chief, squashing the vision pit and crushing his Pipe and buffalo robe.

That Super Indian barely escaped with his life. He ran down the hill in a panic, as if being pursued by the Great Water Monster. He rushed into the sweatlodge, where three medicine men were waiting for him, and stammered, "That boulder wanted to kill me. It has smashed all my sacred things, flattened the vision pit, uprooted trees!"

The medicine men went up the mountain. They found everything intact. The pit, the Pipe, and the trees were untouched. The boulder rested in its accustomed place. Then the medicine men told that Super Indian, "Be humble. Don't boast. Step lightly. Respect nature. Then maybe you'll have better luck next time."

When I was twelve years old, my grandfather took me to the mountaintop. As I sat there praying, I felt myself flying across the sky, looking down at the Earth, gyrating in a swirl of sparkling rainbow colors. It seemed all very real. I had no other vision but this, and I did not know what it meant. At about the same time, lightning struck a spot near where I was sitting, and the same night I dreamt of horses. When I told this to three of our elders, they said, "You're a *heyoka* now. Do something backward every day!" It was fifteen years before I went on another Hanblecheya, and it changed me completely, from a *heyoka* into what I am now.

I was already past thirty when I went on what I consider my first real Vision Quest. I was keeping company with my father, who was visiting a friend in California. He went there to bless this man's place. Then something urged me to tell my father, "This is a good time for me to go the mountaintop. Would you take me?"

My father looked at me and smiled. He loaded the Pipe and said, "I can't take you. I don't think anyone can take you. You must take yourself. Go on!"

This was a little sad and puzzling to me, but I waved goodbye to him and climbed up. I stayed on that mountain four days and four nights but did not receive a single vision. Then, on the last day, just as I was about to go down, I suddenly felt my spirit leaving my body.

Before I knew it, I was up in the top of an oak tree looking down on my body, which was lying on its back. As I watched, a strange, indistinct shape came up from the South and talked to me in Lakota. The apparition told me, "We have come after you, and we are going to take you with us."

The apparition was pulling hard at my body, and I started to laugh. My body was in the earthly dimension, and my spirit, up in the tree, was in the spirit dimension. For this reason, the one who was jerking my body around could not see me, and that seemed funny to me up there among the leaves.

Then from the North came two more shapes. I knew that the first apparition was Nagi, the Shadow or Ghost. The second was Niyah, the Spirit or Breath of Life. And the third was the Spirit of the Sky and the Clouds. The first one was still tugging at my body, but the two others from the North said, "Leave him alone. He is one of us. His work is only beginning now, but one day his work will be done and then the three of us will come and get him, for that is the way it is." They left singing and laughing, going toward the North.

Next I saw my father sitting below me with his head down and his old cowboy hat pushed way back. And all of a sudden, my spirit reentered my body. I looked again, and my father had vanished, as had the log he had been sitting on. I was very scared, even though it was only five o'clock in the afternoon and the sun was still up. That first apparition, I knew, had wanted to take me to the spirit world.

I ran all the way to the foot of the mountain, jumped into my car, and drove as fast as I could to the house where my father and I were staying. I ran into the house. My father was sitting at the fireplace, exactly as I had seen him in my vision.

He looked up and smiled. "I made some coffee for you just now. Here, have some *pejuta sapa*, some 'black medicine.'"

I took the cup of steaming coffee. My father lit a cigarette, and I sat down next to him. I was about to say, "Let me tell you what I experienced on my Vision Quest," but he stopped me as soon as I opened my mouth.

"There's no need to tell me anything," he said. "I was there. My spirit was there. I have seen them, and now I know what you are. You have experienced this spiritual power. It flowed from me to you, and it will flow to your son. It will be passed on from generation to generation as long as there is one Lame Deer left. There's no need to explain. For me it's time to go. I'm ready."

A month and a half later, my father got into that car accident. He was grievously hurt and never recovered. He lingered on, but in the end he heard the owl calling him.

I came back from that Vision Quest with the gift of being able to see in your face what is in store for you. It does not always work, but most of the time it does. I look at you, but I don't tell you that your woman will leave you or that your family will break up. There may be two among you who won't be around when I come through the next time, but I am not allowed to tell of these things. I have to keep this knowledge within myself.

Women, too, sometimes have this gift. My father once told me that a girl can obtain a vision by wrapping up her first moon flow and putting it into the crotch of a tree.

When my father told me that our old ceremonies and beliefs have been handed on in our family from generation to generation and that I was one more link in the chain of passing on the flame, he knew what he was talking about. When my son John was eleven years old, he told me, "Dad, I want to go on a Vision Quest. I have this one problem: here I'm already pretty grown up, and I'm still afraid of the dark. Staying up there for four days and nights will cure me of that fear. I want to do this on top of Bear Butte, which is a sacred place."

When my son told me that, I was so touched that tears came to my eyes. His mother was crying, too. This happened while we were driving. I pulled off the road. I tried to talk him out of it. I told him, "You are too young. Four days and nights, that's a very hard thing for a boy of your age. Wait a year or two."

So I put him on the mountain for one day and one night. The place he selected was like a little fortress, with steep cliffs in front and on all sides, with only one way to enter or leave in the back. Bear Butte is shaped like a bear, and the spot where my son spread his buffalo robe is the bear's head. Right below, surrounded by pines, is the place where the Cheyennes come to pray and hold their Sundance.

I was glad that my son had picked that particular site to cry for a vision.

I made a few jokes to put him at ease, saying, "Son, you love to eat. Maybe you'll have a hamburger vision, a Pepsi vision, or even a French fries vision." But then I ended by telling him, "Now we have to be serious, very serious."

John settled down on his buffalo robe, smoking his Pipe like a man. And again tears were welling up in my eyes as I thought, This is the end of his boyhood.

When his night on Bear Butte was over, John related to me what he had experienced. "Along toward evening," he said, "I got really tired and fell asleep for a while. When I woke up, it was completely dark, and I felt very scared. There was a big owl hooting in a tree very close to me. At first the owl scared me, but I got used to its hooting—except that I was very sleepy and it kept me awake.

"Then came a pack of coyotes. They were prowling around no more than twenty yards away. That *really* scared me. I didn't want to sleep with all those coyotes right there. I held on to my Pipe, and I prayed for what seemed like a very long time. Finally the coyotes left, and I fell asleep again.

"I woke up very early in the morning to see a small herd of black-tailed deer scattered over the hill beside me. One doe came right up to my vision pit, peeked in, and looked at me. Then she turned and rejoined her family."

I said, "Son, you have done what many a grown man would have been afraid to do. Your little sister has a real hero now."

Both my wife and I were very proud of our young son for the qualities he showed us then. With no urging, not even a suggestion from anyone else, he did what he had to do to overcome a weakness. He had the honesty to admit that he was afraid of the dark, the wisdom to know that the only way to conquer his fear was to face it, and the courage to go ahead and deal with it alone. He also proved to himself that he had the faith to pray his way through his fear. After that night, the dark held no more terror for him.

Also, all through the night of my son's Vision Quest, a buffalo bull stayed very nearby. Perhaps this bull had gone near John's vision pit to watch over him and help give him strength.

One time, in March, I was going up to Bear Butte to pray. I had my son and a white friend with me. This friend told me, "I don't feel it's right to go up with you because I'm not an Indian. So I'll stay down here and wait until you come back."

So John and I climbed up by ourselves. I went to the place that is sacred to the Cheyennes, below the pines on the southeast side of Bear Butte. There I loaded my father's Sacred Pipe, offering it to the Creator and the Earth. As I started praying toward the West, my son said, "Look, Dad, there is a man getting ready for a Vision Quest."

As I turned toward the North, about half a mile down the ravine—two or three hundred yards as the crow flies—I saw a tall, slender man with two long braids. He had nothing on except his breechcloth and moccasins. He was strewing the ground around him with sage and putting up a buffalo altar for Hanblecheya. I thought, Why would anybody be doing a Vision Quest at this time of the year? But I had to continue my prayers, so I lifted my Pipe toward the East.

Then my son interrupted me. "Look, Dad, eagles are playing above us!"

I looked up and saw that he was right but continued praying. Then I faced the South, and as I lifted my Pipe, my son said, "Dad, our car is leaving."

I looked to where he was pointing, and sure enough, my car was rolling downhill. It went all the way to the gate, which I knew was closed. (That early in the year, there's nobody at Bear Butte except the caretaker. He had opened the gate for us because he knew that I often went up the mountain to perform ceremonies.) But when I looked again, I saw that my car had somehow gotten through the gate and was now going at high speed along the blacktop toward Sturgis.

I finished my prayer and put away the Pipe. My son asked, "How are we going to get home, Dad?"

I said, "We'll call the police from the pay phone farther down. And maybe we'll call for somebody to give us a ride home."

We went down to the bottom, where our friend was waiting for us. I told him what had happened, but he had not noticed anything unusual. We kept walking and chopped some cherrywood on the way. When we came to the place where I had parked my car, it was still there. My son stood open-mouthed. Again and again he said, "But we both saw our car being driven away."

I told him, "Son, there are things in this life that are hard to explain—especially to people who don't understand the way of the Sacred Pipe and who know nothing of our ancient teachings. They don't understand, and what they don't understand they cannot believe."

I tested the doors of the car. They were locked, and I still had the keys in my pocket. So I said a short prayer and accepted the unexplainable. My son and I had received one of the rarest visions: two people, wide awake, seeing exactly the same thing.

Then I recalled something that had happened a long time ago, back in 1947. My father had taken me to see an old friend of his—Washu Maza (Iron Hail), who was also known as Dewey Beard, a very old man who had fought against Custer at the Little Bighorn. He must have been in his nineties when we went to see him, but he stood erect, and his mind was still clear. He had been a friend of Tashunke Witko (Crazy Horse), and my father wanted to hear his ancient stories about our greatest warrior. Most of all, my father wanted to know whether he still knew Crazy Horse's song. He wanted to learn it.

Dewey Beard told me about Crazy Horse. This great Lakota, who never called himself a chief, had tied a *yuwipi* stone into his horse's mane so that the animal could never be wounded or shot. And he himself always wore a medicine pebble behind his ear, which made him bulletproof. Dewey Beard also described having seen Crazy Horse preparing for a Vision Quest—a slender figure in loincloth and moccasins, with two long, black braids with a slight copper tinge. Thinking back to that time, it occurred to me that what the old man had described was exactly the vision my son and I had seen on Bear Butte.

I also remembered my father telling me that my great-grandfather, Tacsha Ushte, had been one of the two war chiefs who led the Mnikowoju braves against the soldiers at the Little Bighorn, and that my great-grandfather had also been a close friend of Tashunke Witko, who had given him some of his medicine, maybe also a *yuwipi* stone. "We have the power and the way of Crazy Horse," my father said, "and it has been passed on to you." So I wonder whether it was the greatest of all Lakota warriors who sent me and my son this vision.

Visions and Vision Quests are of utmost importance to our people and to myself personally. Through dreams and visions, we receive power and the gift of "seeing ahead," of getting glimpses of the future. A young man's first Vision Quest often determines what kind of life he will lead. Visions are not imaginings; they are messages from the Supernaturals. True visions have a reality distinct from what the white man usually calls "reality." A man who never had a vision is impoverished, indeed.

Always in my mind and heart will remain the words of Crazy Horse's song, which Iron Hail taught me on that memorable day many years ago. The way I translated it may not be the best way, but it was the best I could do:

> My friend,
> They will return again.
> All over the Earth,
> They are returning again.
> Ancient teachings of the Earth,
> Ancient songs of the Earth,
> They are returning again.
>
> My friend, they are returning.
> I give them to you,
> And through them
> You will understand,
> You will see.
> They are returning again
> Upon the Earth.

CHAPTER 17

The Gift of
White Buffalo Woman

The Sacred Pipe was given to us by Ptesan Win, White Buffalo Calf Woman, who taught our people how to live. We cannot speak of our ceremonies without speaking about Chanunpa, the Sacred Pipe. There is no ritual without the Pipe being smoked. In truth, smoking the Pipe is in itself a solemn ceremony. The Pipe is the link between man and the Grandfather Spirit above. The smoke rising from it connects us humans with what is more than human. Power emanates from the Pipe, and we look upon it as something that is alive, not mere wood and stone.

As my father used to say, "The Pipe is the Indian's heart. The bowl of red pipestone is his blood and flesh. The stem is his spine or body, and the smoke rising from it is Wakan Tanka's breath. The *chanshasha*, our Indian tobacco, is sacred, too. It's not the same tobacco that is in a Camel, a Lucky Strike, or a Marlboro; it is something entirely different. With the Pipe in your hand, you cannot lie; you can only speak the truth. 'Talking through the Pipe,' as we call it, you will be believed. You Christians have sold and crucified your savior, but we Indians never betrayed or sold our Pipe."

The Pipe itself is not sacred. It is the way in which we use it and the prayers we say when smoking it that make it holy. A Pipe is a manmade, material thing until it has been used in a ceremony, prayed over, and blessed. Then a Pipe becomes sacred. Then you can feel a Pipe's power and its spiritual vibration as you hold it in your hand.

When White Buffalo Woman came, she brought us the Pipe. The story of her coming has been passed on from generation to generation. Long, long ago—how long we cannot tell anymore—the Lakota tribes came together for their midsummer celebration. They did this every year when the Earth was blanketed with green, the grass was high, and the plains were teeming with game. That year, however, game was nowhere to be found, and the people were starving.

Among the seven tribes assembled were the Itazipcho, the "Without Bows." They were hungry and trying desperately to find buffalo. Chief Standing Hollow Horn chose two young men from among his warriors to scout for game. These two roamed far and wide, without any luck. But just when they had become so discouraged that they were about to give up and return to camp, one of them said, "Brother, I see a buffalo coming from a long way off."

As they watched it coming closer and closer, the other young warrior exclaimed, "This is not a buffalo approaching, but a woman."

It was a woman, indeed—a woman more beautiful than words can describe. Her face was radiant, and she seemed to float rather than walk. She was dressed in unadorned, white, fringed deerskin, which enfolded her like a robe. Her hair was hanging loose, slightly stirred by the wind. Tied to it on the left side was a fringe of buffalo hair.

When this strange woman was no more than an arm's length away, one of the two scouts said, "This maiden is alone. She is beautiful beyond imagination. I shall lie with her."

"Brother, do not do this," said the other. "This is no ordinary woman. Do you not see that she is walking above the ground, her feet not touching the Earth?"

But the other would not heed him and reached out his hand to touch her. At once a cloud descended upon him, and when it lifted, all that was left of the warrior was a heap of bones.

The strange woman addressed the other scout: "Your friend had impure thoughts. For his lack of humility, he was punished. I have been sent by the Buffalo Nation to bring a message to your people, a most important message. Return to your tribe. Tell your chief and the people what has happened here.

"I shall come tomorrow at sunrise to visit your camp," the woman continued. "Tell the people to prepare everything for my coming. Tell them to put up a special tipi. Its door should face toward where the sun disappears in the evening. Have the ground strewn with sage. Make a rack of three sticks—two uprights and one across. In front of this, place a buffalo skull. Also make a square of carefully smoothed earth. Make everything holy. Now go home to your camp without looking back."

The young warrior did as he was told. He related to Chief Standing Hollow Horn what had happened to his friend and what the strange woman had commanded. Helped by all the people, the chief prepared everything for the strange woman's visit. The *eyapaha* (the herald) rode all around camp calling for all the men, women, and children to assemble at sunrise to welcome the Wakan Woman. At the first light of dawn, the Holy Maiden appeared, dressed as she had been the day before. In her hands she carried the Ptehinchala Huhu Chanunpa, the Most Sacred Pipe, made from a buffalo calf's leg bone. This Pipe was not fashioned by man but by Wakan Tanka, the Creator. Ptesan Win, White Buffalo Calf Woman (as she was known from that moment onward), walked over the sage, singing:

Niya taninyan	With visible breath
Mawani ye.	I am walking.
Oyate le	This (Buffalo) nation
Imawani,	Toward it I walk,
Na	And
Hotaninyan.	My voice is heard.
Mawani ye.	I am walking.
Niya taninyan	With visible breath
Mawani ye.	I am walking.
Waluta le,	This red sacred thing,
Imawani ye.	(For it) I am walking.

Ptesan Win entered the lodge that had been prepared for her and sat down in the place of honor. She began to sing, "Take this Sacred Pipe to the center. Pray to Wakan Tanka, the Creator. This Pipe he gave to you." She faced to the West, whose color is black, and lifted the Pipe: "I offer this to the Wakinyan, the Winged Ones. I pray to them."

Then she turned to her right, to the North, whose color is red, and lifted the Pipe: "To the Whirlwind and to all that moves in a circle, to the Wind and to the Sacred Four Directions, I offer this."

Then she turned to the East, whose color is yellow, presenting the Pipe: "The sun is rising, giving us a new day, giving thanks for all that lives."

Then she turned to the South, whose color is white, praying, "I give thanks to the Spirit World, the world beyond."

She completed the circle, then lifted the Pipe upward to the sky above, praying and instructing the people, "I am your sister. We are one people and one spirit. We are the Buffalo Nation." Then she sang:

> I give you this Earth,
> On which you will walk
> In a sacred manner.
> You will walk in balance with Unchi,
> The Grandmother Earth.
> I give you this Sacred Pipe.
> With it you will pray
> For all living things—
> For those who walk, who fly,
> Who swim, and who crawl.

She also told the people, "I will return again some day, and then it will be for always. Then there will be a new life and a new understanding."

Chief Standing Hollow Horn then addressed the Buffalo Maiden: "Sister, you have come to console us when we are in great need. It is our custom to feed our guests, but we are poor and starving and have nothing to give you but water."

So saying, he dipped a braid of *wachanga* (fragrant sweetgrass) into a buffalo horn filled with rainwater and offered it to the maiden. She thanked him, saying, "This is better than any feast you could have prepared for me."

She then showed the chief how to load the Pipe with sacred tobacco, how to light it with a glowing buffalo chip, and how to smoke it in a ceremonial manner. She also gave to the Lakota people their seven sacred rituals: The Inipi or Purification in the sweatlodge, the Vision Quest, the

Sundance, the Spirit Keeping, the young girl's Ishnati Alonwanpi or Puberty Rite, the Making of Relatives, and the Throwing of the Ball.

She instructed the men: "You are the strong ones. You must protect and be kind to those who are helpless—the women and children. You must share your food with those who are too weak or old to hunt and to feed themselves. You must pray with this Pipe. You Without Bows have been chosen to receive it, but it belongs to all the Red Nations."

To the women, Ptesan Win said, "You are weak, yet you are strong. Your strength keeps the family together. You are the life-givers, the nation's womb. You love children. You are kind to all living things. Wakan Tanka loves you."

To the little children she said, "You are small now, but you will grow up to be men and women, walking in the way of the Pipe, carrying the spark to the next generation. You are blessed."

For four days, Ptesan Win instructed the people how to behave as human beings. She taught them everything they needed to know. When her work was done, she told the people, "I must leave you, but follow me to the top of that hill over there, and you shall no longer be hungry." And the Holy Woman walked toward the East.

Awed and thankful, the people followed her at a respectful distance. When she reached the hill she transformed herself into a white buffalo calf and slowly disappeared. Then the people knew for certain that she had been sent by Wakan Tanka. And as they themselves came to the hilltop, they found before them, on the far side, a herd of buffalo waiting to give their flesh so that the nation could live.

This is the story of Ptesan Win and the Pipe, as my grandfather told it to me when I was a boy. I have seen White Buffalo Calf Woman in visions. Four times she has appeared to me, each time with a bunch of sage in her arms.

Two tribal Pipes are kept by members of the Looking Horse family at Green Grass. One of them is the Pipe that Ptesan Win brought. It is kept in a Sacred Bundle, wrapped in buffalo hide and enfolded in old red trade cloth. It is made from a buffalo calf's leg bone, and seven red eagle feathers are attached to it. Its stem is covered with bird skins. The Bundle includes a tamper decorated with porcupine quills. Also in the Bundle are three beautifully carved canoe paddles—a gift from my father's Mnikowoju tribe.

The whole Bundle is lovingly and reverently cared for. It is kept on a tripod and every day is turned to face to the Sacred Four Directions. The Calf Pipe is brittle and fragile now and can no longer be smoked, but I have been privileged to hold it and pray with it, and I have felt its great power fill my whole being. I know that Wakan Tanka's spirit is in that Pipe. Only in times of hunger, distress, and danger to the Lakota tribes is the Bundle opened and the Pipe unwrapped to be shown to the people and prayed over.

The Calf Pipe has been kept by our people for many generations—some say for three hundred years, some say for a thousand. The first keeper, all agree, was Chief Standing Hollow Horn, also known as Standing Walking Buffalo. Then, in succession, it was passed on to Thinking While Walking, Many Wounds, Strikes Fire, Red Earth, Sunrise, Buffalo Path, and Red Hair. For a few generations, it was kept by members of the Elk Head family. Old Man Elk Head died in 1916 at the age of ninety-one. Then Red Eagle and, after him, Mrs. Bad Warrior and Eli Bad Warrior became the keepers. The Pipe then passed to Stanley Looking Horse who, a few years ago, relinquished it to his son Arvol, the present keeper.

Besides the Calf Pipe Bundle, there is a second one in which a very old tribal Pipe is kept, made of red pipestone, or so-called "catlinite." Most of the many Pipes owned and used individually by our people have bowls made of this red stone, which my father called the flesh and blood of our people.

Pipestone occurs naturally in only one place, the sacred pipestone quarry in western Minnesota. Nowadays, only Indians are allowed to dig for pipestone there, but unfortunately, so much stone has been removed in this century for souvenir pipes that very little of this precious material is left. Even now, most of it lies below water, so it is very hard to get at it. In the old days, the quarry was sacred ground to all Indian nations. Even men from tribes who were at war with each other dug for the red stone side by side. Once, on this hallowed ground, all men were friends and at peace with each other.

We also have a black pipestone, which can still be found near Corn Creek where I grew up, about four feet below the surface. This stone is very easy to carve, but today I know of only one man, Seelo Black Crow, who uses a black Pipe. George Eagle Elk, a *yuwipi* man, used and carved black Pipe bowls, but he is gone now.

The bond between the Sacred Pipe and our family is strong and goes back a long way. As far as I know, the 1868 treaty between the U.S. Government and the Lakota was the only one at which the signing was combined with the smoking of the Sacred Pipe. And it was Chief Lone Man and my great-grandfather, the first Lame Deer, who put their marks and thumb-prints on that treaty.

My father's father was privileged to smoke the Buffalo Calf Pipe. (As I mentioned much earlier, his second name was "Let Them Have Enough," because he was a generous man who always shared his food with the poor.) And around 1930, Mrs. Elk Head, the keeper at that time, let my father smoke both the Calf Pipe and the tribal Pipe with the red pipestone bowl. This was the most profound experience in my father's long life.

As my father told it to me, he had a great vision. He heard a voice telling him, "Go and pray with the Ptehinchala Huhu Chanunpa, pray with the Buffalo Calf Pipe!" My father said that following this vision was like sitting in the back seat of a car with the Great Spirit in the driver's seat, taking him to where the Pipe was.

This happened during the winter. Someone who has never experienced a South Dakota winter cannot imagine how terribly cold it can be. With the windchill factor, the temperature often drops to fifty or seventy degrees below zero. It happened on a night like that. On top of that, there was a blizzard, and the snow had turned to ice. Walking on it, my father said, was like walking on a mirror whose touch chilled a man's bones. My father was lucky to survive this trip and make it to the Pipekeeper's humble log cabin.

"The going was very tough," my father remembered. "The icy wind was in my face, and it snowed so hard that I walked on and on unseeing, like a blind man. I don't know how I managed to find that place. I would have been a goner if the spirits had not helped me."

My father expected to find the Pipekeeper, Old Man Elk Head, in the cabin, but the only living soul inside was an old woman who was more dead than alive. This was Elk Head's older sister, who was keeping the Pipe for her brother who had died some time before. My father had not known this.

The old woman was sick and on the point of death. She was so frail and feeble that the slightest puff of wind could have blown her away like a dry leaf in the fall. My father noticed that the room was prepared for a ceremony. The earthen floor was covered with sage. Everything needed was there—a buffalo skull, an eagle wing, sweetgrass, cedar, and sacred tobacco.

My father asked, "Who is running a ceremony here?"

The woman answered, "You are. I have never met you before, but I saw you in a vision. This vision told me that a young man would come here from the South, pray with Pipe, and cure me. You are that man. There is a terrible storm right now, but tomorrow, at daybreak, the storm will cease, and you will come to cure me. My own sons no longer keep the old ways. They turned Christian. So it's up to you now."

My father went to spend the night in Green Grass with some people he knew. He related to them what Mrs. Elk Head had told him, and they said, "This woman is crazy. We heard the forecast on the radio. This storm will last a week." The wind was shaking the house like a cat shakes a rat. There was no sign that it would ever stop blowing.

Shortly before daybreak, my father woke up. It was the stillness, the great quiet, that had aroused him. Not even a whisper could be heard. My father dressed, had a drink of water, and stepped outside. He saw a gigantic sun rising. It turned the whole plain, covered with hard, iced-over snow, into gleaming red. It was as if the whole Earth had turned into blindingly bright, scarlet crystal.

My father went over to Mrs. Elk Head's cabin. He found her, as he had found her before, sitting in the middle of the one-room cabin. She had made the little cabin holy, fragrant with the smell of smoking sweetgrass and cedar, ready to receive the spirits.

My father sat down at the west side of the cabin. He looked around and noticed two large canvas Bundles the size of a human being. He said that the Bundles looked like "two tied-up *yuwipi* men."

The old lady pointed to one of the Bundles and said, "Takoja, unwrap it!"

My father took off layer after layer—rawhide, deer and buffalo skins, and red and blue trade cloth. Then he unwrapped the last layer, and there was the Calf Pipe! It was, he told me, the most sacred thing in the whole universe for him. Looking at it, he trembled with awe and elation.

Old Mrs. Elk Head pointed to the second Bundle. "Grandson, unwrap that one also!"

My father did as she asked and found that the second Bundle contained the holy tribal Pipe with its bowl of red pipestone. This Pipe was big; compared to it, the Calf Pipe was small.

Mrs. Elk Head said, "Takoja, take hold of these two Pipes. Put the Calf

Pipe on top of the red one. Pray with them. I saw you coming here in my vision, and you came. Pray and let the Spirit guide you." The old lady did not talk Lakota but spoke in a sort of ghost language, yet my father could understand her.

My father held the two Pipes in his hands. He felt that they were extensions of himself, part of his flesh. He felt his blood flowing into the Calf Pipe and then back into his body again. The Ptehinchala Huhu Chanunpa became part of his blood cycle. He felt the Pipe come alive in his hands. He felt power surging through every fiber of his being. He experienced a happiness he never guessed could be his. He wept. Tears were trickling down his cheeks.

He loaded the Sacred Pipe and smoked it, and his breath mingled with the smoke. He knew that it was also the Creator's breath. He gave himself up entirely to Spirit, surrendered himself completely to Wakan Tanka, to the air and the winds. He felt himself at the center of the universe. He also felt in his bones that, at this same moment, other Indians smoking their Pipes experienced this same joy and were filled with the same power.

My father said that he experienced all this not with his human mind but in the way a buffalo or eagle might experience the Grandfather Spirit. He felt himself one with all living things, all animals and plants. "This Pipe," he told me, "cured the blindness of my heart." My father might have been the last one to smoke the Calf Pipe, because shortly afterward it was decided that it was too fragile to be loaded and smoked, though one can still pray with it.

After my father rewrapped the Bundles, Mrs. Elk Head got well and lived a few years longer. "Maybe my prayers helped her," my father said later, "but I'll never know."

In 1962, my father took me to Green Grass and to Eagle Butte to open the Calf Pipe Bundle. We sat on top of the hill from six o'clock in the morning until eleven, drinking coffee and looking out over the land while my father instructed me in the ways of the Sacred Pipe. Suddenly, out of nowhere, a huge van appeared, with New York plates, bristling with large cameras and tons of equipment. The people riding in it and a second car had come all the way from the East Coast to televise the opening of the Pipe.

While they started unloading, I stayed on the far side of the shed in which the Pipe was kept at the time. I sat there crying. I did not want the unwrapping of the Sacred Bundle to become a sensationalized media event for curious white people who would only misinterpret what they were seeing on the screens of their boob tubes. I was crying and praying hard—as hard as I had ever prayed—that this sacred ceremony would not be shown on television.

The Pipekeeper, his father, and many elders were sitting inside the Looking Horses' log house debating the matter. My father was in there, too. I vowed that if they let this desecration happen, I would turn away from the Indian way. I might just as well go on hitting the bottle, raising hell, and forget about being an Indian if the Sacred Pipe was to become a tourist curio.

But it seems that somebody heard my prayers, because after a while my father emerged from the house with a big grin. "Come on, let's eat," he said. "We've decided not to open the Pipe under these circumstances."

For a while I didn't say anything; we just sat there and ate. Finally we just left.

"What did you do while I was in there?" my father asked.

I told him that I went down to the cherry thickets, got three branches, and made them into a pipe rack, which I leaned against the Pipe Bundle in the shed.

"*Washte-lo!*" he said. "You did the right thing."

That was the first time my father saw me cry. "I saw you go to war and do crazy things," he said, "and I saw you go through hell, but I never knew you could cry." He was silent for a while, then he concluded: "You are the Pipestem. You are the connection." I didn't say anything; I didn't have to.

In 1979, Stanley Looking Horse sent out a call for spiritual leaders to come to Eagle Butte to talk about the keeping of the Pipe Bundles. Elders and medicine people came, not only from our Lakota nation, but from the Oklahoma tribes, even from the faraway Zuni in New Mexico. Many brought gifts. I donated two cows to be butchered in order to feed those who had come. I also brought my little son, John.

There was good feeling among us. We made a bed of sage, and the Bundle was brought out and placed in its center. The Bundle was not opened; it was there to be prayed over and to inspire us.

Every day, the meeting continued as medicine men and traditional elders took their turns speaking about the meaning of the Sacred Pipe and how to care for it. As the talks progressed, all the medicine men loaded their

Pipes, smoking in a solemn, ceremonial manner. Traditional women were there, too—a dozen of them, dressed in beautifully decorated quilled and beaded buckskin. Compared to these stately, elderly ladies, the men in their faded Levi's, worn cowboy boots, and old, patched shirts looked like hobos who had just gotten off a train. The women had their Pipes, too, and we all purified ourselves and prayed together. In the place of honor sat Stanley Looking Horse and his wife and children, the family whose members kept—and are still keeping—the Sacred Pipes.

Suddenly, before the ceremonies ended, my little boy, John, walked right into the circle and began praying to the Buffalo Calf Pipe. Nobody had told him to do this; he had followed an inner voice. He was only four years old at the time but had already pierced during the Sundance. He came right into the circle and, in his little voice, prayed to the Pipe.

One of the younger medicine men tried to take him away, thinking maybe that it was not fit for a child to intrude in this assembly of elders, but Stanley Looking Horse restrained him, saying, "Let him alone; he knows what he's doing."

My little boy finished his prayer and left the circle, walking toward the East. At once, a horse took his place, coming, it seemed, out of nowhere. The horse stood on the spot John had just left, right in the middle of all the elders. While this was going on, songs were being sung as each medicine man stepped into the circle, lifting up his Pipe, praying to the Creator after his own fashion.

There were thirty-two medicine men at this gathering around the Buffalo Calf Pipe. One of them said, "It's so peaceful and quiet here, but there's a scratching at the door. I see a white boy there with a backpack."

That boy, hardly out of his teens, begged for us to let him in, saying, "My father and my mother taught me nothing. School taught me nothing. Who will accept me? My parents won't."

The elders said, "Let him in, let him in. All people, all living things are one. The White Buffalo Woman taught us this."

And to me they said, "Lame Deer, you talk to him. You have a way with such people. Their technology is killing them, their system is killing them. Now they're coming to us for help, scratching at the door." I spoke to this young fellow, fed him, and gave him a place to sleep.

In August 1987, I came once more to the Buffalo Calf Pipe, again with my son. As we were driving, an eagle swooped down repeatedly over our car, almost touching the roof. I took this for a sign but didn't know how to read it. That year, the Bundles were supposed to be unwrapped by William Red Cloud, the descendant of one of our greatest chiefs. But before he arrived, we had a Yuwipi during which the rock spirits told us that the Pipe should not be opened. Arvol Looking Horse, the son of the Pipekeeper, came to me and asked, "Uncle, can you help us? Will you be the last speaker and interpret for the rock spirits?"

I accepted. I spoke to the elders of the Gray Eagle Society, to the tribal chairman, and to Red Cloud himself, and they all accepted that the Bundles should not be opened. It was on this occasion that Stanley Looking Horse relinquished his position as Pipekeeper to Arvol, who came to me and said, "Uncle, I am still young. Until I get older, will you be a spokesman for the Pipe? You travel much. Teach the people about this holy Ptehinchala Chanunpa." And I answered, "I will do it."

At that meeting, I told Arvol, "I have a Pipe—a beautiful, old Indian Pipe. It was given to me by a man in Europe. He gave it freely. He meant it as a symbol that the spiritual things taken by Europeans to faraway lands are being returned and that their power is being given back to the Buffalo Calf Pipe."

So Arvol took this Pipe, still loaded and sealed with sage, and put it with the Ptehinchala Huhu Chanunpa. It is still there today.

Finally, at that solemn meeting, I sang a song. I told the people sitting around the circle, "This ancient song tells the story of the Sacred Pipe. Our family kept this song for generations. My father taught it to me, just as my grandfather taught it to him, and just as he had been taught by those who came before. I give this song to you, who now keep the Sacred Buffalo Calf Pipe, because it belongs to you. I give it back. You must use this song, because we are the people of the Pipe, and you are its keepers." So these are the bonds that connect me to the Buffalo Calf Pipe.

The whole country is flooded with so-called "genuine Indian peace pipes" made for the tourist trade. Some are not even carved of pipestone, but of quartz, soapstone, or even plastic.

If you want to have a Pipe to pray with, don't buy one from a souvenir shop, or even a museum. You don't know who carved such a pipe, or why, or what kind of person he was, or why he sold it. Such a pipe might have negative powers. At the very least, it would be just a thing without meaning. Instead, get yourself a lump of red pipestone. Carry it around for a long time. Touch it, feel it, sense it. Then maybe you will get a dream telling you how to carve it.

Carve it yourself. Impart to it some of your own spirit. When you have finished it, take the pipe to a ceremony, a Vision Quest or Sundance, and have it blessed by a spiritual man. Then you will have a Pipe that is sacred.

Now, don't say, "This is *my* Pipe." The Pipe doesn't belong to you; it belongs to all living things. You are entrusted with its keeping, entrusted to use it in a sacred manner, whether you are aware of this or not. Don't hang the Pipe up on the wall or display it as an artifact in a glass case. Keep it hidden. Your Pipe is not a curio. Don't carry it around on the street and show it off. With this Pipe, you should have a Pipe bag and a tamper. Tampers are sometimes large and beautifully decorated, but some think that the best tamper is a wooden skewer that has been used to pierce a man for the Sundance. Don't carry the Pipe bag unless you're going to a ceremony.

If you need the help of a *pejuta wichasha* or a *yuwipi* man, you must send him a loaded Pipe. Then he will perform a ceremony for you. That is the only right way. If someone phones me, saying, "Lame Deer, I need your help," I won't come—not unless they send me the Pipe. Smoke the Pipe in a circle and pass the Pipe around clockwise. Each puff is a thanksgiving and a prayer—for the animal world, the plants, the Earth, the fire, the air, and the rocks. You are the living connection, then, between yourself and the spirit world.

The tobacco we use is also sacred when we smoke it during a ceremony. We also use it in our tobacco ties for many ceremonies, and we make tobacco offerings—to the Sundance Tree, for instance. We call it *chanshasha*, which means "red wood." This has given some people the idea that what we smoke is red willow bark, but that is not so. *Chanshasha* is a bush belonging to the dogwood family. It is red during the winter. In the summer, it turns either dark brown or green, and it has little white berries that are not edible.

You must harvest *chanshasha* before the first thunder. After that season, it becomes too strong to use. Also at that time, the tree needs energy to feed the leaves. We take both the outer and inner bark and dry them separately, then mix them together. Sometimes we mix the tobacco with berries and berry roots, which gives it a wonderful fragrance. People usually call Indian tobacco "kinnikinnick," but this is an Algonquian word used by the Eastern Woodlands tribes. Once you have smoked *chanshasha*, you'll never forget its good, soul-lifting, aromatic smell.

All this is not to say that every medicine man has to use the Pipe. My grandfather, who raised me in the Indian way, never carried or touched a Pipe. He was a *pejuta wichasha*, an herb man, a healer. He used the Bear and the Buffalo in his ceremonies, and his great medicine was a sacred buffalo horn. The Pipe was not in his vision. Grandpa was a man of immense inner strength. Some medicine men today use the Pipe like a crutch to lean on, something to give them a sense of security. That was not Grandpa's way.

My own great vision comes from the Buffalo Calf Pipe and nothing else. Its teachings are holy. My father told me, "The Pipe is the last key to the last door. In the red glow of the Pipe is the fire of the sun. I am an old man now, but I have never been able to learn all the ways of the Sacred Pipe. Maybe we are not meant to learn its last secrets. I know that when I smoked the Pipe, I released something of myself that wanted to be free to roam the universe as part of the Circle Without End. With the Pipe, I made peace with my greatest enemy—myself. When the last traditional Indian on the face of the Earth stands with the Pipe in his hand and she swallows him up, then the Earth will go with him."

I understood the meaning of my father's words, because our teachings are one, from generation to generation.

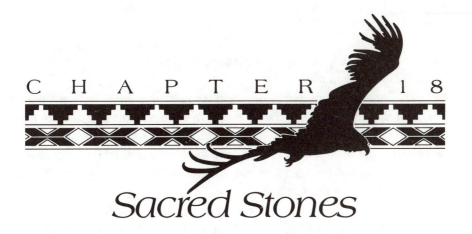

Sacred Stones

We have an ancient chant:

He wami yank, auwe,	They come to see you,
Tunka kin sitomniya,	All the sacred stones,
Wani yank, auwe.	They come to see you.

yuwipi man — one who finds out

This is the song of the *yuwipi* man, the rock dreamer, the "man of flickering lights," the "one who is tied up," the "master of the finding stones." The *yuwipi* man is yet another kind of medicine man I want to talk about—perhaps the strangest one of all, just as the ritual he performs is our most mysterious, awe-inspiring ceremony.

When a child has wandered off and cannot be found, when something is lost or stolen and the owner wants to get it back, when a sick person wants to know the cause of an illness, then it is time to go to the *yuwipi* man for help, because he is the "one who finds out." Spirits will whisper in his ear and tell him what to do. The sacred stones will do much of the work for him. The dog will be the sacrifice.

The person who wants help will send the *yuwipi* man a loaded Pipe. Approached in the proper manner, the *yuwipi wichasha* cannot refuse his help, and he will put on the Hanhepi Wichohan, the night mystery, the ritual we call Yuwipi.

The medicine man receives no fee for putting on this ceremony, but the sponsor must feed all comers. Whenever a Yuwipi is held, there are

215

people besides the sponsor who want to participate, because they also need help. They come in for free.

The Yuwipi is heralded by the night song, *hanlowanpi*; and it is ruled by *hanhepi wasichun*, the mystery power of the night, the sacred spirit of darkness. As always before an important ceremony, the men purify themselves in the sweatlodge, enveloped by the cloud of white vapor that rises from the red-hot rocks as water is poured over them—the white, warming Breath of the Creator.

Yuwipi is also a dog feast. A few hours before nightfall, a dog is sacrificed, usually a young plump one. A red stripe is painted on the animal, beginning at the nose and running all the way down its back. The dog is strangled in such a way that it is killed instantly. The hair is singed off over an open fire, and the body is cut up to go into the kettle of *wahanpi*, "meat soup." It is a privilege as well as a sign of respect to receive the head. The dog serves as a sacred offering, and it is served as sacred food, but whether the spirit of the animal appreciates this, I cannot say.

To perform the Yuwipi, one room in the medicine man's house is emptied out. All the furniture is removed, and all the windows are covered with blankets so that not the even the tiniest flicker of light can penetrate. Things that could reflect light, such as mirrors or pictures in glass frames, are removed or turned with their faces against the wall. Those who attend the ceremony take off their wristwatches and other shiny objects and put them in their pockets. After the room has been stripped bare, only some folded-up blankets or cushions along the walls are left for people to sit on.

Then all is made holy. The floor is covered with sage, our most sacred herb. A rectangle is made, formed from a long string into which 405 *chanli wapahta*—tiny bundles of tobacco offerings—are tied. The number 405 represents all the different kinds of plants in the Lakota world, all the green, growing things that make the Earth beautiful. Some say that this number stands for all the many kinds of animals—the four-legged, the two-legged, the six-legged, as well as the "no-legs."

At the four corners of the rectangle are put large tin cans—Maxwell House coffee cans, for instance—filled with earth, sometimes taken from gopher holes or mole holes. Gopher dust is sacred. Before battle, our great warrior Crazy Horse always sprinkled himself and his horse with gopher dust. But each *yuwipi* man has his own vision of what kind of earth to use.

Into each of these cans is stuck a peeled stick, topped with a colored, cloth flag called *waunyanpi*, representing the sacred Four Directions. The black flag stands for the West, the red for the North, the yellow for the East, the white for the South. Some *yuwipi* men will use two additional flags—a green one representing the Earth and its trees and plants, and a blue one, symbolic of the sky.

In the center, on the northern side of the rectangle formed by tobacco ties, is planted the sacred staff, its upper half painted red and its lower half painted black. In between them is a thin, yellow stripe. Red represents the day, black stands for the night, and the dividing yellow is for the dawn.

To the top of the staff is tied an eagle feather. Wanbli, the Eagle, is the Creator's messenger who will carry to Wakan Tanka the prayers of those taking part in the ceremony. To the middle of the staff is tied the tail of the Blacktailed Deer, which is very sacred.

Next to the staff is a rack on which rests the Chanunpa, the Sacred Pipe. No ceremony can be performed without it. There might be other sacred objects, depending on a medicine man's vision. My brother Crow Dog also uses deer antlers and the head of a bald eagle in his Yuwipi.

In front of the sacred staff is *maka-kagapi*, "that which is made of earth," the altar. It looks like an oval made of red earth, smoothed with an eagle feather. The altar represents the Earth. The design, like the Sacred Hoop, has no beginning and no end. There is also a face in there. It is a spirit but also a human. Four horns sprout from its head, representing the Four Directions. The horns are split at the ends, making four two-pronged forks. The prongs stand for the positive and negative, which are part of everything.

The earth altar is made to cure the sick. I have to stress that this is my father's own personal design; other medicine men might use a different one. Pointing to the horned head, my father told me, "It is a spirit and it is a man, but it is also myself. It is Lame Deer."

On each side of the rock is placed one *wagmuha*, or gourd rattle. Sometimes these are made of buffalo or deer hide, and often they are painted red. Each of these rattles is filled with 405 tiny rock crystals taken from ant heaps. These are the "talking stones," and their sound is the voice of the spirits. Sometimes during a Yuwipi, these rattles fly through the air, moved by spirit power. We take the tiny gourd rocks from the *tajuska oyate*, the "ant people," because these little creatures are wise and know many secrets.

They pick the right kind of transparent talking stones. They are also industrious and selfless and work together. There is something *wakan* in every ant. Embodied in these ant stones is the chief element of *yuwipi* power—Tunka, the Rock.

Tunka represents the power of the immovable. We have an old saying, "Everything living must die. Only the rocks and mountains are forever." Tunka is part of our word for the Creator, Tunkashila, Grandfather of All Things. Tunka has no birth and no death, no beginning and no end.

The *yuwipi* man is a rock dreamer. He works with the sacred rocks, and they work for him. He has a sacred rock, perfectly round, perfect in itself, often painted red, kept in a bundle made of hide and lined with sage. This is a "finding stone." In the old days, we had a special ceremony called Pte Hiko, during which a finding stone pointed out the place where buffalo could be found. Such a rock is *lila wakan*, "most sacred."

During a Yuwipi ceremony, a rock, the gourd rattles, or the spirit voices whispering into the medicine man's ear will tell him where something lost can be found. A man might come and say, "My best horse has been stolen. Get it back for me." And through the power of the rock, the animal is returned to the owner. He might also ask, "Who was the thief?" But the *yuwipi* man will say, "You got your horse back, what more do you want?" The *wichasha wakan* wants no strife or disunity in the tribe, so he does not name those who have done something bad, but just puts things right. In rocks, there is a cry from the womb, a reminder of the Earth's beginnings, a pounding of buffalo hooves, a sacred fire.

There is another word for rock or stone: *inyan. Inyan-sha* is the red pipestone out of which the bowls of the sacred Chanunpa are made. Pipestone is the flesh and blood of the Indian, the subject of many legends. Inyan brought us the buffalo. Ptesan Win brought us the Pipe and taught us how to use it. She taught us how to live. She also brought with her a mysterious, round stone.

Many traditional people still carry their own personal medicine stones in small pouches around their necks. Crazy Horse had a pebble tied behind his ear that made him bulletproof. To us, such stones are active and have a soul.

Prayers and flesh offerings are made to Inyan and Tunka. On the bare-rock mountaintops of the Paha Sapa, the Wakinyan are believed to have their nests. My father always told me that some rocks are covered with spidery lines and cracks, secret spirit writing that only a few can interpret. And there are also the holy rocks of purification, which we use in the Inipi.

Other sacred things used in the Yuwipi are an eagle wing, which is sometimes used to "fan off" a sick person, and an eagle-bone whistle. Beside such ceremonial objects, there is placed, within the rectangle of tobacco ties, the ritual food, the kettle of dog soup, a pail of fresh spring water, fry bread, a kind of berry pudding called *wojapi*, and corn or kidney *wasna*, which the whites call "pemmican." The space inside the string of *chanli* forming the rectangle is sometimes called "Hochoka." It is a sacred space. Nobody but the *yuwipi* man and two helpers who tie him up is allowed to step inside this space. The other participants sit outside it in the narrow lane between the walls and the Hochoka. Often, after the ceremony, one or more of those who want to be doctored may be led into the Hochoka to be "cedared," or fanned with the smoke of smoldering *wachanga* (fragrant sweetgrass).

Some thirty years ago, my father made a number of paintings and drawings showing the start of a Yuwipi from a sort of bird's-eye view. Everything is there—the tobacco ties, the flags, the earth altar, the gourds, and the food. On top, to the right of the sacred staff, sit the drummers and singers. Behind the staff sits a man holding the Pipe. The other participants are sitting on three sides along the rectangle, the women in one place, the men in another. In the center of the sacred space, on a bed of sage, lies the *yuwipi* man, tied up in his star blanket. All the essentials of the ritual are there, but allowance must be made for the fact that these are paintings of my *father's* Yuwipi. Other medicine men might arrange things somewhat differently. For example, while my father placed the colored flags at the four corners of the rectangle, others line them up in a row at the top, with the sacred staff in the middle.

The Yuwipi begins with the medicine man standing in the center. First the helpers tie his hands together behind his back, lacing his fingers together with slipknots. They wrap him up like a mummy inside a star blanket, covering his head and body down to his ankles, so that one wonders how he can breathe or what power keeps him from being smothered to death. A long, rawhide thong is wound seven times around the blanket and the man inside. This is done in such a way that the thong forms a line down his back, secured by seven knots.

When the *yuwipi* man is tightly bound, his helpers lift him up and put him face down in the center of the Hochoka. Then they step outside the string of tobacco ties. All present will put a sprig of sage behind one ear, or fasten it in their hair, so that the spirits will come and talk to them. All the lights are extinguished, plunging everything into the darkest darkness. Then the drums begin to beat, and the Yuwipi begins.

Imagine yourself being thrown into a pool of inky, impenetrable blackness. You feel disembodied and isolated, though you are aware of friends all around you. Imagine the roaring drums and the powerful voices of the singers drowning out all other noises, emptying your mind completely of all that does not matter, making it ready to be filled with wonder.

For those who believe, the darkness is welcome, and they concentrate their minds on the spirit of Yuwipi. To them, the trance-inducing drumbeat is the gladdening pulsebeat of life. On skeptical whites, the effect can be quite different. Sometimes the darkness frightens them, making them feel claustrophobic. But eventually they get used to this "night song." At the end of the Yuwipi, there are few skeptics left.

Suddenly, out of the darkness, come little whisperings—otherworldly talking, muffled sounds. These are spirit voices speaking in a language only the *yuwipi* man can understand. Little sparks of light appear out of nowhere, like so many fireflies—first one, then many, dancing around the people, sitting along the the walls, flitting back and forth over the ceiling. The spirits have come in. Then the rattling gourds fly through the air. Sometimes they hit someone who wants to be cured. This is a good sign; the ones who are touched by the *wagmuha* will get well. The beating of wings and the thin, high-pitched cry of eagles is heard. Feathers caress the faces of some of those who are present. The voices of the singers rise to a crescendo.

This goes on for a long time, sometimes for hours. Then, suddenly, all is quiet. The sparks of light fade away, the whisperings stop. The rattles come to rest in their proper places, next to the sacred staff. Someone turns on the light. The *yuwipi* man sits in the center, unwrapped and untied. He has been dead, but is brought back to life by the prayers of those taking part in the ceremony.

The *yuwipi* man explains what the spirit voices have told him, interpreting what they have said about the cause of a person's sickness or where something that has been lost might be found. He doctors the sick ones, fanning them with his eagle wing, blowing on his eagle-bone whistle, telling people what herbs to use, and maybe giving them some of his special medicines.

Going clockwise, people begin to talk about what they have learned during the time of darkness. They speak about their feelings and problems. The *yuwipi* listens and advises. He might tell of having been hundreds of miles away while lying wrapped in his star blanket. He might identify some of the spirits who had been present—the spirit of Crazy Horse, maybe, or the spirit of some humble, no-account, long-dead fellow. One is as important as the other. The Sacred Pipe goes around, also clockwise. Everyone takes a few puffs and says a few good words as the air is filled with the aromatic smoke of Indian tobacco. They say, "Mitakuye Oyasin—All My Relations," to include all living things in their prayers. This ends the ceremony.

Afterward, as with all Lakota rituals, there comes the feast. Everyone eats the dog and the berry soup, drinks *pejuta sapa* (strong, black coffee), and makes small talk. At last, they all get up to greet the dawn and go back to their homes. Only a few linger until the sun is well up.

What happens during a Yuwipi cannot be explained. How can you explain the unexplainable? What some whites call "supernatural" is quite natural to us Lakota; it just cannot be explained or analyzed by the white man's science. It cannot be explained by a medicine man's science, either, because there are no words for it; you just have to accept it.

Around 1940, the BIA superintendent at Pine Ridge, a white official named Ferraca, did an experiment. He challenged our most powerful *yuwipi* man, Horn Chips, to perform the ceremony in full daylight or in a room lit by kerosene lamps in order to prove that the things taking place during a Yuwipi were not sleights of hand or magic tricks. Ferraca invited a number of white friends to witness the ceremony. He had his tribal policeman tie Horn Chips up and place him face down on the ground. As usual, the gourd rattles flew through the air, the flickering lights danced around like so many lightning bugs, and the spirit voices whispered into the white people's ears. Ferraca had to admit that he had experienced something strange and wonderful that was beyond the white man's understanding. Eventually, he even wrote a paper about it.

George Eagle Elk, an old friend of mine who was found murdered on a roadside some years ago, was another powerful *yuwipi* man who could perform the ritual in a lighted room. When he did so, there was always an overwhelming presence of his medicine animal, the Eagle. You could not see it, but its shrill cries filled your ears as you felt its wings touching you. And the ceiling of the room where you were sitting suddenly widened to become as big as the Western sky.

There are some who tell me they have witnessed the *yuwipi* man floating through the air—"levitating," as the white man calls it. I never saw this, but at one ritual I took part in, when the lights were turned on, the *yuwipi* man was found "sitting" upside-down on his head in a corner. He could not have jumped over the people lining the wall. How could he have done this without somebody noticing? I do not question it; I just accept it.

Once, during a vision, I left my body and floated—or rather, my spirit levitated out of its human wrapping. Being fully conscious, I looked down on my body far below, wondering about how to reenter it. Hovering above, I felt a danger that something might be done to my body, making it impossible for my spirit to return. But return I did.

During one Yuwipi I attended, Brave Buffalo, a friend of mine who passed over to the spirit world a few years ago, was singing beside me, and the Buffalo spirit physically entered the room. When the lights were turned on, a lot of undigested grass was lying all around me. It had been chewed up in the way of old animals with worn teeth, who just suck up the juice and spit out the pulp. That Buffalo spirit left some of this stuff on my head. There was wet grass and foam dripping all over my face. As I was wiping it off, the *yuwipi* man who was running the ceremony said, "The spirit of Ptesan Win has blessed us." In this way, I experienced the tie that exists between this holy animal and our Lakota nation.

In the old days, the rock dreamer did his sacred stone ceremony inside a large tipi made of buffalo skin, and instead of being tied up inside a star blanket, he was wrapped in a buffalo robe. When the fire was rekindled, he was often found, untied and unwrapped, wedged into the poles at the top of the tipi. Whenever I do a ceremony, the Buffalo is always there. So are the Bear, the Blacktailed Deer, and the Eagle. Even the Owl comes around. They appear, not in order to scare people, but to make them understand, to open the eyes of their minds and hearts.

I come from a long line of famous *yuwipi* men, and they began taking me at a very early age to their ceremonies. I still remember it; I was just a little boy. I loved the drumming and singing and the animal spirits coming in. I loved the whispering spirit voices. I loved watching the little lights flitting through the darkness. I didn't understand the meaning of these things yet, but my enthusiasm knew no bounds. I jumped up and tried to catch the little sparks. In the darkness, if I tripped over the Four-Direction flags, somebody would guide me back to the place I was supposed to be. The old people never scolded me. The next day, one of them would take me on his lap and gently instruct me, telling me what and what not to do. These were famous spiritual men and chiefs—Old Man Red Cloud and ninety-year-old Iron Hail, who had fought against Custer and his men at the Little Bighorn.

As I grew older, I became less bold. Sometimes I got scared, watching things being performed by spirits I couldn't see. I was even frightened by the little lights, seemingly about to touch me, dancing close to my face like glowworms on a summer night. But then some of the rock dreamers let me drum for them during the ritual—*yuwipi* men like Sleeping Bear, John Singing Goose, George First-in-Trouble, Horned Antelope, Horn Chips, and Poor Thunder. These were men of extraordinary power, and I was proud to call them "Uncle." They were all relations of mine in one way or another. So, this was my introduction to Yuwipi, and over the years I gradually became part of it.

Until a few years ago, I thought that these sacred-stone ceremonies were performed only by our Lakota People. In my travels around the world, however, I found out that this is not so. In Denmark, an Inuit friend from Greenland described to me nighttime ceremonies performed by Eskimo medicine men called "Angakok," during which they are tied up and wrapped in skins. Just as with our Yuwipi, when the lamps are lit, the men stand there untied and interpret to their people what the spirits have told them.

In France, I saw the dolmens and menhirs of prehistoric people—sacred stone circles and rows of huge rocks aligned with the sunrise. Inside ancient caves, I saw rock paintings like those found throughout America, made by men who lived more than ten thousand years ago. There I also found painted round and oddly shaped pebbles of different sizes, which must have been medicine stones. On one of the cave walls, I saw a drawing of a horned head almost exactly like the one my father used on his Yuwipi earth altar.

Once a man has taken up the burden of Yuwipi, he must be worthy of it. A man cannot perform this ceremony to satisfy somebody's curiosity, but only for healing and finding out. Also, once he has accepted this burden, he cannot just throw it away when it becomes heavy. A man is a stone dreamer for life; he remains a *yuwipi* man until death.

One of my uncles (I will not tell you his name) was a *yuwipi* man for almost fifty years, as were his father and grandfather before him. One day he just got up, took his medicine bundle, his rattles, and his sacred staff and went deep into the Badlands. He threw his sacred things into a narrow gorge—simply threw them away as if they had been so much garbage. He told everybody, "That's it. I don't want to be bothered anymore. I've had my fill. I'm sick and tired of solving other people's problems. I want time for myself."

This man was held in the highest regard, yet there he was, throwing his power away. So his bundle is still sitting in the Badlands. However, after he did this, every time he sat down—whether at a table, in the back of a car, or on a couch—the rattles would appear. They would hit the ceiling and the floor, seemingly trying to tell him something. He kept denying it. He did not want those rattles around. But they kept coming and coming, the sacred ant rocks inside them asking him to go on. They were telling him by their rattling, "You have sons, you have grandchildren. Some of them have to take up your power, continue the ritual, and pass it on."

But he would not accept it, so his wife got sick and died, and some of his closest relatives were taken to the spirit world. Then his limbs were taken away—amputated, one by one—and finally he himself passed on. All because he had thrown away the gift his Creator had given him and refused to pass it on to his children. Yuwipi is not a thing to play with. It is *wakan* and must be treated as such.

A *yuwipi* man never asks anything for himself. He has the power to heal, and he must use it. He does not send you a bill. But when he is old and his teeth fall out, it is not unusual for him to receive a little package with no return address, and inside is a new set of store-bought teeth. Or maybe he totals his car and people hear about it. In the morning, there stands a jalopy before his door, with a full tank of gas, ready to go. Or perhaps there is a side of beef hanging from a tree next to his home. That is the Indian way.

One of the men I most respected as a spiritual person and human being was Ellis Chips, whose recent passing I will mourn for as long as I live. He had his home at Wamblee, on the Pine Ridge Reservation. My father had entrusted his sacred things to Ellis, telling him to pass them on to me. So, on the day I buried my father, Ellis' son Godfrey, a *yuwipi* man, was tied up.

After the ceremony was finished, he explained what he had seen: "I see my cousin Archie walking with a Pipe. He staggers and then comes to a hill. He has a Pipe, and he staggers. He is tripping and falling over rocks, and he comes down from the hill. He is walking through a forest, and he gets lost. He is walking in a fog, but then at the end, he comes out of it. He stands above the fog, and he smiles at the people."

After this young man had told of his vision, Ellis Chips, son of the great spiritual man Horn Chips, handed me my father's Sacred Pipe and sacred bonnet, passing his burden on to me.

This is a serious chapter that talks about many mysteries. Let me end it with a smile. Once, my friend Richard Erdoes' apartment in New York City was full of Lakota people who had come visiting. Among them were Old Henry Crow Dog and his son, Leonard, a young *yuwipi* man. The young man had had a dream so compelling that they decided to do a Yuwipi to find out its true meaning. They had everything they needed to perform the ritual except the dog. Richard's apartment was on the eighth floor, overlooking Broadway. Henry took Richard to the window and pointed to a man on the street, walking his dog.

"Look at that fat young dog," said Henry. "Go, get him."

"No way," said Richard. "Over my dead body!"

Henry insisted, "Go tell the man what an honor it is. Tell the dog what an honor it is. Tell him we'll do him right—paint him with sacred red paint."

Richard said, "Henry, this is a New York dog. It has no sense of honor." So they had to use beef instead.

C H A P T E R   1 9

Eagle-Bone Whistles

Every year, at the height of summer, a song is heard on the Sioux reservations—Rosebud, Pine Ridge, Standing Rock, and Cheyenne River:

Wakan Tanka unshimala ye,	Creator, have pity on me,
Wanikta cha lecha mu welo.	I shall live; that is why I am doing this.

The high, quavering voices rise to the sky. Men sit in a circle pounding on a big drum until its rhythm becomes the pulsebeat and heartthrob of all those present—a thousand hearts beating as one. The deep thudding of the drum fills both body and mind, making bare feet stomp to its rhythm. Mingled with the chant is the twittering of a hundred eagle-bone whistles, making a sound like the high-pitched cry of eagles, filling the air, reverberating back from the hillside. These are the sounds of Wiwanyank Wachipi—the Sundance, the most sacred and solemn of all our ceremonies.

The Sundance has been misunderstood by the white man and misrepresented by the media. As I mentioned, in movies such as *A Man Called Horse*, the (white) hero is depicted as undergoing the Sundance piercing in order to prove his courage and be adopted into the tribe. This is all wrong.

We pierce and suffer and pray for the renewal of all life in order to honor the women who suffer in bringing forth new life. For this reason, very traditional women do not do the Sundance, except for extreme reasons and/or when there is no man in the family to do it—for example, in time of war or when there are heavy alcohol, drug, or health problems in the family. We pierce and offer our suffering for our families and for the life of the

Sundance

226

Sacred Hoop. In other words, we "pierce" in order to help someone. We undergo the pain of piercing because this might take pain away from someone we love.

A man goes into the sweatlodge to purify himself and pray. He tells the medicine man running the Inipi, "My mother is sick. If you make her well, I will sundance for four years." So he makes this solemn commitment. Recently, a grandfather made a vow to pierce his flesh, hoping that it would bring his grandson, a soldier in the Gulf War, home alive and in one piece.

As my father used to say, "White Christians let Jesus do the suffering for them, but Indians give of their own flesh, taking the suffering upon themselves, making a sacrificial altar of their own bodies. If we offer the Creator a horse, tobacco bundles, food for the needy, we are making him a present of something he already owns. Everything on this Earth has been created by Wakan Tanka and is a part of him. It is only our own flesh, our blood and pain, that is a real sacrifice, a real giving of ourselves. How can we give anything less?"

My father also told me, "Wiwanyank Wachipi is also a dance dedicated to Ptesan Win, White Buffalo Calf Woman, and to women generally. When a sundancer feels the pain of the skewers," he said, "he also feels and understands the pain a woman endures during childbirth."

A man might vow to have his chest pierced in two places, the skewers attached to the top of the Sacred Tree by long rawhide thongs. At the right moment, he will tear himself free. Or he may have decided to hang from the Sundance Tree, or to drag buffalo skulls attached to skewers in his back. My cousin Crow Dog had himself pierced in four places—two in his chest and two in his back. Ropes were tied to the skewers, as well as to four horses. The horses were then "fanned off" with eagle wings, and they galloped away in four different directions. Traditional men may prefer not to be pierced with wooden skewers but by an eagle claw or a bear claw, or even by a badger's sharp, rigid penis.

Two years after my father died, I resolved to become a sundancer. I felt that I could never run this great ceremony until I myself had been pierced, so I made the vow. That year, a Sundance was being held at Davis, in Northern California. There were a lot of Indians at the university there, with many Lakota among them. On the first day of the dance, I was dragging eight buffalo skulls, and it was hard for me. I was forcing myself, step by painful step, around the Sundance circle, using every ounce of strength in my body to pull the heavy skulls, which weighed about twenty-five pounds each.

I completed the first round. This one is always for the people and for their survival. I knew that I had to walk round and round three more times. As I went to the South, Old Sam Moves Camp's wife came and prayed over the wounds in my back. I went on, pulling, pulling—blowing all the time on my eagle-bone whistle to the beat of the drum. Suddenly, the skewer on one side tore itself out. That was at the West door of the black flags. I stopped and asked for my father's Pipe. My friend Dennis Banks brought it to me, and that was a help.

I struggled on. Now the going was even harder, as all the weight of the skulls was hanging on one skewer, pulling me to one side. The rhythm of the drum and the whistles, as well as the pain, put me into a trance. I was looking to the North and saw a woman coming toward me. She was dressed in old-style, fringed buckskin, without any beadwork or quill decoration. Her long, black hair was flowing in the wind, and she was beautiful beyond words. She stopped in front of me and said, "Cinksh, my son, we taught you the Inipi, which is the first step. We told you to wait until we guide you to the next one. You are going too fast. Slow down. Remember these . . . " She stretched out her arms, and two sweatlodges appeared before her. "Cinksh," she continued, "remember well. When this dance is ending, look to the North and behold a fire. Do not go to it, but know that I am there, and I am real."

I did not know what she meant, but continued pulling the buffalo skulls that were attached to one side. As I got to the red flags in the North, the last skewer broke through and I was free.

On the last day of the Sundance, as they passed out *wasna* and *chankpa hanpi* (pemmican and cherry juice), someone shouted, "Fire!" We looked toward the north, where eight sweatlodges stood in a circle. The northern-most lodge was on fire, and before anybody could extinguish it, it burned to the ground.

There had been no sweatlodge fires going at the time; they had all been put out the night before. This fire had not been started in a natural way. I realized that the woman who had appeared to me was the same messenger who had appeared to warn me of my stepmother's approaching death, and who had shown me a vision of the sweatlodge long ago. I knew then that this was White Buffalo Calf Woman.

Years have gone by since then, and I have continued with the Sundance. In 1986, I came full circle. I was traveling in Europe, sitting alone in someone's house. I felt bad, thinking of what was happening to my people, and I started to cry. All of a sudden, it grew very dark outside, and the room was plunged into blackness. A light came into the room, and I found myself sitting on a green mountainside. Below me was a strangely beautiful valley, and on the far side rose a tall mountain.

A cloud formed in front of me and turned into the shape of a giant man reaching to the top of the mountain. The cloud then became an enormous hand that smashed the mountaintop, transforming it into a mirror. Then again, the hand assumed the shape of a man, towering above the land, the valley, and the mountain. Where the man's face should have been, there was a hole through which I could see the sky. The hair and forehead of this "cloud man" was there, but the face was not.

This apparition took the flat mirror, which had been a mountaintop, and with it picked up the rays of the sun and reflected them into my face. I fell over backward. As I did so, I returned to the room I had been sitting in, and the lights were turned on. In that moment, I found that I was holding a Sacred Pipe in my hands. All doubts and disbeliefs that I had ever harbored vanished, and I heard myself talking to the Grandfather Spirit.

"Up to now I did not truly acknowledge your existence," I said. "It took me that long to know that you are real. I denied you on a mountaintop. I looked upon myself as your equal, and now I realize that I am nothing. You are stronger than all things."

Months went by before I moved back to South Dakota. Very early each morning, I would go outside with a cup of coffee, offer a little to the spirits, and pray. One morning, as I stood on my porch, the mysterious woman again appeared to me, walking toward me from a row of trees. She raised her hands and spoke to to me: "Cinksh, my son, I am back again. I come in a good way, in a sacred manner. Look at me."

I was forced to look at her face, and I was numbed by its unearthly beauty. It was the radiant face of a young woman. She said to me, "Don't let my face fool you. Look at my hair." As I looked at her hair, it went from black to red to yellow and, at last, to white. She said, "Know that whatever the color of the hair, the blood runs red, like the good Red Road of your grandfathers. Behold!" And as I looked, she turned herself into a white buffalo cow and walked around me.

"Watch me," she said, walking away. From the tip of the buffalo's nose, the white started to turn brown, all the way to the tip of the tail. "Upon this Earth," she said, "there will be buffalo again, and I will return to make myself known to the people." And with that, she slowly disappeared northward over the hills.

With this fourth great vision, I had come full circle. Such visions occur to us traditional native people during ceremonies, or whenever we are in a right frame of mind to receive them, for our senses have not been dulled to receiving messages from the spirits.

Between 1890 and 1940, the Sundance, as well as all other native ceremonies, were forbidden under the Indian Offenses Act. One could be jailed for just having an Inipi or praying in the Lakota way, as the government and the missionaries tried to stamp out our old beliefs in order to make us into slightly darker, "civilized" Christians. Many historians believe that during those fifty years no Sundances were performed, but they are wrong. The Sundance was held every year, just as before, but it had to be done in secret, in lonely places where no white man could spy on us.

In 1939, when I was a small child, my grandfather took me to the biggest powwow that I had ever seen at Corn Creek. As far as I could see, there were tipis and tents and wagons—no cars, just wagons and horses. This powwow was held to draw attention away from a Sundance that was being performed nearby.

Up until the fifties at these big powwows, the young men of the tribe used to put on a spectacular mock attack before the dancing started. They painted their faces black, as for war, and they rode bareback, wearing only breechcloths. They also intertwined wild grape vines with their horses' manes and tails. They did everything in the old way, just as they would have done a hundred years ago when setting out on the warpath.

At that 1939 powwow, we assembled under the huge brush arbor and waited and watched the hill where the attack was to begin. We heard a mighty shout of many men, followed by the thunder of hooves. What must have been two hundred warriors came over the crest and charged down the hill at breathtaking speed, whooping and yelling in a swirling cloud of dust.

As they came off the hill onto the flat, they began the first of four circles around the arbor—all at a dead run, which made the Earth tremble.

"Takoja, Grandson," my grandfather said to me, "take a good look, for you will never see the like again."

Looking back, I believe that these riders had been taking part in preparing the underground Sundance, because in the old days, young men put on black face paint and counted coup on the cottonwood selected to become the Sundance Tree. They did this just as if the tree were an enemy. Later, on the Sundance ground, there was always the great *uchita*, a big parade on horseback in front of the Sacred Tree.

That same year, Grandpa took me to a place near the home of Asa Jones, not too far from the powwow, where the hidden Sundance was being performed. This was my first Wiwanyank Wachipi. It was also to be my last for many years to come. There were no other young people present; I was the only child there. Only three very old men were being pierced— the Oglala chief American Horse, Turns Twice, and Iron Hail. These were all famous warriors who, as young men, had fought General Crook at the Rosebud and Custer at the Little Bighorn in 1876. The whites called these fights "massacres," while they call the killing of unarmed Cheyenne women and children at Sand Creek and the Washita "battles."

There was no drum at that Sundance, which might have attracted the police or the missionaries. Instead, they used a dried, folded buffalo hide, which they beat with cherry sticks.

Security was tight at this Sundance. All around on the hills, men were watching, making sure that the BIA police would not get wind of what was going on. They did a good job. The ceremony went on safely and without interruption, and it was beautiful and awe-inspiring to my young eyes.

After the dance, the old men talked of many things. They said that for a few years to come, our people would turn their backs on our sacred Sundance, but that in a short time it would come back stronger than ever, openly performed in many places on the several Sioux reservations. They said that, in time, the Sundance and the Purification would become one with all of our other ancient ceremonies at a secret place known only to a young man who would be guided by a spiritual power.

Iron Hail talked about Crazy Horse, who had been his friend. He talked about the great warrior's horse, which had brought him his sacred medicine.

Before Crazy Horse went into battle, he would pray and talk to his horse as if it were a human being. He would also tie a sacred herb to his animal's mane, covering its body with hailstone and lightning designs. He painted the same designs on his arms and chest, and, as I said, he wore a special pebble behind his ear that made him bulletproof.

Iron Hail chanted one of Crazy Horse's sacred songs:

> My friend,
> They are coming back.
> In a sacred way,
> All over the universe,
> Behold, they are coming back.
> The whole universe
> Moving in a sacred way.
> Behold, over there,
> From the spirit world,
> They are coming back.
> Over the whole universe,
> Behold,
> They are coming back.

"Crazy Horse received his song during a vision," Iron Hail said. "When he opened his eyes to see who was singing this song, he saw that it was a spirit who turned into a rabbit, which hopped away. Crazy Horse was a very spiritual man, and some of his powers were given to me."

Later the old chiefs came over to my grandfather and shook his hands. I was proud that they were his friends. I will never forget this first Sundance of mine.

The Sundance is the most holy of all our rituals. My father called it the "granddaddy of all Indian ceremonies." It goes way back to the beginning of our history. The way the old people tell it, some two thousand years ago, there was a famine. All the game had disappeared. One man received a vision that he should drag a huge buffalo skull fastened by a thong to the flesh of his back so that his people would survive. He did what the vision told him to do. He kept walking and walking without stopping, eating, or drinking. No storm, no stream, and no mountain could stop him, and after four days he broke loose. This, according to the legend, was the first Sundance.

Every year since 1979, I have helped run the Sundance at Crow Dog's Paradise on the Rosebud Reservation. There are always two leaders to conduct the Wiwanyank Wachipi: the intercessor, or *kuwa kiyapi*; and the director or dance chief, the *itanchan*. I act as the intercessor, and the medicine man Leonard Crow Dog, whom I look upon as a brother, acts as the director.

As intercessor, I am like the stem of the Sacred Pipe lifted up to the sky—a living link between Wakan Tanka and those who have come to participate in the dance. The intercessor is a messenger from the Creator to the people. But in another sense, he is like the seed that goes from the man into the woman. He is as high as the sky and as low as the Earth of which he is a part. He is the "man-in-between," the one who does the praying. He must concentrate his mind, explain the meaning of the dance to those who do not know it, and answer questions. During the Sundance, the intercessor must stay by himself in his own tipi and eat only traditional food. He is enveloped by his own thoughts and prayers. He performs the ritual's spiritual part.

The director runs the Sundance in all its practical aspects. You could almost call him the choreographer. He motions the dancers to their proper places. He sees to it that all are doing the right thing. He knows the songs and supervises the drummers. Both men are needed to run the dance, as one man alone could not do everything that is necessary.

The intercessor and the director support and complement each other. They also enter the dance circle together, side by side, in front of the dancers. The intercessor is on the right, carrying the Pipe; the director is on the left, carrying the buffalo skull with its muzzle pointing forward. Only during the Sundance do I wear my father's old bonnet, both to honor his memory and so that people can see me in the crowd. After a week of preparations, the Sundance itself lasts four days. It always takes place at the height of summer—at Crow Dog's, it goes from August 1 through August 5.

In 1970, during the Sundance on the Pine Ridge Reservation, the ground was so hot that it blistered the soles of some of the dancers. Our oldest medicine man, Frank Fools Crow, asked my father for help. "My son," he said, "do something, for the dancers are suffering from the worst heat ever."

My father smiled and went to the center of the dance ground, where the Tree of Life, the Sacred Sundance Tree, was standing. He asked the dancers to form a circle around him. As soon as they did, my father began to pray. As he prayed, a little black cloud formed and became bigger and bigger. At the same time, a man came from the west, carrying a basket filled with hailstones, which he threw at the people while running around the dance ground counterclockwise. Then he left the sacred area and went into a tipi. The people followed him in, but they found nobody inside.

Simultaneously, it was hailing all around, except at the Sacred Tree under which my father was still praying. The whole area was white with hail. Then the cloud disappeared and the hail evaporated in the returning sunshine, but the ground remained moist and cool. My father said to Fools Crow, "Is that what you wanted?" Then he left the dance circle, went into his tipi, and we did not see him again for the rest of the day. This was a part of my father's *heyoka* power.

One summer, I went to a Sundance at Seelo Black Crow's place. On the second day in the afternoon, a black cloud appeared in the west—a very big cloud. With it came lightning and thunder. Two of the medicine men present said, "This will finish the dance for today. They jumped into their cars and drove away in different directions. The Sundance director came over to me and said, "Uncle, this huge cloud is coming. What shall I do?"

"Go on dancing as before," I told him. "Don't interrupt the sacred ceremony. I will go to the Sacred Tree, led by this young girl who carries the Pipe, the one who represents Ptesan Win. I don't want to go alone to the Sundance Tree."

The young girl took her Pipe and led me to the center. I prayed and held a Pipe ceremony. The cloud divided into two parts, and the thundering ceased. I told the men, "Finish the dance, then go and purify yourselves in the sweatlodge. After that, go into your tipis, close the flaps, and prepare yourselves for a big storm. Later during the night, the weather will clear up."

So they danced until evening, ending at the proper time and in the proper way, without interruption. I ran two or three Purification ceremonies in the sweatlodges, and then we went into our tipis. One of the dancers turned to me and said, "Thank you, Uncle, for dividing that cloud so that it wouldn't rain on us. It must have been the power that Old John, your father, gave you."

"I didn't divide the cloud," I told them. "The two medicine men who ran off took the clouds with them."

Everybody laughed. "Seriously," I said, "don't forget the young girl carrying the Pipe. During the Sundance, as long as she represents Ptesan Win, she also has the power of the Buffalo. And then I felt still another power, a spiritual presence that was hovering around the Sacred Tree."

I also told them, "Get ready, because in fifteen minutes it will be raining so hard you won't be able to see your hand in front of your face. If you have to use the outhouse, go now, because for the next two hours you won't be able to leave your tipis."

The storm burst upon us with tremendous force. The rain came down in sheets. But soon it cleared up, the stars came out, and the rest of the night was magnificent. In the morning the sky was blue, with not a cloud in sight. Normally, the weather is always good while there is sundancing. If it rains, it does so during the night when there is no dancing. If there is a threat of bad weather, there is usually someone present who has the power to protect the dance. I once witnessed one of our holy men making the sun shine on a few acres of dance grounds while it rained buckets across the rest of the state.

There is even a special Sundance song to ensure good weather:

Anpetu wi tanyan, hinapa nunwe	May the sun rise well,
Maka ozazanyan tanyan,	Brightly shining upon the Earth.
Hinapa nunwe.	

On the evening before the dance, the tree for the Sundance is cut. This tree, which is set up in the center of the dance grounds, represents the Great Tree of Life. It is chosen by young scouts who go looking for a tall, perfect cottonwood. In 1991, the Sundance Tree was especially large—about as tall as a six-story building and two feet thick at the base.

The cottonwood is sacred above all other trees. The white fluff from its seeds represents downy eagle plumes, and its heart-shaped leaves are like the heart of the nation. In the wintertime, when there is no forage for the horses, bark stripped from cottonwoods can keep them alive.

A young virgin representing White Buffalo Woman makes the first four chops in the living tree with her axe. After that, anyone present—man, woman, or child—can step up to "give the trunk four licks." As the tree falls, it is caught by the dancers. It must not be allowed to touch the ground. The tree is then trimmed of its branches, but the leaves at the very top are left, because that is where the tree's spirit dwells. Smaller branches and leaves are picked up by those present, for prayer and good luck. After the tree is trimmed, it is carried to the Sundance ground by dancers walking in pairs, its top pointing forward. In 1991, they had to walk two miles.

The Sundance ground is a huge circle formed by the "shade," an arbor made of poles and pine boughs. The circle is left open at the East, where the dancers enter. Nobody is ever allowed to sit or stand there, or even to pass across the East door. At the center, a large hole has been dug in which the tree will be planted.

The trunk of the tree has water inside. When you cut down a cotton-wood of this size, there is an still an average of four or five gallons of water in it. You have to let the water run out. You catch it in a bucket and use it for healing after the dance is finished. At the end, when the sacred food is distributed, the water is given to the old people as a cure for their illnesses. If the tree is put in the ground with the water still in it, it seals up and gets hot, and in that state it could be struck by the Thunderbeings.

The Sundance Tree always ends in a fork made of two large branches, reminding me of a human stretching out his arms toward the sun. This Tree of Life connects the people standing on the Earth with the sky and the Creator above. Before the tree is erected, tobacco offerings and dozens of colored banners are tied to its top. A crossbar the length of a man is also tied across the crotch, together with a bundle of chokecherry sticks and leaves. Some people also hang their medicine bundles there to be blessed by the power of the Sacred Tree and the dance.

The dancers also put "food for the Sacred Tree" into the hole in which it will be planted: buffalo fat, corn *wasna*, kidney pemmican, chokecherries, and water. This food offering is made as a prayer both to ask that the food may be plentiful for the people and to give thanks for that which we already have. Then, with four strong ropes and the help of many people, the Sacred Tree is slowly raised upright. When it finally stands there in all its glory, a shout goes up and the women make the tremolo, ululating the "brave-heart" cry.

Offerings are tied to the tree trunk—black, red, yellow, and white strips of cloth representing the Four Sacred Directions and the four races of mankind. There are blue flags for the sky and green ones for the Earth. Many tobacco offerings are tied to the trunk.

Small figures of a man and a bison, cut from buffalo hide, hang from the Sacred Tree. These are depicted with huge male parts, because the Sundance is also a rite of renewal and fruitfulness, a prayer for more children and more buffalo to be born. The missionaries did not like this, so these figures had something missing at the commercialized Sundances they held on Pine Ridge. At our traditional Sundances, we did not submit to any white-imposed prudery.

Because this dance is also a rite of rebirth, there is a lot of humorously obscene banter going on at this time. Some of the things we hear from otherwise respectable, modest ladies on this occasion are really quite embarrassing to us. This is all in Lakota, and it is all a part of this ceremony of the renewal of life.

To the west of the Tree is a holy place called Owanka Wakan, made of smoothed-over earth and a buffalo-skull altar. There is great power contained in both. There is also a special Sundance tipi where the leaders and elders take counsel before and after the dance. Finally, up to twelve large sweatlodges accommodate the many dancers, and special Inipis are also held for the women.

The Wiwanyank Wachipi at Crow Dog's place is the only really traditional Sundance left. There are no hot-dog stands or kiddie rides here, no fancy-dance powwows, no entrance fees, no curiosity seekers or tourists with cameras. There are no nonparticipants, either. All present, including those standing in the arbor, are dancing barefoot in rhythm with the drum, waving bunches of sage.

Several times a day, the dancers will hand their Pipes to some men and women standing in the arbor, and groups of five or six will form around each Pipe, smoking it and praying as it goes around. Also, those who do not dance gather sage, chop wood, haul water, get rocks for the sweats, or help with the cooking. Everybody is involved; there are no idle spectators. It takes about $5,000 to feed the more than a thousand people who come to this dance every year, and this sum is usually raised by donations.

The Sundance is common to all Plains tribes—to the Cheyennes,

Arapahoes, Assiniboines, Crows, Pawnees, Shoshones, Utes, and Kiowas. The Mandans have their own version of the dance—the Okipa, which is performed a little differently from the way we do it. You can get an idea of what the Okipa was like from the 1831 paintings of George Catlin and Karl Bodmer. These are reproduced in many books dealing with Native Americans.

It is said that, in the old days, the Mandans and Cheyennes underwent the most severe kind of self-torture. Nowadays, the Cheyennes dance without piercing. Their holy ground is Bear Butte, at the northern edge of the Black Hills, a place where my family and I often pray—after tourist season ends. The Kiowas never pierced, as for them the sight of blood during the Sundance is a bad omen.

Nowadays, people come from as many as fifteen different tribes to dance at Crow Dog's place, and some of them come from tribes that never had a Sundance. In some cases, their own ceremonies have been suppressed and forgotten, so they come to sundance with us Sioux to "become Indian again," and we are happy to help them find their way back. They want to go back to the traditional way, and taking part in this sacred ritual is one way of doing it. So we have Navajo, Pueblo, Apache, and Iroquois dancers, and many even come from south of the border.

Tlacael, an old Aztec medicine man from around Guadalajara, comes every year to pierce. He always brings with him ten to twenty young Indians from Mexico—Zapotecs, Huichols, Nahuas, Maya, Mixtecs, and Tarahumaras. One of these men walked on foot for three months to join the Sundance, starting somewhere in Oaxaca. Tlacael always dances in his own way, all by himself, at the edge of the circle. Once a young fellow appeared dressed in Mexican peasant fashion with a poncho around his shoulders. He said that his Nahua name was Warm Southwind. Our young men, with their peculiar sense of humor, immediately dubbed him "Mild Disturbance."

Our Lakota prayers always include all of humanity and every living being on this Earth. The Sacred Hoop is all-embracing. The black, red, yellow, and white flags waving from the top of the Sacred Tree of Life represent the Four Directions of the universe. And because of the universality of our prayers, many people now think of these colors as representing the different races of mankind.

So how can we forbid our non-Indian friends to sundance? There are many reasons for this. As I said, we allow other Indians from all over America to sundance—this includes Mexico and Central America. Many of these people have survived a genocide so thorough that their own religion was destroyed. Many have their old religion, but simply wish to share in the self-sacrifice and the prayers for all life on Earth.

We have had black medicine men from Africa who have become sundancers. There is a Japanese monk who has sundanced with us for many years. But these are people who come from a lifelong spiritual discipline—people who have lived their lives close to the Earth, respecting her balance and learning the true meaning of inner spiritual growth.

Our own people are born and raised in our tradition. Our sundancers go into this ceremony with a lifetime of preparation behind them. Not all Indians, not all Sioux become sundancers. The Sundance is not a step along the way like confirmation or first communion to a Catholic. The Sundance is an extra-special ceremony, an extra measure some decide to give—and usually for a very strong reason. The vast majority of non-Indian people do not understand this.

The Sundance is not a rite of passage, as many people mistakenly believe. It is not a rite of acceptance into some "spiritually elite" group. It is not a "higher degree" in "Lakota divinity study"—there is no such thing. Sundance is a matter of the few giving an extra measure in prayer for the good of the people.

In 1991, we finally allowed one white man to dance and to pierce. He is a man from France who has been with us in our spiritual ways for many years. He has learned with us and prayed with us, showing the greatest respect and patience for many long years. Above all, he is proud of his own heritage. He knows he will never be a Lakota, and he doesn't want to be one. He wants only to find his way back to the Earth, to the religion that includes the value of the Earth and all her life forms. This is why he sundances, to pray for the reconnection to our mother the Earth. He told me that while piercing, he felt *grand pouvoir*—"a great power."

This man had previously taken his Pipe to the Keeper of the Buffalo Calf Pipe, where it stayed for seven years. After this period of time, Arvol returned the Pipe to our French brother, who in turn brought it to Leonard

Crow Dog and me and asked us in the traditional way for permission to sundance. We and other chiefs and elders agreed.

Some other people have allowed non-Indians to dance, but giving indiscriminate permission for non-Indians to sundance has had very bad results. Sometimes these white people say, "Why dance for four long days? Let's make it two days!" Traditionally, Sundance participants do not eat or drink during the day while the dance is going on, but at some dances they have gallons of water to drink after every round.

These days, Sundances are going on all over the place—at Eagle Butte, Sisseton, Santee, everywhere. On the Rosebud Reservation alone, they run three or four dances and let almost everyone participate, as long as they come across with some *maza-ska*, or "green frogskins," as my father called them.

I think there should be only one dance on each reservation. I also think that it is not right to take this most sacred of our ceremonies to strange places where it has never been performed. We made an exception, sundancing at Big Mountain in Arizona's Navajo country, but this was a special case. The traditional, sheepherding, hogan-dwelling Dineh people living there for generations were being evicted by the government to be "relocated" in city slums, which they looked upon as a fate worse than death. They came to us with tears in their eyes, asking us for help, asking us to bring the Sundance to them for spiritual support. The Dineh people in northern Canada have had a Sundance and kept it alive through many years of tradition. So we introduced the dance to the Navajo people and ran it for them for a number of years.

However, I was outraged to learn that some men, pretending to be shamans, were running "Sundances" in Europe for whites only, charging each person $1,500 to participate. In these days of the New Age movement, all kinds of fake medicine men come crawling out of the woodwork, putting on fake Indian ceremonies and thereby giving Native American spirituality a bad name.

All this has led to some very strange doings. One radical feminist group put on so-called Sundances "for women only." This, of course, is wrong, because the ritual is all-inclusive. You can't reject somebody on account of his or her sex. Then there were mostly white lesbian dances and, most grotesque of all, an all-white, gay "Sundance" during which men capered around stark naked, engaging in all kinds of sadomasochistic rites, which they called "the original piercing." This is a gross mockery of our beliefs. We Indians have always been tolerant and understanding of our *winktes*, since we believe that men and women are what the Great Spirit made them. But a homosexual "Sundance" is a contradiction in itself, as the Wiwanyank Wacipi is a rite for renewing the life of the people.

The most tragic happening occurred in 1988, when a man appeared at one Sundance (not at Crow Dog's) claiming to be an Indian who had made the vow to pierce. At that time, medicine men used to pierce a number of dancers in succession with the same knife. This stranger turned out to be a criminal on parole who had contracted AIDS in prison. He was not even an Indian. The knife that had his blood on it was used on others, who then became infected with the HIV virus. Thus, this terrible disease came to the Lakota people.

Now every dancer has to bring his own knife. For those who don't, we have dozens of surgical scalpels donated by the reservation hospital. I know of one man who goes so far as to use surgical gloves when he pierces a dancer. It leaves a sour taste in my mouth that such things are used in this very ancient ritual. Very bad things happen when a Sundance is put on in a wrong way.

And then there are the hordes of white people trying to force their way in to "get a piece of the Indian spiritual action." They usually lecture us: "Don't eat meat; it's full of negative energy and cholesterol. Fry bread is fattening. You're drinking too much coffee; it's bad for you. Use crystals instead of the Pipe." And on and on. Soon they'll be serving sage tea on airlines. But enough of this; while speaking of the Sundance, one should have no negative thoughts.

Like all our ceremonies, the Sundance is always preceded by a Purification ceremony in the sweatlodge. I run some of these Inipis, while Crow Dog runs the others. Some dancers can conduct Inipis for themselves. Elderly, experienced ladies lead the women's Purifications. When I run an Inipi as a ceremony in itself, I always do four doors—that is, four rounds. This can take a long time, up to two hours. At the Sundance, I run two doors in the morning and two doors in the evening, making four in all.

Our people today are not as strong as our grandfathers. They can't go on dancing all day, from morning to night, without eating or drinking,

and undergo two four-door Inipis on top of that. We don't have the stamina
of our forefathers. Also, I make these Inipis cooler than usual. Many
dancers from other tribes have never experienced a real scorching—a six-
ty- or one-hundred-rock Sioux Inipi. So I have to go slow. I want to purify
them, not cook them.

The dance itself is a beautiful and inspiring thing to behold. It is *all*
the people communicating with *all* the spirit powers. It could be called a
religious drama, like a Christian passion play. It is prayer in motion. It is,
as one man said, an expression of emotion in rhythm. It is going beyond
yourself into another world. It is the Hanbleceya of the whole Sioux nation.

The Wiwanyank Wacipi is a mystery, full of Indian symbolism. The
dance ground represents the universe, the Circle Without End. The Sacred
Tree is a unifier, connecting the people on Grandmother Earth with the
sky and the Great Spirit above. The buffalo altar represents our brother,
the bison, who gave of his flesh so that the people could live. The Owanka
Wakan, the holy place to the west of the tree, stands for the essence of life.
In the crotch of the cottonwood lies the nest of the Thunderbirds. The eagle-
bone whistle, with its soft, downy plume, symbolizes the Eagle, the
Creator's winged messenger. It also represents the cry of the Thunderbirds. The little figures of a man and a buffalo stand for giving new life.

The men are all dressed alike. They are naked to the waist. Below, they
wear a red kilt reaching to the ankles, not unlike a South Sea sarong. Their
long hair is left to fall loosely to their shoulders. Around their heads, wrists,
and ankles, they wear wreaths of sage, an herb that is pleasing to the sun.
Often, two upright eagle feathers are stuck into the head wreath, one on
each side. In the old days, the dancers also wore a *wapegnaka*, a hair or-
nament of buffalo fur, as a symbol of our close connection to this sacred
animal. There is even an old song:

Anpe wi kin, kola wa yelo.	The Sun is my friend.
Changleska le, koyag mayelo.	He made me wear a hoop.
Wanbli wan, koyag wayelo.	He made me wear an eagle.

This song refers to the head garland of sage and the eagle feathers stuck in it.

Most dancers wear their medicine bags dangling from their necks. Some
have red spots painted on their chest and back to mark the place where they
want to be pierced. Some of our elders, old men who don't sundance any-

more, help out, marking the dancers, sometimes painting them with the design of a Thunderbird, sun, moon, star, or eagle. (Speaking of our elders, the oldest dancer piercing in 1991 was a man of eighty-seven years.) Being the intercessor, I wear a differently colored skirt every day, in tune with the colors of the Four Directions.

The climax of the Sundance is reached with the piercing. Up to about 1975, the piercing was always done on the fourth and last day, but now there are so many dancers that we have to do some piercing every day.

As the dancers enter the circle, each raises his arms to the Sacred Tree, saying a prayer. Those who have made the vow to suffer enter the circle in a solemn manner, their eagle-bone whistles hanging from their necks. Often these whistles are beautifully decorated with braids of porcupine quills wound around the stem, to which is also tied a sprig of fresh sage. Fastened to the whistle's tip is a white eagle plume, which is stirred by the dancer's breath whenever he blows on it. The sound of the whistle is a prayer for wisdom and a further understanding of the Creator. The men blow their whistles intermittently throughout the entire dance, in rhythm to the drum. And so the dance goes on for four long days.

Many years ago, the knives used for the piercing were made of buffalo bone. We splintered the leg bone of a buffalo and shaped it into a very sharp knife. We also used bone skewers and well-cleaned and polished eagle claws. Around the turn of the century, awls were the preferred instrument. Up to a short while ago, medicine men used ordinary pocket knives. My father's special jackknife, which he used for piercing, had the blade honed to a point.

A dancer can choose the one who will pierce him, but Crow Dog and I do most of it. In 1979, it was Leonard Crow Dog who showed me how to pierce. He was doing it to one man right in front of me, saying, "Look, you do it like this. . . . " He ran his knife through so quickly that the dancer felt no pain. "Of course," he went on, "that's the way your father did it. And you'll do it the same way. Now you know how." Crow Dog had watched my father piercing many times, but I had never seen it.

Leonard then showed me his way of piercing, which was different. Some medicine men would take the flesh and skin of the chest, above the nipple, between their teeth and bite down hard. This was supposed to make the spot numb so that there wouldn't be much pain.

But they also did this for a more important reason. Back in 1965, I asked my father, "Why do you have to bite a man before you pierce him?"

He told me, "You got to know where the blood vessels are. If you grab one with your fingers, you can feel it. Then you bite down on it. This makes the vein underneath very flexible, and it goes back against the flesh. After that, all you have in your hand is the skin and part of the sinew. That's what you pierce. In this way, you miss the vein altogether, but you must know exactly what you are doing." I have never pierced a man who continued to bleed, but I have stopped a lot of bleeding when someone was badly pierced.

Most dancers are pierced while lying on their backs, but some prefer to have it done standing up. Some specify that the skewers should be carved of chokecherry wood. A rope made into a Y-shape with loops will be attached to these skewers; the other end of the rope is attached to the Sacred Tree. After the dance, the skewers may be given to friends to use as pipe tampers.

Dancers choose one of several different ways in which they want to be pierced. The most common is to be pierced in two places on the chest above the nipples. These men dance three times back from the Sacred Tree until the flesh is stretched far out, almost to the breaking point, then tear themselves free on the fourth try.

Others have made a vow to drag buffalo skulls. In that case, the skewers are inserted in two places in the flesh of the back and then connected with cords to the skulls. A man may choose to pull two, eight, or even twelve skulls. In 1991, we used a large buffalo hide, fur side up, upon which we placed the skulls, tying the cords to the hide rather than to the skulls. This load was very heavy to pull, and some dancers had to use a heavy staff, planting it into the ground to help pull themselves slowly forward. This is a very hard way and takes a strong belief in the mystery of the Wiwanyank Wacipi. Here, too, the dancer uses the sacred number and goes around the circle four times.

Sometimes, when a man dancing with buffalo skulls is completely exhausted, his friends will grab him under the arms and help pull him along. Sometimes small children from the dancer's family are made to sit on the skulls to make the load heavier. This makes it easier for the dancer to free free himself. Often the skewers are so deeply embedded that a dancer's friend may even have to make cuts in his flesh to make it easier for him to break loose.

Still others have made a vow to hang from the Tree of Life. They, too, are pierced in two places on the back. Cords attached to the skewers are thrown over the crossbar, high up on the Tree, and then connected to a horse that has been brought in close. The rider then moves his animal for a short distance, thereby slowly hoisting the dancer aloft. There are usually two riders, which means two dancers are suspended at one time.

A heavy man has it easier than a skinny one, because he will break free and fall to the ground in a shorter time. If a dancer hangs too long, the rider, making his horse quickly trot to and from the Sacred Tree, jerks the dancer around so that he breaks free. If this does not do it, friends simply grab the man by the legs and pull him down. I have seen men hanging from the Sacred Tree for up to two hours.

It takes a very brave man to dance "standing tied." Such a man stands upright between four poles. He is pierced in four places, two in the chest and two in the back. Cords connect the skewers to the four poles. The cords are short, leaving the dancer little room to move. While other dancers can jump or run backwards to tear themselves loose, the one who is "standing tied" has to work himself free slowly and painfully. I have seen a young *winkte* do this. He was swaying to and fro for over an hour, gracefully— like a ballet dancer—with an otherworldly smile on his face.

The most severe form of piercing was endured by some men during the 1991 Sundance. They pierced on the first day. They "danced with the Sacred Tree"—that is, they pulled so hard in rhythm to the drum that you could actually see the top of the tree sway. They were careful to get near the breaking point without actually pulling themselves free. In the evening, they took the thongs off the skewers but left the wooden sticks in their chests. In this way, they spent the night on the Sundance ground, never leaving the sacred circle. The next day, they reconnected their skewers to the Sacred Tree and danced in one spot from dawn to dusk. This they did for four long days until, at the end of the last day, they finally pulled themselves free.

Whether a dancer suffers much, little, or not at all depends on many things: his state of mind; the strength of his belief in Wakan Tanka; the ecstasy that overcomes the agony; and *wi-ihanbla*, or "sun-dreaming"— that is, receiving a vision and being in a trance.

A ten-year-old boy told me, "Uncle, pierce me deep." I did as he wished, but he felt no pain. I know one dancer who normally cannot stand the sight of blood. He faints and actually keels over whenever he sees a hypodermic needle. But at the Sundance he does not even blink when the skewers are inserted. Another young man told me, "Uncle, I was in another beautiful world. I was not even aware of tearing myself loose. I felt no pain, only great joy!" Some do not even feel my knife going in. It is all part of the great mystery of the dance.

Just as a sundancer sometimes experiences the pain of his wife in labor, so it sometimes hurts a woman when her man is being pierced. And nowadays, some women also suffer the pain of the Sundance more directly. The first woman I pierced was a widow with four children. She came to me and said, "I want to be pierced. There is no man in my home. I want to set an example for my children." I pierced her on the upper arms, on each side. She pierced for four years running, as is the custom. Now her sons are teenagers, and they also sundance.

For some years, women were pierced only on the arms and wrists. When women come in long dresses and sleeves, we cut the cloth and then pierce them. From 1977 on, some women began to pierce at the collar bones.

Some years ago, at Big Mountain, Mary Brave Bird, who at that time was married to Crow Dog, was pierced in four places, in front and back. The cords leading from the skewers were attached to four horses, which at the proper moment were "fanned off" to the Four Directions. The next year, she was hanging from the Sacred Tree. One of the two skewers in her back tore through, and she spun wildly, suspended at one side only. "I didn't mind," she told me. "I was busy having a beautiful vision."

Whenever a man or woman pulls free, all the women watching from the arbor make what some people call "the *li-li-li* sound," the high-pitched, ululating sound that makes the hairs on your back stand up. The dancer then runs once around the circle, together with all the friends and relatives who have supported him during the ordeal.

Many of the nondancers will come to the Sacred Tree to pray and make a flesh offering. Tiny pieces of skin, from twenty to a hundred, are cut from their upper arms. My teenage daughter, Josephine, made such an offering, the cuts on her arm forming a circle.

It is our custom to include the children in all our ceremonies. Little girls are brought to the dance ground to have their ears pierced by a medicine man. My father performed this task many times. In the old days, this piercing was done with a sharp, pointed bone, but now we use awls. If a child is sick, the parents might make a vow to have its ears pierced to help it get well. Having this done during a Sundance also brings good luck. A little girl undergoing this ceremony is honored just like a grownup dancer who has pierced.

After the piercing, we seal the wound with sage or put tobacco on it. If you use tobacco, you have to use the right kind. It must be the purest tobacco you can find. You can also put a whole green leaf of tobacco on the wound; it purifies it and stops the bleeding. Don't use the packaged tobacco that comes in plastic bags; it has chemicals in it and does more harm than good. I knew one old *pejuta wichasha* who sealed wounds with a special soil taken from gopher holes.

It is thought that the sundancers, immediately after the ritual has ended, have a certain healing power to cure sicknesses. So after the Sundance, we ask those who want to be healed to come up to the dancers to pray with them and to be fanned with a feather or a sprig of sage. This is actually an exchange: the ones who are sick give their thanks and good feelings to the dancers, and the dancers in turn give back some of the strength and power they have at that special moment. Also, at some Sundances you will see a huge root shaped like a human being, with "arms" and "legs." This is a species of American ginseng that has healing power. After the dance, it is cut into small pieces and distributed to all who want it.

So many unusual things happened at the 1991 Sundance. For example, a woman went to the outhouse and found a huge rattlesnake with fourteen "buttons" on its tail crawling on the seat. It politely slithered off. During one night, there came the strange, ghostly cry of an animal that nobody had ever heard before. Also, for the first time ever, we had Old Glory waving from two poles at the East door.

I had mixed feelings about this. For generations, to us Indians the Stars and Stripes had meant oppression. White soldiers had carried that flag when they came to kill us; and we had used it, flown upside-down, as a sign of distress. Ghost dancers had wrapped themselves in such upside-down flags. And now it was waving over us, right side up. But I accepted it, because at this Sundance we flew it to honor the many Native Americans who had fought and died under it.

Besides myself, there was one other man at the dance who wore a bonnet: Chief Spotted Tail. He came and he pierced deeply. More than a hundred years ago, my brother Crow Dog's great-grandfather had shot and killed Spotted Tail, the head chief of the Rosebud Sioux tribe and this dancer's great-grandfather. As Leonard Crow Dog always said, "For four generations, this blood has been dripping on me. Only my children will be free of this burden." But here was today's Chief Spotted Tail, dancing at Crow Dog's place! We honored him, just as he honored us by his presence. I was moved by this, seeing it as one more proof that the Sundance is also a peace-making ceremony, creating friendship out of ancient enmity.

Heyokas also came to take part in the dance and be pierced. I am proud to have brought about their acceptance at our Wiwanyank Wacipi and to have made them welcome. One of these contraries came dressed like an old woman in a black wraparound and brown skirt, his face shrouded so that one could not see it. He pierced and then suddenly vanished, as if the Earth had swallowed him up. One *heyoka* came in from the West. Half his body was painted white, the other half black, and he was covered with hailstone designs. After piercing, he went into a sweatlodge and just disappeared. One half-Indian, half-Hispanic contrary came in a strange outfit with a feather headdress and a multicolored skirt. He danced in a grotesque way and later hung suspended from the Sacred Tree, waving an eagle feather. Afterward, he went to the loudspeaker at the drum and said a long prayer in both English and Spanish.

In the pause between rounds, everybody has the privilege to come to the drum and say something. Once, during such a pause, I heard a voice over the loudspeaker: "Somebody has donated a cow. We need some guy who can shoot a cow, a guy who can knock her on the head, a guy who knows butchering." Another time, a man was making a plea in Lakota and then in English: "Pray for the sick, for those who suffer from cancer or AIDS. Put yourself in their shoes, in their minds. You'll be better men for it." When I heard this, I got a lump in my throat because it truly expressed the spirit of this dance.

I was even more touched when some singers intoned "*Tahcha Ushte Wiwang Wachielo*," the "Song of Lame Deer," my father's song. I was also moved when a Mapuche Indian, all the way from southern Chile, said, "I take the power of this dance home with me to my people." Likewise when an Onondaga from upstate New York told the dancers, "There is truth in this sacred ceremony."

My son John, who was sixteen in 1991, has been sundancing since he was five years old. For the big yearly Rosebud Powwow, my wife and I spent a whole year putting together our son's first powwow regalia, including his feather bustle and headdress. The headpiece is called a "roach" and is made out of porcupine. It was a great outfit, and John loved dressing in it when we came to the powwow.

At that powwow, John watched a little boy who was dancing in tennis shoes and Levi's, naked from the waist up. The kid had no dance outfit. John, five years old at the time, kept staring at the boy. Suddenly I heard my name called from the announcer's stand. They wanted me to come up there. I did, and by the loudspeaker was my son and this other little kid. John said, "Dad, I want to give my outfit to this boy, because he doesn't have an outfit to dance with. I don't think I should dance in a powwow when I am a sundancer. I want him to have my outfit, because I have my Sundance skirt and Pipe and everything."

We listen to our children, even if they are only five years old. I was proud that my son had already caught the spirit of the Sundance. As long as there are Lame Deers, there will be a Sundance, and as long as there is a Sundance, there will be Lame Deers. Crow Dog's son, Pedro, has also been sundancing from childhood and is already running ceremonies. And at every Wiwanyank Wachipi, we see boys of eight or ten piercing so that our ceremonies and beliefs will live forever.

It is indescribably beautiful and heartwarming to see 150 men dancing in long red skirts, waving their eagle wings, moving in rhythm as one body. It is just as though a centuries-old painting has come to life. It is both heartwarming and heartbreaking to see so many women sundancing. Women will do this because of very heavy family problems or because there is no man in the family who can (or will) do it.

When it is over, all the nondancers form a long line, and all the dancers who have pierced walk along it, and they all shake hands with each other. The Sundance unites us, makes us one. After we leave, the Sacred Tree with its flags and offerings is abandoned to the elements, just as the bodies of our warriors were left on their funeral scaffolds to the sun, the winds, and the birds. But their ghosts, and the ghosts of the Sacred Trees of times past, are still with us. As long as we dance, we will survive as a people and the nation will live.

Tunkashila, hoye wayinkte.	Grandfather, a voice I will send.
Namahon yelo	Hear me!
Maka sitomniyan	All over the universe,
Hoye wayinkte.	A voice I am sending.
Mitakuye obwaniktelo.	With my relatives I shall live.
Epelo.	I am saying this.

CHAPTER 20

Taku Wakan

Taku Wakan means "Something Holy," "Something Mysterious." The sacred world of our Lakota people, the world of God and the Supernaturals, is Taku Wakan. At the head of cosmic existence stands the Creator, Wakan Tanka, literally the "Great Mystery." We also call the Creator Tunkashila, the "Grandfather Spirit." Wakan Tanka is the Everywhere Spirit. He has no form. He is not shaped like a human being, and humans are not made in Wakan Tanka's image, as in the Christian Bible. He is like the air we breathe—invisible.

Wakan Tanka never rests. He is always moving. He is all pervasive. His power dwells in everything that lives. I remember being in the mission school at St. Francis, and the priest who taught us said, "God created the world in six days, and on the seventh day he rested." I knew better. I thought, "What kind of lazy, laid-back fellow is that Christian God? What is he doing resting?"

Also, my grandfather had taught me that Creation has no beginning and no end. Wakan Tanka never stops creating. He created the Wakanpi, the "Sacred Ones," the "Sixteen Great Mysteries" or supernatural spirits that some white anthropologists refer to as "gods" or "godlikes." Some of our elders say that Wakan Tanka is not perfect, because nothing in the universe is or should be perfect—not even the Christian God or Jesus.

Wakan Tanka made a big mistake when he created the fifteenth of the Great Mysteries—Sichun, "the Intellect." *Sichun* also means "power" because, in a way, intellect and power are the same. Intellect was given to man and was misused. This is why the world is in such sorry shape. But everything is negative as well as positive; this duality is central to our beliefs.

The Sixteen Great Mysteries are all different aspects of the Creator, because, as my grandfather used to say, "Wakan Tanka is like sixteen different persons." Christians who believe in the Holy Trinity should have no trouble with this concept. Wakan Tanka is the sun, the sky, the rock, a brook, or a tiny flower. To speak about the Creator and his Great Mysteries, a man should be a *wichasha wakan*, a spiritual man who speaks the sacred and secret language of Hanbloglaka, whose words come from the dream world. He must see with the eye of the spirit rather than with the two eyes in his head. He should speak "through the Pipe"—that is, nothing but the truth. To make all this easier to understand, I have made a chart of what

(handwritten margin notes: "duality central to beliefs", "16 great mysteries all are God")

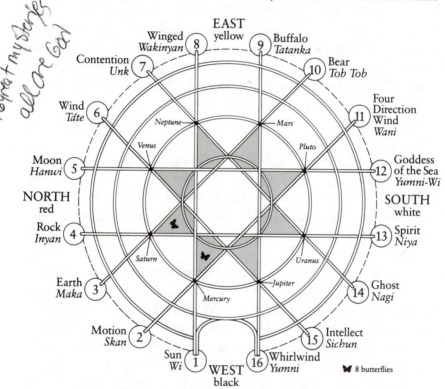

The Sixteen Great Mysteries. *These spirits are all contained within the universe of the the sweatlodge, whose intersecting willow loops form an eight-pointed star.*

you might call the Lakota cosmology, a "map" of the Sixteen Great Mysteries.

These Sixteen Supernaturals are divided into four Superiors or Chief Mysteries called *Wakan Akantu* (in our language meaning "the Highest"); four Associates or *Wakan Kolaya*—that is, "Spirit Friends"; four Subordinates called *Wakan Kuya* or "Lesser Mysteries"; and four Inferiors called *Wakanlapi*, those who are "Like Something Sacred."

The Universe created itself. Wakan Tanka created himself; then he created the Sixteen Great Mysteries. First and foremost, he made Wi, the Sun. Wi is the Great Life Giver, the Light Bringer, the Heat Provider without whom the Earth would be only a great lump of icy rock, "bald and without hair"—that is, without our green relatives, the plants. Wi stands for courage and generosity. We pray to the Sun, the blinding orb around which our Earth revolves. We dance in Wi's honor. And yet, though Wi is the first and mightiest among the Great Mysteries, he derives his power to transmit heat and light from Taku Skanskan, the "Power That Moves Everything," which propels him along his designated path. So Wi is powerful, indeed, but not all-powerful. And Wakan Tanka created Hanhepi Wi, the "Night Sun," or Moon, as a wife for Wi.

Taku Skanskan, or "Skan" for short, comes second after Wi. He is Motion. He is the "Power That Moves Everything." He is energy personified, a force that moves things magically. Taku Skanskan quickens the seed in plants, animals, and humans. Some old people say that Skan stands at the edge of the world showing the spirits of the dead the way over the Spirit Trail to the spirit world. It is said that Skan gives the newborn its first gasp of breath. He causes the arrow to fly and the waters to flow. Skan is also thought to be the sky because his color is blue. Sometimes the powers we call Wakan Tanka, Wi, and Skan seem to be interchangeable so that it is hard for us poor humans to tell which is which. Skan teaches us that in the universe nothing is immobile, that there is motion even within a rock.

The third Superior is Maka, the Earth, the "All-Mother" whom we also call Unchi or Grandmother. She is the great nourisher who feeds all—who makes the plants, trees, and corn grow. From her breasts flow all the things we need in order to live. She is the good red Earth of the Indian nation, at the heart of which stands the Turtle Continent, the home of all Native

Americans. She covers our planet with her "green hair"—the trees, plants, herbs, and grasses. Unchi hugs us to her bosom, teaching us the secret knowledge of how to save this planet. We would share this knowledge with all the world, if only the world would listen!

Together with the Sun, the Moon, and the sky, Unchi-Maka represents roundness—the Sacred Hoop, the Circle Without End, the womb, the belly of a woman big with child, the pot full of water, the ball used in the Ball-Throwing ceremony.

We believe that we humans are merely caretakers of the Earth; that we must revere her and leave her unharmed as we pass her on to future generations. We do not believe that the Earth belongs to humans; we believe that we belong to the Earth. We believe that Grandmother Earth is one and indivisible; that she is there for all and cannot be owned or sold in little pieces. That is why we resisted being put onto reservations and made into farmers.

The Earth is full of sacred places in which dwell unseen powers. Our little dome-shaped sweatlodge represents the Earth as well as the whole universe. The little sacred earth mound outside the sweatlodge stands for Unchi, the Grandmother. We use earth altars during the Sundance, the Yuwipi, and other ceremonies. When swearing to tell the truth, we touch the Earth to be a witness. Should we lie (so our elders taught us), our horse will stumble and throw us.

The ghost dancers of a hundred years ago thought that by performing the Ghost Dance and singing certain songs taught to them by Wovoka, a Paiute shaman and prophet, they could roll up the white man's earth like a carpet, together with its stinking factories, artificially bred pigs and chickens, and barbed wire and telegraph poles. They believed that underneath this rolled-up mass of spoiled soil would reappear the good red world of the Indian—a world alive once more with herds of buffalo, teeming with game of all kinds, and covered with tipis inhabited by people who had been killed by white soldiers. This dream was shattered at Wounded Knee, where hundreds of our men, women, and children were massacred by the Seventh Cavalry, Custer's old regiment.

The fourth of these Superiors is Inyan, the Rock. Inyan represents the everlasting nature of the Creator. As one of our proverbs has it, "Only the stones last forever; men must die." An older word for the Rock is "Tunka," one of the shapes it has pleased Wakan Tanka to assume. Therefore, we also address the Creator as Tunkashila, or "Grandfather." Tunka knows all secrets and finds that which is lost. Inyan is the "All-Father Spirit." All stones are alive and hold within them secret powers. Certain rocks can penetrate the shadows of a person's thoughts. Amethyst, for example, will enter the right or spiritual part of the brain, while transparent crystal works on the left side, influencing thoughts about science, technology, and religion.

Inyan, or Tunka, plays a major part in our most sacred ceremonies. This spirit is present in the hot, purifying rocks of the sweatlodge, in the "finding rocks" of the Yuwipi, and in the tiny crystals gathered from anthills that speak to us from within the gourd rattles used in many of our rituals. Perfectly round stones are used in many of our individual medicine bags as protective charms to ward off evil. As I mentioned, Crazy Horse carried a magic pebble behind his ear to make himself bulletproof. One of the gifts White Buffalo Woman brought to the Sioux nation was a round, bright red rock upon which were engraved seven circles, representing the Seven Sacred Rituals of our people.

I interrupt the story here for a moment to talk about the fact that there is magic and mystery also in the Lakota language. *Winyan*, for instance, our word for "woman," is a combination of the words *wi* (sun) and *inyan* (rock), indicating the connection between woman, sun, moon (*hanwi*), and rock. *Wakinyan* (literally, "sacred rock") is our term for the Great Thunderbird. *Ikche Wichasha* (literally, "natural man of the Earth"), our old term for the Sioux people, combines the word for "natural" with the word for "man." Actually, *Ikche Wichasha* contains five different Lakota words: those for "natural," "penis," "sun," "step," and "red." You can read all kinds of meanings into this.

Or take *Wasichun (Sichun)*, the sacred power of the intellect. Oddly enough, we use the same word for the "fat taker," the greedy white man. One could philosophize that this is no coincidence but a combination of both the intellect and the white man's negative natures. I spend much time pondering the subtle, hidden meanings of Lakota words and phrases.

Next come the four Associate Spirits. First is the Moon, Hanwi, which literally means "Night Sun." Hanwi waxes and wanes, symbolizing that everything living is born, grows, and dies. Hanwi is a woman, the wife of Wi, the far-shining Sun. She lights up the night. She sees all that happens on Earth. Hanwi is the Supernatural of women. As some of our elders say,

Hanwi is connected to every woman and every female four-legged by a "magical, invisible umbilical cord." She controls a woman's monthly flow.

When a woman menstruates, we say that she is "on her moon." At this time, a woman is magically strong—"in the moon power," as we say. This power is so strong that it temporarily wipes out a medicine man's power. Our old people used to say that if a woman tans a bearskin while menstruating, she will take on the disposition of a bear, at least for a short time. Also, as I mentioned, a girl who is becoming a woman should wrap up her first moon flow and place it in the crotch of a tree. She may then experience a great vision.

The second Associate Spirit is Táte, the Wind. Táte is the Sun's younger brother. He always was and always will be. His tipi stands at the end of the world, in the Land of Wasichunpi, the region of northern lights. He controls the seasons and watches over the Wanagi Tachanku, the Ghost Trail, which leads to the spirit land. Táte has four sons, the Winds of the Four Directions. There is also a fifth, small and puny son, but this one might not be Táte's child. Táte's wife Ite (the name simply means "face") is one of the most beautiful women in the world.

The third Associate Spirit is Unk, Contention, the Father of Evil. Unk is the negative aspect of Wakinyan, the Thunderbeing. He is known as the One who Kills and can change men into beasts. The Creator punished Unk for his evil ways by turning him into Unktehi, the Great Water Monster. He has four legs and a great horn, which he can draw into his head or stretch out into the clouds. He also has long, mosslike hair and a powerful tail. He lives in dark lakes and swamps. His power rests in his huge tail, which he uses to kill all who get in his way.

People encounter Unktehi in their nightmares. It is said that this monster loves dog meat and that, if you throw him a white dog, he will devour it, giving you a chance to escape. The female Water Monster is called Uncegila. If a powerful spirit could manage to cut their tails off, it would render both Unktehi and Uncegila helpless. Strewn all across the Badlands of South Dakota lie the huge bones of long-extinct animals. Some of the old folks say these are the bones of Unktehi.

The fourth Associate Supernatural is Wakinyan, the Thunderbird. He stands where the sun rises. His voice is thunder, and the light of his eyes turns into lightning. Wakinyan sometimes lives inside a rock. He is the spirit who creates electrical energy. He wears a robe of clouds and engages in eternal combat with Unktehi. Each interaction of Wakinyan's thunder power on the ocean surface creates a wave. Each of these "frictions" creates so much energy that it is sufficient to light up all the light bulbs on this Earth.

Wakinyan sits on a gigantic nest of dry bones containing an enormous egg out of which young Thunderbirds continuously hatch. He swallows his young, and they all turn into so many of Wakinyan's selves. His symbol is that of forked lightning, representing the positive and the negative powers of lightning. Those who dream of Wakinyan, or any of his several attributes, thereby become *heyokas*—upside-down "contraries."

The first of the four Subordinate Powers is Tatanka, the Buffalo Spirit. Tatanka is not just an animal; he is a holy spirit, the Indian's brother, the giver of health, food, and life. We Sioux consider ourselves part of the Tatanka Oyate, the Buffalo Nation, so closely are we connected to this wonderful Supernatural. Tatanka means "that which reaches highest; that which excels."

The buffalo skull is *lila wakan*, "very sacred," an altar to pray to and to pray with. A certain part of Tatanka's shoulder meat represents the universe. That is hard to understand. The image of a buffalo, cut from its hide, is suspended from the Sundance Tree, a symbol of the renewal of life.

The Buffalo Spirit is part of all our sacred rites. The ball used in the Tapa Wanka Yap, the young girl's Ball-Throwing ceremony, is made of buffalo hair covered with buffalo skin. According to our legends, when the white man began to exterminate the buffalo herds, which once covered the prairie by the millions, the survivors vanished into a big cave in the side of a great mountain. Our prophecies say they will one day return.

The second Subordinate Spirit is Tob Tob, the Bear, the wisest of all spirits. Tob Tob created the four-legged beings. He is Great Medicine, the Healer of Wounds who teaches medicine men the secret language of the shaman. Tob Tob, also known as Mato, stands for love and bravery. As I mentioned earlier, there are very few Bear doctors left. Such doctors, when on the job, used to cover themselves with bear skins. They cleaned wounds with bear claws and were also skilled at setting broken bones. At a recent Sundance, some of the dancers were given bear meat to make them strong.

The third Subordinate is Wani, the Four-Direction Wind. Wani is the energizer and weather maker. He represents the power of the Four Sacred Directions. He is a messenger from the Holy Ones.

The fourth Subordinate is Yumni-Wi, the Goddess of the Sea. She is also the goddess of love, sports, and games. Yumni-Wi, representing the power of the feminine, is a very important spirit whose presence is necessary to restore balance in the world.

The first of the four Inferior Spirits is Niya, which literally means "the Spirit." Niya is the personification of life, sometimes called the Breath of Life. He is a person's essence, one of the four souls who dwell in every human being. Niya leaves the body after its death. He is a guardian spirit who can talk to humans and who gives a newborn baby its first breath.

The second Inferior is Nagi. In one sense, the word *nagi* can be used in the same way white people use "ghost," as a roaming spirit of the dead. My father knew the ghost song of a man who jilted and betrayed the girl who loved him and who, after he was killed in battle, was condemned to roam over the prairie, haunting campsites and singing his eery, mournful song. As a Supernatural, however, Nagi is one of a person's four souls. He is a presence. He is inside an animal, a stone, a tree, or a stream.

A human's ghost is called "Wicha Nagi," while a four-legged's ghost is called "Wamaka Nagi." Nagi is the shadow of everyone and everything. He is the spirit that goes with a man into the spirit world. Nagi never dies. A man knows what he sees with his own eyes, while Nagi knows what has been and what will be. Whenever we sit down, we put aside a few morsels of food for the Nagipi, the ghosts of our departed friends and relations. It is thought that the incense of sage and sweetgrass is pleasing to the ghosts. Nagi can cause men and animals to talk to each other.

In the old days, when a beloved child died, the grieving parents often decided to keep its soul, its *nagi*, with them for a number of months, usually a year. In that case, a ceremony called Wanagi Yuhapi, or "Soul Keeping," was performed. A bundle was made, containing a braid of sweetgrass, a lock of hair from the dead child, and some other small object connected with it, wrapped in red cloth and buckskin. The bundle was dressed in clothes, like a doll, and kept in a little ghost tipi.

The bundle was lovingly cared for in a ritually prescribed way, and the child's nagi was regularly fed. The dead little one's soul resided in this doll-like bundle. After the proper time of soul keeping had elapsed, the child's *nagi* was finally released in a solemn ceremony—free to go to the spirit world.

The third Inferior is Sichun, "the Intellect," an innate power dwelling inside every man or woman and one of a person's four souls. Sichun embodies knowledge and a special power given to every newborn child by the Supernaturals. It is a power to guard against evil, but, like everything else, it has both a positive and a negative nature.

The fourth Inferior, and the last of the Sixteen Great Mysteries, is Yumni. Yumni is all that is immaterial—the orphan who was never born, the swirling air, the little whirlwind, the impish messenger of the Supernaturals.

There are four-times-four sacred things and symbols that complement the Sixteen Great Mysteries: four bird skins—the eagle, the swan, the red-tailed hawk, and the red-headed woodpecker; four animal skins—the buffalo, the blacktailed deer, the mole, and the badger; four roots or herbs—smartweed, licorice, snakeroot, and prairie-dog weed (for cramps, influenza, poor appetite, and asthma); and rocks of four different colors—red, black, yellow, and white.

There are eight Supernaturals who represent the Negative Powers. As I mentioned, Anung Ite, the Two-Faced Woman, is incredibly beautiful and horribly ugly at the same time. The daughter of Waziya, the Wizard, and Kanka, the Old Woman Witch, Anung Ite is both cunning and malicious. She is a temptress who can hide herself anywhere—even in a gopher hole—and who can hear people whispering from a mile away. She loves to scare pregnant women and cause painful menstrual cramps. "Two-Face" incites strife and is gossip in the shape of a woman. Smoke from burning cottonwood branches will drive her away.

Also as mentioned, Iktomi is the wicked trickster, Spiderman. He is the smartass who often outsmarts himself, the glutton, the ever-horny woman chaser, the player of practical jokes. Iktomi has a dual nature, being at the same time powerful and weak, proud and humble, smart and stupid, good and evil, young and old. Iktomi can transform himself at will into human, animal, or plant, but he usually appears in the shape of a spider.

Kanka is the Old Woman Spirit, a witch who taught useful things to pre-human beings who lived underground before they emerged into the above-ground world to become real people. Kanka is the wife of the Old Man Wizard of the North. She is a prophet who foresees the future. But don't imagine Kanka as a white man's Halloween witch riding on a broom; the Indian idea of "witch" is very different from a fairy-tale white man's witch.

Ksa is the Water Goddess, wisdom turned into negative cleverness. Some people say that Ksa is just another different shape that Yum was pleased to assume. Some legends also have it that Ksa was hatched in a mysterious way from a Thunderbird egg.

Wazi, or Waziya, is the Wizard, the Sorcerer. Wazi brings cold and death. His bone-chilling breath turns into Yata, the North Wind, who freezes the marrow in people's bones. He walks around in a robe made of wolf skin. When a man is stingy, we call him a *waziya*. The missionaries made Wazi into Santa Claus, which shows their ignorance.

The other three Negative Powers are Tob Tob, the Bear; Táte, the Wind; and Yumni, the Whirlwind. These I have already described when talking about the Sixteen Great Mysteries. All these Supernatural spirits resemble the Greek gods of ancient mythology because they behave in many ways like human beings.

Wakan Tanka, the Creator, the Great Mystery who is timeless, envisioned the universe into existence. It took eons of time for the universe, the Supernaturals, the Earth, and the humans on it to evolve and assume their final shapes.

At first, all was immaterial and invisible, drifting in endless space. During the first stage of world making, Wakan Tanka created Wi, Skan, Maka, and Inyan—the Sun, the Power of Motion, the Earth, and the Rock. (I realize that these English words do not convey the spiritual meanings of these names, but I have to use the words that are available to me. English is a poor language when it comes to talking about mysteries.) The Grandfather Spirit created the Sun first and the everlasting Rock last. With that, the first phase of world making was accomplished.

The four Superiors were given the power to be creators in turn. After an interval of uncountable years, the second phase began. Wi, the Sun, created Hanwi, the Moon, to be his wife. Skan, the Motion Power, created Táte, the Wind, who is himself a motion giver. Maka, the Earth, created Unk, who is Contention and Passion personified—both the passion between man and woman and the many kinds of passion we have in our lives.

Inyan, the Rock, created Wakinyan, the Great Thunderbeing, the Winged One who controls lightning and electricity. In this way, the four Associate Supernaturals came into being, and that concluded the second phase of Creation.

After another eon of time, during the third phase, the Associates helped to bring the four Subordinates into being: Tatanka, the Buffalo Spirit; Tob Tob, the Bear Power; Wani, the Wind of the Four Directions; and Yumni-Wi, the Goddess of the Sea. This does not mean that the Buffalo and the Bear were created materially, like the buffalo and bears we see in zoos. They existed at first as noncorporeal spirits. One could say that in the beginning, they existed as thoughts in Wakan Tanka's mind.

During the fourth and final phase of Creation, the four Lesser Powers came into being. These were the "Without Body Spirits" who were (and forever remained) invisible and untouchable: Niya, the Spirit; Nagi, the Ghost; Sichun, the Intellect; and Yumni, The Whirlwind. These spectral powers made their presence felt in many mysterious ways, even though they were immaterial "mind dwellers."

Now Wazi, the Old Wizard, and Kanka, the Old Witch, had a daughter called Ite, or Face, because hers was the most beautiful face in the world. She was given to Táte, the Wind, to be his wife. Ite bore her husband four sons: Yata, the North Wind, a cruel, ill-tempered giant; Eya, the West Wind, a giant seen only in visions; Yanpa, the East Wind, who lives on an island resting on a bed made of duckdown and goosedown; and Okaga, the South Wind, a friendly, life- and warmth-giving power.

Actually, these four Supernaturals are quadruplets, but they emerged into the world in the order indicated here. Because Yata was such an unpleasant, quarrelsome son, Táte took his birthright away and gave it to Eya, the second son. Therefore, in the order of the Four Directions, the West comes first, followed by the North, the East, and the South. Seeing Eya put ahead of him, Yata wept with rage.

Old Man Waziya and Old Woman Kanka still lived underground beneath the Earth's surface. They were jealous of the higher powers, the Sixteen Great Mysteries. The Old Wizard and the Witch longed to obtain greater status and to sit among the Sixteen Great Supernaturals.

Iktomi, the evil Spiderman, always eager to cause mischief, saw here his opportunity to make trouble. "Why don't you use your daughter's beauty to advance your cause?" he asked Waziya and Kanka. "Ite is so much more beautiful than Hanwi, the Moon. Let Wi, the Great Sun, first among the mystery powers, just get a glimpse of Ite, and he will send Hanwi away and take up with your daughter."

Wazi and Kanka thought this was a very clever idea. If Wi, chief of all the Great Mysteries, would take Ite as his consort, then surely their daughter could use her wiles to induce him to elevate her parents in rank. When they told Ite of their evil plans, she was willing to go along with them, even though she was already married and the mother of four sons.

So Wi gave a great feast to all the other fifteen Supernaturals. While the feast was being prepared, and before the guests arrived, Iktomi managed to smuggle Ite into Wi's tipi. And before anybody could stop her, she took Hanwi's (the Moon's) seat beside the Great Sun. Wi was smitten by Ite's beauty and had eyes only for her. Unk (Contention) now saw his chance to do evil by magically arousing passion for the beautiful temptress in Wi's heart. When Hanwi arrived upon the scene, she saw that her place next to the Sun was occupied by another, and she hid her face. Iktomi laughed at her, and so did Wazi and Kanka. Hanwi cried for shame.

Ite became pregnant and gave birth to her fifth son. Because this son was conceived in adultery, he was born unnaturally and prematurely. He was named Yumni, or Whirlwind. He turned into a puny, shriveled spirit, a little dust devil dancing along the road.

Skan was appointed to sit in judgment. Ite was punished by having her sons taken away and put in Táte's care. Skan struck Ite on one side of her face, and that side became ugly and horrible to look upon. The other half of Ite's face remained as beautiful as before. She was condemned to roam the Earth, shunned and friendless. Sometimes she tempts men with the beautiful side of her face; but when they embrace her, she lets them see the ugly half, making them flee in horror. She was henceforth known as Anung-Ite, the Two-Faced Woman.

Wi was punished by having Hanwi taken away from him. From then onward, Wi ruled the day and Hanwi the night. During daylight, whenever Hanwi comes too close to her former companion, she hides her face.

Wazi and Kanka were banished to the end of the world, wandering around its rim where there is nothing but icy cold and the howling of snowstorms. Kanka, however, was given the power to do good to those who deserve it while bringing misfortune to those who transgress against the Great Mysteries.

Unk was punished by being transformed into Unktehi, the Great Water Monster, to dwell in slime, mud, and morasses. Iktomi was chastised by being hated by all the Supernaturals, but he said he did not care. And that was the end of this phase of Creation. What had been immaterial had been made material, and Maka, the Earth, took on her present shape and body.

At first, Maka was without water. Táte gathered water out of space, the Water of Life, and blew it all over the Earth, thus creating oceans and huge lakes. But the Earth was cold and the waters froze. Then Wakan Tanka ordered Wi to give warmth to Maka, thereby creating conditions for life on Earth.

Everything in the universe moved, but Maka stood still. Earth remained rooted in her place. Then Skan put the Earth into motion so that she began to spin from left to right. Now all that Skan puts in motion turns from left to right—clockwise, as the white people say. And that is why we always enter and leave the sweatlodge from left to right, why we enter and leave a tipi that way, and why the Pipe goes around from hand to hand in the same way. Throughout all these eons upon eons, Wakan Tanka has kept on creating and recreating himself, appearing in all his various manifestations—the One in Many and the Many in One.

At one time, something shining fell through the smoke hole into the lodge of Táte, the Wind. It was a shooting star or a meteor that took on the shape of a young woman more beautiful than Ite had ever been. This woman had long, flowing, shiny black hair and delicate movements. But, unlike the Two-Faced One, she was pure and undefiled. This Supernatural was Wohpe, sent by her father, the Sky, to do great deeds.

Wohpe brought with her a never-empty sacred bundle, full of food fit for gods. And from out of this medicine bundle, amid the scent of sweetgrass, she offered food that Táte and his sons had never tasted before. Wohpe also made a splendid robe of buckskin for Táte to wear. She could do anything and everything. Táte and his sons stood in awe, watching her creating useful things never seen before out of nothing. Wohpe called Táte "Father" and Okaga, the benign South Wind, "Little Brother."

Okaga fell in love with Wohpe and played a flute she had made for him as a sign of his love. But Wohpe was a pure spirit whom neither god nor man could possess. And Táte and his sons realized that she was the gentle side of themselves, because every man and every woman has a masculine and a feminine nature. Wohpe was the goddess of love, of play, and of knowledge.

Under Wakan Tanka's instructions, the Sixteen Great Mysteries created plants and trees to cover the Earth. They also created the winged, the four-legged, and the crawling ones. At first, Wazi, Kanka, and Anung-Ite were the only humanlike beings on Earth, but finally, as the last act of Creation, Wakan Tanka made beings who walked upright on two legs and who were placed above all other living things.

At first, these upright walkers could still talk with the plants and other animals, but when Wakan Tanka gave them Sicun (Intellect), they became separated in mind and fact from their winged and four-legged relatives. An old man once told me, "I think the Creator made a mistake giving intellect to human beings, because they will only use it to destroy themselves." I never wanted to believe this, but as I contemplate the world today, it occurs to me that he might have been right.

The newly created people inquired of Wakan Tanka, "Will we live forever?" He answered, "You are just tiny parts of a circle within a circle within a circle within a circle, part of the Sacred Hoop that has no end. Life dies and renews itself forever and ever." With this answer they had to be content.

At first, the people did not know how to live. They were like the beasts in the field. They had no beliefs to cling to. Then Wohpe reinvented herself as White Buffalo Calf Woman and descended from the sky as a link from the Ones Above to the ones below, and she brought to the people the Sacred Pipe and the Seven Sacred Rites, and made them brothers to the buffalo, as I have already taught.

You may take all this as the naked truth or as a beautiful legend. But I tell you that whenever we purify ourselves in the right way and the Pipe goes around and Wakan Tanka's breath flows from its bowl, the Sixteen Great Mysteries will be with us inside the sweatlodge, and you will feel their presence. Sometimes they fill my whole being so that I want to cry.

When the Four Superior Powers instructed the Four Associates, they kept 10 percent of their secrets for themselves, and when the Four Associates taught the Subordinate Spirits, they withheld some of their knowledge. The

Subordinates did likewise when teaching the Inferior Spirits. So when the people received their knowledge from the Inferiors through White Buffalo Woman, they received only 60 percent of the sacred universal knowledge. And when I tell you about the wisdom that was given to me, I also must hold something back, because we never should reveal all.

And that is as it ought to be. The humble upright-walker should not be all knowing. We are already too smart for our own good—very clever but seldom wise. And that is all I have to tell. I have spoken.

E P I L O G U E

The World of Archie Fire

You might want to know what I am doing as the twentieth century nears its end. I am still running Sundances and ceremonies for my people. I make my living as a teacher of Indian culture—as the white man might put it, I am a lecturer.

I did not have any education that would enable me to "make it in the free-market world"; instead, I grew up in the great oral tradition of our people, and I am a good speaker. So I tell Indians and non-Indians about the beauty of the ancient Lakota way of life and religion. This is really the only thing I want to do. Clearing up misunderstandings and prejudices in this way, I believe I am doing a service to both Indians and non-Indians. I do a lot of my lecturing in Europe. I didn't plan it that way; it just happened.

Of course, these days there are many people on the lecture circuit. But there is one problem: many fake "Indian medicine men" and so-called "shamans" giving people like myself a bad name. Some of these lecturers are blond and blue-eyed but call themselves Sioux, Cherokee, or Seneca. Some claim to be reincarnations of Crazy Horse, Geronimo, or Tecumseh. They give themselves fancy names to impress their audiences: "Buffalo Grazing on the Mountainside," "Free Soul Soaring to the Sky," "Stands by the Water Straight as a Willow." When you come across such Hollywood names, watch out. One of these characters, during a TV interview, said, "Shit, man, I'm an Indian because I *say* I'm an Indian."

Real Indian names are not invented for publicity's sake. I was born in the middle of the night in the wintertime when the nights were short, so my mother gave me my child's name: Hanhepi Chikala, or "Little Night." This was the old way.

There are fake Indian "medicine women" and "princesses," too. Scores of these New Age "gurus" are coming out of the woodwork. None of them speak an Indian language. They could not run a ceremony on a reserva-

269

tion, but they impress the white people with weird rituals of their own invention. They are usually glib talkers. They wear fringed buckskin jackets and Stetson hats. They cover themselves with beads, feathers, and turquoise jewelry.

They have discovered that there is easy money in the phony medicine-man business, charging maybe three thousand dollars for an "Indian Wisdom Seminar" or a thousand bucks to participate in a sweat. One guy, claiming to be a member of a nonexistent tribe, teaches "sacred Indian sex" in group sessions at a nifty fee. Another will make you, in one weekend, into a "genuine Lakota medicine man," complete with a pretty, signed diploma, for a mere two thousand dollars.

Unfortunately, some *real* Indians are also doing this. As a result, many Native American spiritual men are often tarred with the same brush. I do not sell Indian religion. I am not paid for performing ceremonies. I am simply a lecturer on Native American culture and beliefs. I do so with a sense of the importance of my mission, but also with a sense of humor. Often I make fun of myself as well as my listeners. There is a time for everything—a time to be serious, a time for prayer, a time for jokes. I don't want adulation. I don't want to be put on a pedestal. I am not a guru or a maharishi. I don't walk on water. I call myself an "echo chamber," meaning that I try to be an instrument of the Creator.

Some of our younger medicine men are being spoiled by the white people's admiration. It goes to their heads. That's Iktomi business. I don't like people calling me "Chief" or "Mr. Shaman."

"How're you doing, Archie? That's how *I* want to be greeted. Some of these fake medicine men strut around wearing huge bonnets of colored turkey feathers. I do not wear a bonnet on my travels. If the Creator had wanted me to wear feathers, he would have made me a chicken or an eagle. I walk around in a pair of old Levi's, an ordinary shirt, and cowboy boots. In this respect, I am like my father, who often conducted Indian marriages and other ceremonies in an undershirt to show that a medicine man has to be humble, not putting himself above other people.

In the old days, a healer or *yuwipi* man was sometimes given a horse or a large chunk of buffalo meat for his services. I am paid for my lectures in dollars, marks, and francs. No horses or buffalo meat for me; I have to go to the supermarket for my groceries. I live in a modern house with all the usual conveniences, including a television set and an electric coffee maker. But the difference between myself and most white folks is that I still have the knowledge to survive without such things and can always solve my problems by going up to the mountaintop, crying for a dream. My father always told me, "Son, let the Earth be your bed and the clouds your blanket." He meant this to be my way of life, and my father lives in me.

Though I am broke most of the time, my life is rewarding and satisfying. My father's horizon was formed by the reservation. Mine encompasses the whole world. Always a strictly traditional Lakota *wichasha*, I find myself one among a growing number of spiritual teachers from many countries with many different beliefs. We all share the same goal—to save the white man from himself and thereby also save the native peoples of this world.

To give you just one example of what my tribe and I are up against, the Rosebud Tribal Council, against the will of our people, has signed a contract with a Connecticut firm to set aside five thousand acres as a dump for waste and garbage from around the nation. For a fee of one dollar per ton, the contract gives this firm the right to dump whatever kind of waste material they want on a still-unspoiled prairie not far from the mass grave at Wounded Knee—the grave where some 350 Lakota men, women, and children lie buried, massacred by American soldiers a hundred years ago. As one old man told me, "They'll dump the white man's shit on our sacred land." The same thing is happening on other reservations. Spiritual men throughout the world are fighting similar outrages in their own countries.

The white man is very clever, able to give birth to the most sophisticated technologies and weaponries, but he is so unwise that he is unable to control them. He is a helpless slave to the monster gadgets that are his proudest creations. He makes a billion-dollar spaceship, and the malfunction of ten cents' worth of rubber and wire sets him back on his heels while the Thunderbeings laugh at his follies. I try to bring the white people back to Earth, to respect the Grandmother who nourishes us all.

In Europe, I talk to all kinds of people—young folks from the Greenpeace movement, old members of the resistance, Jews, and repentant Nazis. I talk to workers, beggars, and whores, but also to generals, prime ministers, bishops, presidents, and the mayors of big cities. They are all the same to me. The poorer and humbler they are, the better I relate to them.

Big shots do not intimidate me. Once I had a discussion with the pope, and I was disappointed in him. Whenever he arrives at some place, he kneels down and pretends to kiss the Earth. But in reality he places a handkerchief on the tarmac and puts his face close to it. He does not want honest dirt to get on his lips. His is only a make-believe Earth kiss.

I wanted to talk to him about peace, the Earth, and the animals, but he was only interested in his church and his politics. I asked him to have a good, purifying Inipi with me to open our minds to each other, but he would not do it. Instead, he indicated that my audience with him was over and held out his hand with a big ruby ring for me to kiss. But now I was the one to refuse. We shook hands politely, and then I was on my way.

On the other hand, I was privileged to meet the Dalai Lama, who *did* go into a sweatlodge with me and whom I look upon as a friend. During the Inipi, I told him, "I am sorry to say it, but I just saw in my mind that you will be the last Dalai Lama."

"I have seen it, too," was his answer.

I first met the Dalai Lama near my former home in Santa Barbara. He sent for me, and a limousine picked me up. When I got to the place where he was staying, there were people fawning on him, kissing his feet—wealthy people, jet-setters in fancy evening dress, covered with jewels. The Dalai Lama was squirming with embarrassment. He came over to me and smiled. He made a gesture toward those "beautiful" people as if to say, "What can I do about it?"

I said, "Let's sneak out of here and hide in some quiet place." We did, and together we shared a hunk of bread and cheese. He smiled again and told me, "You must always rescue me from my friends." Since then our paths have crossed many times.

The Karmapa of Tibet was also my close friend. He is gone now to wherever departed Buddhists go. Maybe he attained nirvana. He gave me many precious insights, and I still mourn the loss of this holy man who meant so much to me.

I feel a special kinship with the Sami people (also known as the Laplanders) because they are so much like my own people. They, too, have a Purification ceremony, and they have tipis just like ours, which they call *kotahs*. After two thousand years of interbreeding, many Samis have light hair and light eyes, but still you can see their prominent cheekbones and Oriental features.

They gave me a feast of reindeer meat, which tasted very much like buffalo. We Sioux once were nomads, following the buffalo herds on which our survival depended. The Samis are still nomads, wandering with their reindeer herds from one grazing ground to the next.

The Samis also have medicine men just like ours, wise elders who know the uses of curing herbs. Instead of the Sacred Pipe, they have a magic drum with which they drum themselves into a trance or a vision. And when they sing, they sound just like us.

Their chief, Mickel Eiders, a good friend of mine, once gave me a big feast. It was a banquet of chiefs. Each of the Sami chiefs was about half my size, and I felt like a giant among them. They put a huge mess of reindeer meat before me, including racks of barbecued ribs. It seemed like a whole side of reindeer was looking at me. I split it in half and started eating.

One chief said something in the Sami language, and everybody laughed. Mickel translated for me: "He said that the Chief of the West eats like a Sami."

"No," I said, "the Chief of the East eats like a Sioux!"

Looking at these kindred folks in their beautiful blue-and-red costumes, I was overwhelmed by a great feeling of affection.

I love my Danish friends who introduced me to the Sami people, and I love Denmark. Denmark is a country without an army, where you can see the king pedaling through the streets on his bicycle. He is protected not by a swarm of Secret Service agents, but by the love of his people. I wish for a day when I will see an American president riding down Pennsylvania Avenue on his bike. That to me would mean that our country was finally becoming civilized.

I visited the mounds and ancient burial sites near Lemvig, on Jutland, made by pre-Christian people thousands of years ago. I performed a ceremony there and got good feelings from the Earth. On the humorous side, I went to a small town in Denmark, where I saw a gigantic statue of Sitting Bull constructed entirely of thousands upon thousands of little Lego blocks.

In 1990, I was asked by a Danish friend to introduce some buffalo into Denmark in order to start a herd there. So I bought one bull and seven cows—at six hundred dollars per cow and seven hundred for the bull. We got them to Chicago with horse trailers and then flew them out with a huge Lufthansa plane. My friend accompanied them all the way.

They made a stop at Frankfurt. There, he wanted to transfer the buffalo to a smaller plane, because the airport at Aarhus, in Denmark, was not set up for jumbo jets. He was informed that the buffalo would have to be quarantined at two thousand dollars a day per animal because "they might be diseased."

"As soon as they touch German soil," he was told, "those buffalo will be seized."

"OK," he said, "I will transfer them by crane to the smaller plane so that their hooves won't touch your damn tarmac."

"Oh, no, you won't," they said. "As soon as they leave that plane, into quarantine they go."

My friend told the pilot, "Fly on to Denmark!" And he did. Of course, the Aarhus airport couldn't accommodate the big 747. The plane overshot the runway, landing in a mudbank beside the Baltic Sea. The pilot had to climb out of the cockpit and fell down a ladder and sprained his ankles. They also had to cut the plane open with acetylene torches to get the buffalo out. One cow had died, but one calf had been born on the way.

Our little herd was put on 350 acres of land, where they could roam around, and I held a ceremony there. Since then, more calves have been born, so there are now thirteen buffalo there instead of eight. My friend who arranged all this would have been totally impoverished, because the costs of his mishaps were enormous. But the Danish crown prince picked up the tab and promised to visit me during his next trip to the states.

Another of my Danish friends has founded an Eskimo theater company. He introduced me to the members of his group, Inuit people from Greenland. These "Keepers of the North Gate" were young, high-spirited, and full of laughter. They performed wonderful masked dances, and we instantly took to each other.

As previously mentioned, I found out that the Inuit have a ceremony much like our Lakota Yuwipi, in which a medicine man is wrapped up in a fur blanket tied around with rope. When the lamps are lit at the end of the ritual, he appears untied and relates what the spirits have told him.

Once I went to Stonehenge, in England. There, among the sacred megaliths, I participated in a ritual performed by four white-clad Druids, old men speaking an almost extinct Celtic language. They did not utter one word in English, but somehow we communicated. Among them was still alive the knowledge of sacred rocks and of a god or spirit within the stone—the god we Sioux call "Tunka," who was there before all else.

The ancient Celtic people received visions of plants and animals and observed the movements of planets and stars. They were among the first victims of Christianity. So here was a mutual recognition of ancient beliefs held in common, of meeting up with something you have always known in your dreams.

Afterward, French Druids came from Brittany to meet me. They also spoke a half-forgotten language, different from French but similar to the speech of Welsh Druids. They asked me to take part in their spring equinox rituals among rows of huge, upright, star-oriented rocks called menhirs. The Druids' symbol is the Oak Leaf. That is their Sacred Pipe.

When Druids meet you, they put oak leaves around your wrists and invite you to their homes. If you say, "Yes, I will come," they take the leaves back. If you say, "No, I cannot come," they make you a gift of the leaves and go their way. In this case, I said, "Yes, I will be very happy to pray with you among your star rocks." Smiling, they took the leaves from me, and I followed them across the channel to the Land of Megaliths.

Altogether on this equinox journey, I went to sixteen sacred Celtic places: to dolmens and magic caves; to the giant upright Stone of Kerdef near Carnac; to the Menhir de Kerouezel; and to the twenty-five-foot-tall, foot-shaped rock at Penmarch. I felt the presence of spirits at the Dolmen de Crucuno. Awed and mesmerized, I wandered among mile-long rows of upright megaliths. I taught at these sites and, at the same time, was taught—teacher and pupil at the same time. It was a walk through eternity, from the distant past to the distant future.

During this equinox march, I came to a place called "Les Deux Corbins," so named because it was overseen by a Druid with a crow on one shoulder and a raven on the other. This Druid told me he was positive one day, negative the next, and then positive again. He was a *heyoka* in the best sense of the word—a great, almost prehistoric shaman.

I felt power surging through me inside the more than ten-thousand-year-old caves of southern France, whose walls are covered with the images of shaggy, big-tusked mammoths, huge buffalo, short-legged wild horses, and hunters with spears and stone axes. You can see the same kind of images painted and scratched into the rock walls in the plains, deserts, and mountains of the American West. There are even some of the almost-extinct buffalo called wisent, or aurochs, left in some remote corner of Poland, together with a small herd of wild Przewalski horses—sturdy and short-legged like those depicted in the prehistoric caves of France and Spain.

When I first came to the Netherlands, the people waiting for me looked disappointed. I do not wear a costume. I don't want to be taken for a circus performer in a Wild West show. Those Dutch people stared at me and asked, "Where is your feather bonnet?" I answered, "And where are your wooden shoes?" That broke the ice, and we all started laughing and talking.

In 1981, during one of my stays in Holland, I testified before the Bertrand Russell Tribunal, which concerns itself with human rights, Earth rights, and the protection of endangered groups of humans. There I met native people from all over the world: Hawaiians, Xingus from the Amazon, Mapuches from Chile, Nicaraguan Misquitos, Hopis from Arizona, Puyallups from Washington state, Onondaga clan mothers from New York, and Inuits from Greenland and Alaska. There I also met Gypsies, Kurds from Iraq and Turkey, Samis from Scandinavia, and Malays from Timor—all representatives of oppressed minorities just like us Native Americans. Here, too, I taught and was taught in return. The Russell Tribunal made headlines throughout Europe but was totally ignored in the United States.

I am also very fond of the Swiss people. They have a winter solstice festival with masked and horned dancers capering around, dragging along an oversized, fake billy goat—one man in front and one man in back under goat skins sewn together. This, too, goes back to pre-Christian days. These dancers reminded me very much of Hopi kachinas and Navajo *yei*. Whether the Swiss are aware of this, I don't know.

I have participated in the Sacred Bear ritual of the Ainus, who live on Hokkaido, Japan's northernmost island. They tie a bear in the center of their ritual place, dance around it, and pray to it. The bear is regarded as a human being and is later sacrificed, just as we sacrifice a dog during our solemn dog feast.

I have studied the ceremonies of my wife Sandy's tribe, the Chumash Indians of California. Their totemic animal is the Great White Shark, whom they call the "Eagle of the Sea." Chumash children swim in waters where Great Whites are sometimes seen, but the sharks never bother them. During the spring and fall equinoxes, when the sun is going down and the moon is full, the Chumash go down to the ocean, offering tobacco to the water, giving thanks to the bountiful sea, taking the Pacific's power to the land. In the fall, they also offer earth and grass to the waves.

I have related to thousands of people the stories, legends, beliefs, and way of life of my people. I have listened with respect and wonder to the things that holy men from many nations have related to me. There is a bond between us. We are all engaged in a common fight to save the Earth and all the living things that dwell on it.

I tell the people of Europe, "Some of you live in small countries with borders all around you, and that puts borders around your minds. Europeans, Asians, Africans, and Americans all live inside their little bubbles. You must puncture these bubbles. Break them. Break down the fences between countries and between peoples. Stop using words that separate you— 'commie,' 'capitalist pig,' 'leftist,' 'rightist.' Forget such words. If you don't play your part in nursing the little herb of peace, who will? If you don't protect the Earth, who will? Don't be a chicken if you have the potential to be an eagle!"

My grandfather once told me, "You will see the day when the door to your tipi will be opened." I see this day now. I see the day when the doors to *all* tipis will be opened.

We Indians always have our children participate in our ceremonies and the life of the grownups from the earliest moment. Therefore, I have taken all my children with me to Europe on my lecture tours.

Once I took my daughter Josephine to a prehistoric cave near Les Aziz, in France. This place moved me in an indescribable way. There was a presence there—a whispering of power, a sweetgrass of the mind. The keeper told me that, in ancient times, a priestess dressed in white came out of this cave to teach the people Earth wisdom and plant wisdom.

You can imagine how I felt as, deep inside that cave, I found the image of a buffalo carved out of the living rock with water from a sacred spring flowing from its mouth. While I was contemplating this, I heard Josephine holler, "Daddy, quick, come here!" She had inadvertently caused some moss to fall from the cave wall and found there revealed a face exactly like the one my father always used during his Yuwipi ceremonies: a horned head with slits for eyes and mouth, a design that forms a circle without end, the horns representing lightning and ending in positive and negative forks. There it was, right in front of us. My daughter said, "Grandpa's teachings were much older than all other teachings." (*See drawing on page 267.*)

Then our guide said, "All this goes back thousands of years before Christianity." I was wondering whether it was possible that White Buffalo Calf Woman had also taught *these* people at the dawn of humanity, in the days of the mammoth and buffalo hunters.

Our guide was a spiritual man. He raised a special breed of black-and-white horses and kept the image of a dark-skinned prophetess that nowadays is called the "Black Madonna." He told me, "They called her and her sisters witches and burned them at the stake."

"I know all about this," I said. "They called our medicine men witch doctors and shot them dead for the same reasons."

He went on, "This here has survived. Few have been inside this cave. You have been chosen."

I thanked him and told him that, as far as I was concerned, the people who had lived and worshipped here were our brothers—people who guarded the Earth and prayed to the spirits of animals, rocks, trees, and springs. I said that I felt the spirit of White Buffalo Calf Woman moving in this cave. But I wasn't sure. "Maybe she never came here," I said. "Maybe my imagination is running away with me."

"Maybe not," he answered.

When my eight-year-old son came with me on one trip, we met a man near Freiburg, Germany, who kept eagles. The man himself looked like an eagle. He had a small head, a huge beak of a nose, and eyes like those of a bird of prey. His wife had a bird's face, too.

The man showed us his eagles, and one of them soared high into the sky, circling in the clouds above us. Then it flew in smaller and smaller descending circles, hovering above my son. Finally it dropped one of its tail feathers. The feather floated slowly, slowly in the air, also moving in circles, hovered motionless for a moment, as if suspended, and then settled gently upon my son's head. I took it as a gift and a sign.

Archie Fire Lame Deer is a full-blood Sioux, a medicine man and the son and grandson of medicine men. A lecturer on Sioux religion and culture, he travels around the world teaching the ways of Native American spirituality, often by performing healing ceremonies.

He has been instrumental in bringing Indian religion into jails and in reforming laws so that medicine men can go into prisons to conduct ceremonies. "My next goal is to tear down the barbed wire in every prison," he says. He has also been very active in recovery programs for Indians who are alcoholics.

Archie has joined the ranks of other spiritual leaders, such as the Dalai Lama, in the quest for world peace, while always remaining a traditional Sioux medicine man. He is the *kuwa kiyapi*, or intercessor, for the yearly Lakota Sundance and is the official representative for the Sacred Buffalo Calf Pipe at Crow Dog Sundance.

After many years of adventure and travel, Archie has returned to his native South Dakota to make his permanent home among the Sioux people with his wife, Sandy, and their three children, John, Josephine, and Sarah. He is bringing up John to be his successor as healer and teacher; already he runs sweats and has "pierced" in the Sundance. Thus, generations of Lame Deers have followed, and will follow in the future, the way of the Lakotas.

Richard Erdoes is the coauthor of *Lakota Woman* (to be made into a film by Turner Broadcasting), *Lame Deer, Seeker of Visions*, and *American Indian Myths and Legends*, and author of *A.D. 1000: Living on the Brink of Apocalypse, A Sound of Flutes*, and *Crying for a Dream*, as well as more than twenty other titles. His most recent work is *Tales from the American Frontier*.

Richard is an Austrian-born historian, ethnographer, and artist, and has contributed illustrations to many magazines, including *Time, Life, Fortune, The New York Times, Smithsonian,* and *Saturday Evening Post.*

His photographs have been printed in books published by Time-Life, National Geographic, and Reader's Digest. He and coauthor Mary Crow Dog received the 1991 American Book Award for *Lakota Woman* from the Before Columbus Foundation.

Richard has pursued the protection of indigenous people in North America throughout his life.